IMPERMANENCE

Also by Sue Leaf Published by the
University of Minnesota Press

The Bullhead Queen: A Year on Pioneer Lake
Portage: A Family, a Canoe, and the Search for the Good Life
A Love Affair with Birds: The Life of Thomas Sadler Roberts
Minnesota's Geologist: The Life of Newton Horace Winchell

IMPERMANENCE

LIFE AND LOSS ON
SUPERIOR'S SOUTH SHORE

Sue Leaf

University of Minnesota Press
Minneapolis
London

Map on pages x–xi by Patti Isaacs

Photographs on pages xvi and 236 by Tom Leaf;
page 48 courtesy of Library of Congress; page 104 by Sue Leaf;
page 152 copyright Michael McKenzie (CC BY-ND 2.0).

Lines from "Erosion" copyright 1988 by Linda Pastan from *Carnival Evening: New and Selected Poems, 1968–1998* by Linda Pastan; reprinted by permission of W. W. Norton and Company, Inc.

Published by the University of Minnesota Press
111 Third Avenue South, Suite 290
Minneapolis, MN 55401-2520
http://www.upress.umn.edu

ISBN 978-1-5179-1525-4 (pb)

A Cataloging-in-Publication record for this book is available from the Library of Congress.

Printed in the United States of America on acid-free paper

The University of Minnesota is an equal-opportunity educator and employer.

32 31 30 29 28 27 26 25 24 23   10 9 8 7 6 5 4 3 2 1

We are slowly
undermined. Grain
by grain . . .
Inch by inch . . . slippage.
It happens as we watch.
The waves move their long row
of scythes over the beach.
. . .
We wake to water.
Implacably lovely
is this view
though it will swallow
us whole, soon
there will be
nothing left
but view.

—Linda Pastan, "Erosion"

CONTENTS

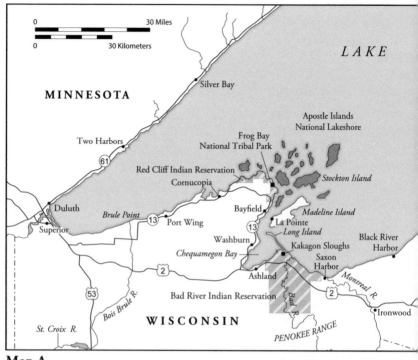

Map A

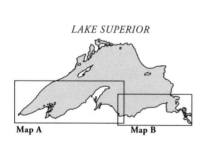

LAKE SUPERIOR

Map A   Map B

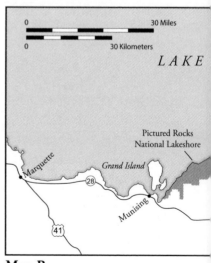

Map B

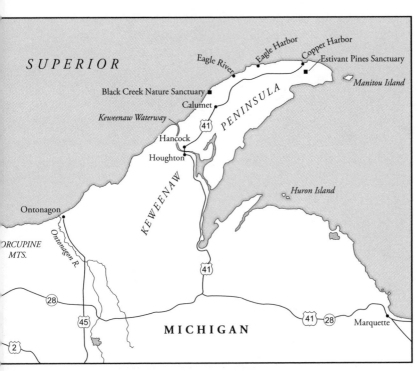

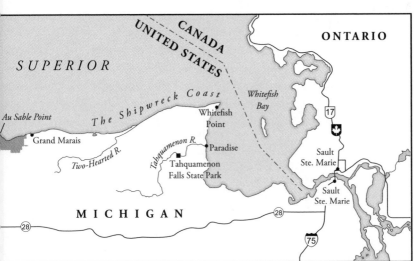

INTRODUCTION

Loving and Losing the South Shore

Down at the beach, the view across the lake this morning is shrouded by mist that hangs low on the water. Some days the Minnesota shoreline, twenty-two miles away, is visible, and other days it is not. When it is clear, I can see the town of Two Harbors with its water tower and some big building, maybe an arena. At night, the Two Harbors light with its distinctive flash pattern punctuates the darkness.

At other times, like today, fog hangs heavy, sometimes near in, sometimes far away, obscuring the horizon. Whatever thoughts of eternity that a long view might offer are veiled and vague. I just never know what Lake Superior will offer me.

For thirty-four years, our family has owned a rustic cabin on Superior's South Shore, outside of Port Wing, Wisconsin. We have spent our summers walking the sand beach, skipping stones, swimming to sandbars, and lounging at water's edge in low-slung chairs, unread books on laps, contemplating the horizon and the distant shore.

When I was a child, Lake Superior's North Shore was all I knew. My family made short visits up and down the shore, stopping at waterfalls, scrambling on the immense rocks, and gawking at the freighters streaming under the Aerial Lift Bridge in Duluth when we stayed in town visiting relatives. Lake Superior's watery expanse was thrilling but cold, and held at arm's length.

It was also unchangeable. Rock formations look remarkably similar today to photographs taken in the 1800s.

That is not true for the South Shore. Its features change season to season, even hourly, if a storm is raging. The explanation lies in the bedrock. The North Shore's bedrock is volcanic, arising over a billion years ago as the earth parted in a midcontinental rift and lava spewed forth, crystallizing as basalt and granite, gabbro and rhyolite, hard, igneous rock.

The South Shore's origin is much later. Some exposed rock is red sandstone, formed in the Cambrian in ancient seabeds, the rosy color a nod to the iron deposits laid down when its volcanic rocks were formed. Some of it is yellow sand beach, spread broadly as a skirt edging mixed-wood forests. Much of the South Shore is edged by red clay cliffs, glacial lake sediment left behind as the last glacier retreated and pooled meltwater receded. The sand and clay are erodible, and the shoreline changes as Superior's wave action readjusts it to its liking.

The North Shore's rock formations rising high above the water make the lake inaccessible in most places. The water is deep and cold immediately offshore. There are few opportunities to swim or boat. The lake is a backdrop for human endeavors on land.

On the South Shore, people interact with Lake Superior. They boat, sail, paddle, and kayak. The shallow water in the bays warms sufficiently for swimming and wading. Anglers ply the water in vessels bristling with rods baited with gaudy lures. When South Shore residents speak of the lake, they use personal terms. They say, "The lake is a misunderstood Beauty." Or "The Lake is the Boss." They refer to her as "she."

During the past decade, the red clay cliffs of the South Shore have been eroding at a fearsome rate. When we first went to our cabin, the previous owners told us to expect an erosion rate of about a foot a year, and for more than twenty years that rate held. But recently, Lake Superior has been at record-high levels, for complicated reasons, but excessive rainfall due to climate change undoubtedly is a factor. The water now laps at the toe of the cliffs more often than not. It stains terra-cotta with suspended clay, soil particles coming off the cliff, causing the shoreline to recede ever closer to the cabin. We have lost twenty-six feet in the past three years. A sense of futility wells in me as I understand that this is a loss I cannot shore up.

The accessibility and impermanence of the South Shore exact a psychic toll on those of us who linger here. While we delight in the immediacy of her charms, the sense of transience is pervasive.

Whether a bobber venturing out on unstable ice or a lakeshore owner ruing the loss of a recently built dock, we know that all that we love about Lake Superior is momentary pleasure. Everything fades, everything passes, everything gets battered by the wind and the waves.

Two weekends ago, during a cabin stay, my husband, Tom, and I went down to the water to walk our beach. The day before there had been cobbles there, but now a twenty-foot-wide sand beach had appeared overnight. A strong northwest wind had pushed the sand toward us. A sandy beach meant that finding agates was less likely, but we might come upon animal tracks, and we did: possibly a bobcat, perhaps a coyote.

It was the cliffs, though, that arrested me. They were wet and oozing from the night's storm. They looked raw and wounded in a way they had not when we were young parents, with small children playing in the sand beneath them. I wondered how this erosion would finally resolve and if we would be around to see the endpoint.

Enchantment with Lake Superior's South Shore takes many forms. In this book, I recount how my husband and I were introduced to the South Shore as young people and how we came to own a cabin here. I tell of the pleasures of our summers on the beach and the pain of loss, as climate change accelerates the natural process of erosion, taking beloved trees and beaches as it intensifies.

I speak to my contemporaries who are likewise caught in the big lake's thrall. I relate stories of people who swim, fish, and work on Superior. I go back in history and ponder what drew people in initially and what fruits their labors bore. I ponder how the beauty of the shore was diminished and what people did to repair the damage.

Above all, I write of the transitory nature of human endeavor that is reflected in the changing aspect of the South Shore. There is no refuge here, no illusion of permanence. We are just passing through. We are at the mercy of the One True Lake.

PART I

The Top of the World

YOU CAN'T TAKE IT WITH YOU

1977

The Greyhound bus rolled into Ontonagon, Michigan, on a Friday night in August and dropped us off under a streetlight next to a sign advertising the Gitche Gumee Oil Company. The driver climbed out of his seat, opened the bus's underbelly, and pulled out our two bike boxes and multiple packs, the panniers that we would hang over our rear bicycle wheels.

The air was cool and the main street was empty, save for little knots of pickup trucks clustered at intervals around the several bars. Laughter and noisy rock music emanated from the open doors of the bars, but it seemed distant and not connected to us in any way.

Working under the streetlight, Tom, my boyfriend of two years, fished his wrench out of a pack and began to assemble our bicycles, adeptly attaching front wheels to frames, hooking up brakes, adjusting seats. The previous summer he had cycled the full breadth of the continent, dipping his back wheel in the Pacific Ocean on the Oregon coast and pedaling across to the Atlantic at Connecticut. He had taken the entire summer off to do this, saving his meager salary as a hospital orderly, savoring his last months of freedom before beginning medical school in the fall. Tom was a tall, lanky man, six foot four, with a shock of curly blond hair, and the cross-continental trip had made him quietly self-assured.

Now, a year later, he had one year of gross anatomy and one cadaver dissection under his belt. With one month of vacation, he had talked me into this bike trip along Lake Superior's southern shore. We were twenty-four years old. Our destination was Duluth, 185 miles to the west.

As Tom worked on the bikes, I wrote. He had yet to learn that I could scribble for hours. There was a bank across the street with a digital clock flashing the time (11:27) and the temperature (58 degrees), and a bit of advice: "You can't—take it—with you—but try—going—somewhere—without it—SAVE!"

I wondered if there was a deeper message in this slogan. We were going somewhere, but what was the "it" that we needed? We had a little money—very little. We had had a layover in Ironwood, Michigan, earlier that evening, enough time to catch supper downtown. I had spent $1.90 on a pasty and $1.25 on *Glamour Magazine*, to while away the last hundred miles of the trip. I was enumerating each cash outlay. The bus ticket from St. Paul to Ironwood had cost us $15.30 each, with an additional $4.00 to get to Ontonagon.

Or maybe we needed perseverance to get somewhere? I had never undertaken a bike ride longer than thirty miles. It seemed straightforward, though—one pedal stroke after another, racking up the miles all the way to Duluth. Tom had done it. Why couldn't I?

Perhaps the bank was urging us toward fidelity to a cause. And what was the cause? Life on a shoestring? The self-sufficiency of traveling under our own power? The freedom of touring with only the small packs? Immersing ourselves in the nearness of the greatest lake, the blue expanse of Superior?

"You can't—take it—with you—but try—going—somewhere—without it!"

A young man strolled out from his apartment. He had been watching us as Tom labored in the weak light, and he was curious about our destination. He was amiable and casual, our first encounter of the trip. He was the first of many to chat with us. The kindness of strangers? Was that what we couldn't take with us?

At 12:00 a.m., the bank's message disappeared, and twenty-five minutes later Tom and I headed off into the darkness. We lacked front headlights but had little plastic leg lights strapped to our calves that moved up and down as we pedaled. These were effective in town, making us visible to cars, but did nothing to light up the pitch-black road. A couple times, I dismounted to feel about for the shoulder, making sure I was still on the road.

The city of Ontonagon maintains a campground a mile out of town, right on the shore. The campers were all asleep when we arrived, but we found a spot and, using a flashlight, pitched the tent, a small orange Eureka backpacker. We found a water tap, brushed our teeth, washed up, and crawled into our sleeping bags. It was now one o'clock, the darkest of nights, with glittering stars, and the big lake shimmering to the northwest.

"You can't—take it—with you—but try—going—somewhere—without it!" Money, perseverance, fidelity, friendship? Perhaps what we really needed on this great adventure was joy.

Ontonagon, Michigan, like nearly every community on the South Shore, had seen better days. But what exactly does that mean? The clues of a more prosperous past were hidden in the elegant buildings lining a main street, banks and schools, city halls and churches that seemed too large, too presumptuous to stand next to the exhausted frame structures that showed their age more frankly. "Better days" implies a more moneyed existence, but it was an open question whether life on the South Shore had been better in the past than it was now.

Ontonagon's economic base was first copper mining, then white pine logging. Extensive stands of old-growth trees were mined, like the copper, in a onetime frenzy of wealth production. The Ontonagon River flowing through town provided a way to ship logs out. The U.S. Coast Guard built a lighthouse at its mouth to mark the harbor, showing the route into port. The handsome structure was constructed of yellow brick with black shutters at the windows.

Sandstone quarries were far from Ontonagon; the red rock architecture that distinguishes Ironwood, Houghton, Calumet, and Marquette is absent. Ontonagon's prosperity was marked in wood. Seventy years later, it was fading as the features of an aging beauty.

But Tom and I didn't tour the town. After our late arrival the night before, we slept in until midmorning. When the walls of the orange tent glowed impossibly bright, we got up and considered how to pay for our site. We couldn't see a paybox or a campground host, so we simply took down the tent, packed it, and stowed our belongings in the panniers, agreeing to breakfast along the shore.

We each had two back panniers strapped to a bike rack bolted over our rear wheels. In these we stashed clothing and equipment. On the rack, we strapped our sleeping pads and bags with bungee cords. I had a front pack as well that was anchored in place by elastic bands that hooked on to the hub of my front wheel. It functioned as a purse, in which I kept my wallet, my glasses, my reading book, my binoculars and, of course, my journal. After a trip to the Red Owl in Ontonagon, it also carried lunch.

Tom had used a little Svea one-burner cookstove on his bike trip the previous year, and we carried that for one-pot meals. Before we left, I had bought a lightweight cook kit designed for backpacking, consisting of two kettles, two bowls, and a little coffeepot. We didn't share the cost of this (it had been considerable, more than fifteen dollars) because I had fallen in love with the aesthetics of the tidy design, and I wanted to keep the kit if things didn't work out between Tom and me. We discovered at our first breakfast that the coffeepot sat precariously on the Svea, a fact Tom pointed out with a disgusted snort. Obviously, he didn't appreciate it. I was glad that the kit was mine alone.

But the remarkable aspect of that first morning was neither the stove nor the little pot but the scenery—a yawning expanse of glittering blueness, Lake Superior, edged by a vast beach of amber-colored, fine-grained sand. Tom and I had both grown up knowing Minnesota's North Shore, with its rugged basalt outcrops and its frigid waters. When I had been quite small, my mother had told me that "no one swims in Lake Superior, Susan, ever."

And yet here we were—on the distant shore of *our* great lake, blueness all around, and miles and miles of sandy shoreline, tiny pebbles where the waves lapped the sand, and the clearest water imaginable. A lake that beckoned swimmers. I kept thinking, "How odd that they (Michigan) have sandy beaches on *our* (Minnesota's) lake!"

OUR DESTINATION that first day was the eastern end of Porcupine Mountains Wilderness State Park. We had only seventeen miles to travel, and there was a shoulder to the highway and few hills: life was good. White yarrow, orange and yellow hawkweed, early goldenrod, and tiny electric-blue asters, the wildflowers of late summer, bloomed in great profusion.

The Union Bay campground in the state park had a spot for us. We set up the tent, donned our suits, and pedaled back a quarter mile to the lake for a swim—a swim! I was still stunned by the fact that Superior was so inviting. On the North Shore, there were rocks to scramble over and an occasional beach with coarse pebbles, but it was a hike to get to accessible places, and the water was deep and dark beyond the rock ledges. Here, one could walk into the water from the sand and start swimming immediately, so I tried it. I surfaced with a gasp. The lovely, clear water was beyond cold, colder by far than the only comparison I could make, our family's summer cabin on a sandy-bottomed walleye lake in central Minnesota. One could swim here, yes, but not for long. Nonetheless, it was perfect. A swim in a cold lake after a ride under a hot sun was a perfect existence.

Back at the campsite, Tom and I practiced playing house. I made Kraft spaghetti and served it with a tossed salad and buttered Ry-Krisp and peanut butter cookies. I rejoiced in the abundance of wildlife, and I especially loved small rodents. At the campsite chipmunks and red squirrels checked us out, but later in the evening, a third species appeared, striped skunks (plural), who were not shy. Tom was reading *The Brothers Karamazov*, a serving spoon in hand, and to my alarm, he would interrupt the story to bang on the cook kettle to warn the skunks from coming too close. We actually watched one startled skunk back up, turn, and make a dash for cover as Tom thumped on the pot.

My twenty-four-year-old self thought this was a glorious way to spend ten days. We stashed our food in a pannier, strung up the pack in a tree, then went to bed.

I WOULD NOT BE TRUTHFUL if I did not admit that cycling thirty miles a day, a very modest mileage for true cyclists, was grueling for me. I had not trained. I didn't know the meaning of the word, and Tom had greatly overestimated my strength, having previously taken trips only with male companions. We skirted the southern boundary of the state park, avoiding truck traffic but not, alas, hills. On this road, we were far from Lake Superior but immersed in the northern hardwoods that mark the Upper Peninsula of Michigan.

Although the U.P. had extensive stands of pine and, in low areas, hemlock, much of it is sugar maple, either in pure stands, with thousands of tiny maple seedlings growing under their parents, or mixed with conifers. Hiking the next morning in the dense woods of Porcupine Mountains State Park, we had identified a Black-throated Blue Warbler, an eastern species not easily found in Minnesota, and a life bird for both of us. In the decades to follow, we would see very few Black-throated Blues and would remember this bird as a singular chap.

On the boundary road, on bicycles, we followed a Broad-winged Hawk, who flew ahead of us through the leafy tunnel created by overhanging branches. He had been perched atop a telephone pole, and our approach had startled him. At no time did he dart into the woods for cover, and I wondered if the thick growth hindered even a woodland hawk's passage through it.

Even as my legs complained, I relished being so close to the living world, to being part of it. The maples were turning in mid-August, and elms were dying. The Midwest was experiencing the first pass-through of Dutch elm disease in the 1970s, and even trees far from others of their kind were succumbing. It seemed that soon there wouldn't be any elms left in what had been called in my college ecology class the "Maple–Basswood–Elm Forest."

After passing through Wakefield and Bessemer, we regrouped in Ironwood. It had been a long, exhausting day of thirty miles, and I had complained enough that Tom offered to box up my bike and see me off on a Greyhound bound for home. The offer wasn't made out of anger but as a way to end my suffering. I had written of "gut-wrenching hills" in my journal, and my weak legs had trembled on the downhill coasts. He would still be my friend if I decided to go home. He might even still be my boyfriend.

But I was loath to leave. Biking was not fun. I freely admitted it. But moving about by such light and modest means charmed me. On a bicycle, there is no barrier between you and local residents, and we found them more likely to talk to us.

Most of all, I thrilled to the sight of Lake Superior day after day, in shining moments, in dull, surly times. We were catching sunsets, watching the water sparkle at noon, both of us under the spell of what I called in my journal the "big sea-water," echoing Longfellow.

We camped and showered at Curry Park on the western edge of town, and I began to perk up. For the first time, we splurged and bought supper at a small café across the highway. I told Tom I didn't want to go home. Getting on that Greyhound felt like giving up. Traveling with all that we needed on our bikes gave me a sense of freedom. And besides, the next day we would have Lake Superior in view once more. That would surely help my disposition. The direct route west to the big lake was via Highway 2. I chose the route: it was only thirty-three miles to Ashland, Wisconsin. One day.

HIGHWAY 2, THEN AS NOW, is the main artery across the Upper Peninsula and northern Wisconsin. Because it is a U.S. highway, the hills have been smoothed out, sort of, and sight lines are open. I did not really ponder what these facts meant before we started out. I should have thought that cars would thunder by us at sixty miles per hour. After three vehicles breezed by, I realized this was a busy, busy road. We would be jostled by high-speed traffic the entire day. The cars were alarming. The many semitrailer trunks were terrorizing. With my heavily laden bike, I clung to the narrow shoulder—a shoulder not designed for cycling—and told myself I could see this challenge through. I did this for eleven miles.

Then, a monstrous truck roared past and seemed to suck Tom, who was ahead of me, into the vortex it created. Horrified, I watched his form wobble toward the traffic lane before he recovered and headed back to the shoulder. With this, I lost my cool. I braked to a screeching halt, emitted high-pitched wails, on the verge of tears. Just like that, Tom changed the route.

We had recently passed the turnoff to the bucolic Wisconsin town of Saxon, whose white-steepled church could be seen in the distance. The county roads leading to the town, and also to Copper Falls State Park, were hilly, and six miles were gravel, but the countryside was dotted with grazing cows, ripened yellow grain, and extensive woodlots of maples and basswoods.

At lunchtime, we picnicked in an oat field that had recently been cut. The meal was a feast of Wisconsin cheese and nectarines, with hard rolls from the Ironwood bakery. The day was sunny, and we savored the warmth and quiet away from Highway 2.

We pedaled on toward Copper Falls State Park. The Bad River flows through the park on its way to Lake Superior. A break in the bedrock in this region marks all rivers that flow into the lake with significant rapids or waterfalls. The Bad River's response is a spectacular falls through a narrow basalt canyon. White pines jut out from rock fissures, leaning precariously over the river. The falls itself is a frothy yellow-brown cascade of twenty feet, hence the name Copper Falls. On a minor scale, the landscape here is reminiscent of Yellowstone or a Rocky Mountain stream.

We were late to the campsite. Tom had to true a wheel, and we ate dinner as the sun's rays filtered through the tree boughs. Then we were intent on washing dishes and getting the food in the pack and ready to hang in the trees, out of reach of bears. Caught up in domestic minutiae, we nearly missed the main attraction—the falls, the descent of the Bad River in glory. They were not far, and we walked in the twilight to the river. In the dusk, Tom was unable to take a photograph, but we agreed that this park was worth a second visit.

THE NEXT DAY, cold and clear, brought us to Ashland, Wisconsin, the largest town we had passed through in a week. Ashland is the home of Northland College, a small liberal arts school that was in that decade crystallizing its focus as an environmental college. The Sigurd Olson Environmental Institute, affiliated with the college, is also based there. Olson had spent formative years in Ashland.

Tom and I were both avid fans of Sigurd Olson, one of the heroes in the fight to protect the Boundary Waters Canoe Area Wilderness, and we had read all his books. I had heard of the institute and thought we should pedal past it. Tom patiently acquiesced, but visiting the place was lower on his agenda than washing clothes and finding a good bakery. We laughed when we saw the institute: a plain, dun-colored, converted old house. A handsome, modern building worthy of its namesake was still several years in the future.

The Snow White Bakery was much more impressive. It was housed in a modest storefront on Main Street and labeled with what I thought was an odd name—what did Snow White have to do with bread? Perhaps "Snow White" was the description of bleached white flour bread, once considered the Cadillac of baked goods. Tom was an enthusiastic consumer of chocolate eclairs, and Snow White's were champions, he declared. The pastries were good, and the hard rolls, a lunch staple for us, the best we had had.

In all, we decided Ashland was a very nice town. The people had been friendly in the laundromat, it had a lovely park with a band shell overlooking Chequamegon Bay, the Main Street bustled, and there were many imposing red sandstone buildings. Shade trees arched over the residential streets, which were lined with comfortable, well-kept homes. Like Ontonagon, Ashland had seen more prosperous times, but we chose not to dwell on that or how it might affect a community. We were, after all, only passing through.

Chequamegon Bay, which I had never heard of (it's pronounced She-wa-meh-gon), is shallow and clear. The name is an Ojibwe word for "a sandbar place" and refers to the spit of sand extending out into the lake from the bay. Ashland has two public beaches on the bay, and the water warms enough in the summer for comfortable swimming. The town also had a massive ore dock extending out into the bay. Ore from the Gogebic Range to the east once had been shipped out of there, and though the mines of that range no longer produce, Ashland residents were very proud of their dock. The high school team is the Ore Dockers, and a silhouette of the dock is emblematic of the town. We agreed with the town: the ore dock gave Ashland status.

We finished the laundry and grocery shopping early and pushed on to Washburn, following the plan to cycle around the Bayfield Peninsula and on to Duluth. The notorious Highway 2 was the route out of town but only for a few miles, when we turned north on Highway 13, a state highway curving around the tip of the peninsula and following the shoreline, more or less, to Superior, Wisconsin. From there we would go over the big bridge into Duluth.

To my dismay, Highway 13 was even busier than Highway 2 had been, and narrower, with twists and turns and zero shoulder. Mid-August is the height of the tourist season, and cars were traveling to and from Bayfield, with its fudge shops and souvenir stands. Washburn was not far up the road, but I fell once with my panniered bicycle, leading me to imagine how much worse it could have been if I had fallen toward the traffic lane. At a bar, we asked about back roads.

There were some, yes, we were told. We were also informed that we could expect twelve miles of road construction on Highway 13 between Washburn and Bayfield, with heavy traffic slowed by the gravel road.

I was torn. I couldn't endure more traffic—there was little courtesy for bicycles, I had discovered. And I didn't want to go home without completing the trip. Tom, though, was adamant: if I was going to be scared to death, we could not pedal Highway 13. We discussed options, and in the end, we decided to conclude the trip at Washburn. We would spend the night at the city park, bike back eleven miles to Ashland, and figure out how to box our bikes and catch the bus out of town.

Washburn, on Chequamegon Bay across from Ashland, is, like other South Shore towns, a mere ghost of its former self. Having a natural harbor, it was founded for railroad access to the Great Lakes. The community grew up around sawmills, mining the virgin pine of the Bayfield Peninsula, and within a decade was the site of active sandstone quarries—seven, in the town's heyday. The quarries produced the handsome red sandstone that was a hallmark of the Richardsonian Romanesque architecture dating from the 1880s, and Washburn itself boasts a splendid sandstone former bank building.

We continued our introduction to the landscape of the South Shore. Craggy white pines and serene red pines grew at the campground, and sandstone cliffs rose above the water. In Washburn, the lake had a sandy beach in some areas and not in others. We gazed far out over the water at Long Island, with its lighthouse.

Rain blew in as we settled into our tent at Memorial Park. From across the bay, Ashland's lights twinkled, and in the sky above, a brilliant electrical storm flashed peach and yellow bolts of lightning. The next morning, in the aftermath, migrating warblers had blown into the park. In mid-August, Nashville and Black and White Warblers were already winging south.

Two days later, on day ten of our adventure, we were once again on a main street of a South Shore town, Ashland, and once again watching a bank clock flash the time and temperature: 6:05 a.m. . . .

45 degrees. Tom, manning the crescent wrench, took off the bikes' pedals, the wheels, and the seats while I taped the bike boxes that we had gotten free of charge from a local business, Bodine's Marina.

A taxi idled at the curb, and eventually its driver got out, ambled over to us, and struck up a conversation. He got up at 4:00 every morning, he said, and acted as the town's local wake-up service. At 4:15, he called the hospital receptionist at her home to make sure she was up. Then he called the travel agency girl at 5:00 to wake her up for work. By 5:35 a.m., he was at the bus depot awaiting the first bus. Today was Sunday, so he was taking someone to St. Agnes for mass at 7:00, and then, he beamed, he would go home and his wife would fix him pancakes.

"Oh," said Tom. "You can't miss that!"

The bus pulled up to us with a bellow, and the driver got out to stash our bikes. "Here," said the taxicab driver, handing us business cards with a hand-scrawled name and telephone number. "Anytime you come back to Ashland, call me and I can help you!"

So we left, with a friend and an assurance of a future welcome. We thought our big adventure was over. My little nesting cook kit was stowed deep within my pannier. I didn't know then that Tom and I would pack it on camping trips for the next forty years. And we never dreamed that our love affair with the South Shore had only begun.

THE TOP OF THE WORLD

Ashland, Wisconsin

Tom and I visited Ashland in 1983 to consider the town as a permanent home. It had been five years since we had bicycled through the town. That had been in summertime, but on this return trip, it was the dead of winter. Snow was piled deep along the highway, and icy patches slicked the surface. We motored through the bare Wisconsin woods, aware that we were hurtling far from the center of our universe. Earl, Seeley, Cable, Drummond. All these were communities so slight that if you turned your head at the wrong moment, you'd miss them. The only signs of life were curls of wood smoke rising from brick chimneys.

Passing Drummond, we descended to a low area that we would later know as the Bibon Swamp. It seemed immense. The pristine wetland went on for miles without much human structure. No roads, few houses, sparse pastures. We were unfamiliar with northern Wisconsin, but this seemed as remote as anything in Minnesota.

We emerged from the swamp—the drive was endless—when unexpectedly, the highway formed a T and the shimmering expanse of Chequamegon Bay spread out before us. Startled, I caught my breath. I felt like we had been traveling through a tunnel, dark and snowy, and at that moment, we had arrived and were seeing the top of the world for the very first time.

What would life be like, I wondered, if we lived on top of the world?

OUR LIVES HAD CHANGED significantly since Tom and I were in Ashland on our 1977 bike trip. In the intervening years, we had married and had a child, a little boy, who was snug in his car seat as we reached the top of the world. Tom had finished medical school and was winding up his three-year residency in family practice. I had taken a master's degree in zoology and was working on my doctorate. If we moved to Ashland, I would write my thesis there.

Tom had the enviable luxury of looking for jobs nearly anywhere. Generalist doctors, the low people in the medical hierarchy, were needed everywhere and particularly in smaller towns. We were considering two other communities. Ashland differed from them in that it was a medical hub to northern Wisconsin with a new, self-sufficient hospital.

There were three family practice clinics in town. The one Tom interviewed at had been founded by a man who was nearing retirement age. The offer was to have Tom work a transition year, in which the older doctor would ease himself out of practice, turning over patients and gradually relinquishing responsibilities. A second partner in the clinic was not ready to retire but looked forward to more time off to pursue his passion, fly-fishing.

Tom hit it off with both doctors. The older doctor's wife, a mother of nine, held a dinner party for us, and we were taken by the warmth and liveliness of the gathering. We considered Ashland an ideal community for all the reasons we had noted on our first exposure: it had a vibrant downtown; it had a small liberal arts college, Northland; the opportunities for outdoor activity (skiing, hiking, canoeing) were vast; and because of Lake Superior, the winters were said to be emphatically snowy. The doctors told us that since Duluth was a full hour away, the hospital treated more complicated cases than similarly sized hospitals closer to an urban area. (For young doctors wishing to expand their skills, this was a definite draw.) Because of the remoteness, the emergency response teams were very good.

And of course, there was Lake Superior, which drew the eye no matter where you were in town. It was impossible to ignore the great lake.

Later in February, Tom told the doctors he would be ready to start September 1.

At age thirty, Tom and I knew a fair amount about academic science but little about real life. We couldn't begin to know what life would be like in a community that was no longer prosperous but not depressed. Ashlanders had told us that since there was a diversity of businesses in town, it wasn't subjected to crippling layoffs, but the town never boomed. For reasons we never understood, there was no rental housing available. We were forced into buying a house—with no savings and whopping student loans. On the positive side, the modest house cost only thirty-five thousand dollars, a price unheard of in Minneapolis—though our mortgage loan was at 13 percent. Even this we viewed as a bargain, the lowest rate for home loans in five years.

Reflecting much later, we both agreed that the best thing about buying the little story-and-a-half house in town was acquiring its next-door neighbor, Don Dickert. We met him the first day we moved in. He was our first friend and remained our most influential guide to life in the South Shore community for our entire stay.

Don was a sixty-year-old bachelor, a retired electrician. He had lived his whole life in the little yellow house to the west of ours. In fact, he had been born there. His family had owned it since 1892. Don seemed too young and too able to be retired, and we never found out exactly why he was no longer working his trade. We acquired a vague understanding that the union was involved in some way. Privately, we discussed how it could be that he lived without a paycheck. He lacked one of life's biggest expenses, a mortgage, but still there were electric bills, gasoline for his big truck, and sundry other expenses.

He heated the house with a wood-burning stove, as did many Ashland residents. (On still winter days, the air quality in town would become quite bad.) He scavenged the wood, so there was no heating expense. And he grew much of his own food, shot deer and froze the meat, and canned the fish he caught—the filets of pale northern pike or walleye captured in mason jars, squirreled away on his pantry shelf.

Don wasted nothing. He rescued a piece of Christmas cactus from the floor of the local grocery store, rooted it in soil, and presented it to me as a healthy plant months later—a plant I continue to nurture thirty-five years later. Seeds from pumpkins were saved to dry and roast for snacks. Items discarded on the highway were captured and brought home to be put to use—tarps that had flown off of pickup beds, furniture left by the roadside, five-gallon pails.

He had traveled very little, and I don't believe he served in World War II, possibly because he was the sole support for his mother. He was widely read, and we soon discovered, at our first dinner together, that he could hold his own in any conversation. Sharp as a tack, with a keen memory, he opined on many things. Since his chief source of political opinions was the American Legion magazine, we were often at odds with him, but we didn't care. Exposed heretofore to only our egghead college-educated world, Tom and I had never met anyone like Don. In the next eighteen months, he dug our potatoes, shoveled our walks when it snowed, helped us in our flooded basement when the sump pump broke, and took us high-bush cranberry picking in the marshland surrounding town. As our toddler, Andy, began to walk, he followed Don about in the garden, picking squash and pumpkins, and in the spring helped him plant potatoes.

Don exemplified the life of many people in the northland. Making do with very little, he lived almost entirely off the land, supplemented by his garden. Residing in a building provided from his past, he lived fully in the present but did not have the resources, neither monetary nor personal (since he never married), to build out into the future. He seemed never to consider that. His life was rich and full in his modest style, and that was sufficient. We could tell he loved it.

TOM AND I SETTLED into a routine in our little house on Tenth Avenue. He was not particularly busy during clinic hours, a change from being a beleaguered resident, but when he was on call every third night, the telephone rang constantly, and he made frequent trips to the hospital.

I was able to hire someone almost immediately to care for Andy several mornings a week so I could work on my thesis. After a morning's writing, I then was free to explore the town. I often took my bicycle, Andy bundled in a snowsuit riding behind me.

Lake Superior, yawning to Ashland's north, dominated everyone's existence. One of the quirks of northland life was that we couldn't get the *Minneapolis Tribune* delivered to our door. The *Ashland Daily Press* provided us with local news, but in the days before the internet, we needed national and international news, so we and other Ashland residents ordered the *Tribune,* which was dropped off at the drugstore downtown. Every day, Andy and I made the ten-minute trek to pick up our paper, sometime in midmorning after it arrived, LEAF scrawled on the front page. As we traveled along Main Street, which paralleled the shoreline of Chequamegon Bay, there was a distinct temperature difference between the blocks of storefronts, shielded from the wind, and the streets open to the lake. Even on the mildest days, we could be hit with an eye-watering blast of air.

There was also, we soon noticed, a peculiar lightness of sky over the bay and the broad expanse of lake beyond it. Cloudy or clear, the northern sky seemed lighter and brighter. I began orienting myself to the lake.

One morning in early November, while out and about, we passed one of the Catholic churches in town, St. Agnes, a big complex built of Apostle Island sandstone, with a school and parish house, the predominant congregation in town. I raised my eyebrows as I read on the church sign that there would be a memorial service for the crew of the ore boat the SS *Edmund Fitzgerald* on November 10.

The *Edmund Fitzgerald* had been loaded with taconite, heading downlake on Superior, when it disappeared during a storm on November 10, 1975. Like all Minnesotans, we learned of the disappearance and probable shipwreck of the freighter the next morning in disbelief and horror. Tom, in fact, had been in Tofte, Minnesota, the night it went down and had witnessed the fury of the lake. Within a year of the wreck, singer Gordon Lightfoot had immortalized the event and its loss of twenty-nine people, the entire crew, in a song.

That is how I thought of the *Fitzgerald* and its fate eight years before—mythic and fabulous—not, somehow, real and shot through with heartache. The clinic staff, though, told Tom that several crew members had lived in Ashland and its environs and had grieving family and friends in town. Two crew, in fact, had been retirement age. The year 1975 was to be their last season. Family members would be present at the memorial mass at St. Agnes.

The people of Ashland spoke in warm, affectionate terms of the men who went down with the *Fitzgerald*. Some had grown up with them. Gone to high school with them. Had a beer with them on winter nights when they were in town, when shipping on Superior had shut down for the year. A *Daily Press* column informed me that, in fact, its news editor, Virginia Burtness, had been the first to alert the nation of the tragedy. She had heard of a missing ship on her marine scanner while at home and called the paper, telling them to pursue the story.

I began to see Lake Superior as a living, dynamic entity, a force and not just as a backdrop to picnics, beach walks, and driftwood fires. When someone would remark, offhand, that Superior was not to be trifled with, it seemed somehow less trite. Ashland, in fact, became more interesting when I realized how it was interwoven with Great Lakes shipping.

Another incident connected Ashland's diminished harbor to the shipping world. In October, the freighter the *John G. Munson* arrived at the Reiss Coal Dock bearing unusual "cargo." It had somehow snagged a nineteenth-century anchor and 250 feet of chain off the bottom at Bete Grise, a bay on the eastern shore of the Keweenaw Peninsula. The *Munson* carried this burden hundreds of miles entangled in its anchor line. At Ashland, most of the old chain was removed, but the anchor made the trip across the lake to Two Harbors, Minnesota, where it was finally removed. The well-traveled anchor was then taken by the Coast Guard back to the Keweenaw, where it can be viewed on the grounds of the Eagle Harbor lighthouse. History buffs could never identify the vessel originally carrying the anchor.

ANOTHER PERSON we met soon after moving to town exemplified a different, but not contradictory, way of living in the northland. This was Suzan MacKenzie-Smith, a trailing spouse turned historic preservationist. She thrilled to Ashland's numerous elegant old buildings that were deemed encumbrances to be torn down. With an outsider's eye, she saw a legacy that deserved to be preserved and lauded for its grace and beauty.

Sue came already adapted to historic preservation. As a child she had known and loved a great-grandmother, whose stories gave Sue a deep sense of a living past, an understanding that what was old could also be vibrantly contemporary. She transferred this appreciation of old people to old buildings, and with her husband renovated an Arts and Crafts bungalow in Milwaukee before moving to Ashland.

Once in town, she was drawn to a large Victorian house on Chapple Avenue, an aging beauty on a residential street in town. With a considerable outlay of elbow grease, they turned the dowager into a stunning family home, with a large wraparound porch, refinished woodwork, and period wallpaper.

The timing on Chapple Avenue was uncanny that year. Of the eight houses on the 700 block, five went on the market and were bought by like-minded young families. They proceeded to learn the finer points of Victorian restoration together, sharing tools and helping each other bring the neighborhood back to life.

The family home, then the neighborhood restoration, led her to a focus on Ashland's historic schools, and from there to Main Street as an entity, which was placed on the National Register of Historic Places.

She now talks in terms of the "embodied energy" of old buildings. This is a broad concept that incorporates the cost entailed to construct them and also the money spent to produce their materials— like quarried stone or cut timber—and, too, the incalculable value of virgin wood, so much finer-grained and sturdier than today's plantation-grown trees.

Sue seemed to be the catalyst that galvanized the town into rethinking its relationship to its past and perhaps to standing up a little straighter. The community didn't need to live in a future of pole barns and concrete-block construction: it had a legacy to build on.

ONE OF THE STRENGTHS of Ashland's daily newspaper, the *Daily Press*, was its coverage of environmental news. Undoubtedly, this was aimed at readers from Northland College, which had a robust environmental focus, with the Sigurd Olson Environmental Institute on campus and faculty strong in the biological sciences. But it probably was also avidly received by the general populace, many of whom relished the outdoor life. Paging through old *Daily Press* issues years later, I was amazed at the coverage, far more than in the highly regarded Twin Cities newspaper the *Star Tribune* that I currently read.

The highlighted environmental issues that made the newspaper week after week are ones we don't think much about these days: acid rain effects on the Great Lakes, the possibility of diverting Great Lakes water to irrigate the southern and western United States, and above all the installation of an extremely low frequency system for submarine communication (Project ELF) that was sending low-frequency sound waves through the granite bedrock of northern Wisconsin and was proposed for the Upper Peninsula of Michigan. Project ELF had created widespread dissension. Elected Wisconsin officials Governor Anthony Earl and Attorney General Bronson La Follette had filed a federal lawsuit to stop the program; they did not succeed. The federal government had set up studies to monitor the effect of the sound waves on various aspects of the environment—birds, soil invertebrates, aquatic systems, and the like. The first phase of the monitoring was winding down when we arrived in town.

I wistfully read through these 1983 news articles. How regional the problems were! How limited in scope, how solvable! No layperson was thinking hard about global warming in 1983.

As ice lidded Chequamegon Bay, Ashland settled into winter. We had heard the stories of "lake effect" snow, how storms take on moisture over the open water of Lake Superior and dump it over the land. To our delight (because we are cross-country skiers), those stories proved true. By late November, we had sixteen inches of snow on the ground and were ready to ski. We did not know it at the time, but the winter of 1983–84 was particularly snowy. The *Daily Press* gleefully reported highways shut down, snow depths in feet, and exuberant winter activity.

It was our first winter with a toddler to accompany us on the ski trails. Tom ordered a sled he had seen in the want ads of a cross-country ski magazine. It was called a Tur-Pulk: a wooden sled with a red nylon cover that zipped up around the child, who sat on the sled with a little chair back for support. The sled had bamboo poles extending forward and attached to a harness that strapped around a parental waist. To this day, we have never seen another one on any trails, although a Google search brings up Norwegian sites that feature pulks.

Andy hated it, but with a little cajoling, crackers, and a pacifier, he allowed us to ski for about an hour. We skied two or three days a week, whenever Tom wasn't on call, sometimes hiring a sitter so we could take longer jaunts. The ski trails around Ashland, and especially those at Valhalla, a recreation area on the Bayfield peninsula maintained by the U.S. Department of Agriculture, were the best we had skied. They had dips and hills, hardwood forests, and long, satisfying runs on which skiers flew.

Sometimes we went farther afield. East of Ashland on Highway 2, outside Ironwood, Michigan, are two well-known cross-country ski centers, Wolverine and Active Backwoods Retreat (ABR). ABR was not in existence in 1983, but we came to love the exposed bedrock, conifers, and downhill runs of Wolverine. It had been expressly laid out by skiers for maximum thrill. Between Ashland and Ironwood, Highway 2 rises in a tremendous incline known to locals as "Birch Hill." This is actually a glacial moraine, a margin of the erstwhile Superior lobe and the reason Ironwood receives such reliable snows. Storms coming off the water are laden with moisture. They hit the elevation and drop their snows in the lee. Ironwood was an hour drive for us, but the snow was a big reason we had moved to Ashland. We were going to live fully in the winter.

While we skied to our heart's content, some Ashlanders spent their free time on what we considered a more dubious activity, bobbing. Not to be confused with the little spherical red-and-white floats found in tackle boxes, bobbers were anglers of a type we had never encountered. They spent their leisure hours far out on Lake Superior's ice sheet, fishing deep waters. Pulling their gear in a sled, sometimes with a snowmobile, they would take along a camp stool and perhaps a small tent to shield them from wind, whiling away a Saturday dropping a line into the icy depths. The quarry was the speckle-flanked lake trout, a cold-water fish that prefers water as deep as one hundred to two hundred feet.

It seemed incredibly dangerous to us, and it was. A lot of knowledge went into making a bobber—the ability to read the condition of the ice, the incoming weather, even the habits of lake trout. That winter, and during frequent winters since, we have read about the ice breaking apart, and bobbers trapped on floes, unable to get back to land. Rescue workers in wind sleds are sometimes deployed to reach them.

THE PROXIMITY of such a large body of water to land builds in a great inertia. Spring was slow in coming to the South Shore that year, and every year. Summer was slow to leave in the fall. Late-ripening tomatoes had had a few extra days to redden. In April, it seemed the days would never warm. We had a late, heavy snow on April 30. Migrating robins hopped belly deep in snow, seeming perplexed. In the interval between the ski season and when I could get into my garden, I defended my doctoral thesis and oversaw its printing, binding, and distribution.

When ice-out arrived on Chequamegon Bay, we witnessed another Lake Superior phenomenon, the annual spring smelt run. Smelt are not native to Lake Superior, whose fisheries have been unhinged by two hundred years of Euro-American intervention. Smelt were accidently released into the Great Lakes waters in the early twentieth century when they escaped from an inland lake in Michigan where they had been stocked as forage fish.

They appeared in Lake Superior in 1946 at a time when the invasive sea lamprey had decimated the native lake trout population, a fish that might have acted as a natural curb to the smelt population. In the absence of trout, smelt numbers skyrocketed.

The small (six-to-nine-inch) silvery fish spawn in running water and enter the streams feeding Superior in great numbers. This run became a spectacular event when smelt numbers peaked in the 1970s. Tens of thousands of fish could be taken from shallow water in rivers and streams feeding Lake Superior, on both the North and South Shores. Happy, beer-soaked anglers flocked to the waterways, with seines, dip nets, ice chests, and buckets. Chequamegon Bay has many feeder streams running into it and was an active site for smelters.

The Polish Catholic Church in town, Holy Family, held an annual smelt fry in mid-April, and we were invited by Tom's nurse, a parishioner, to attend. Tickets could be had at three dollars a head, and should the diner not favor fish (and why would you not?), there were ample sides, including potato salad, coleslaw, and desserts. I had never eaten smelt before, but sunfish, walleye, sardines, pickled herring, and smoked cisco were all part of my repertoire.

We entered the crowded parish hall to find long rows of tables covered with plastic tablecloths, everyone at work eating small fish. The scent of grease hung in the air. The buzz of happy eaters filled the hall.

We each got a plate piled high with deep-fried smelt, heads intact, but not the tails. Andy in a high chair was delighted with this new finger food. Wisconsin fish fries, of which this was a variation, are not to be considered fine dining, but the conviviality could not be matched. By now, we were beginning to be known in town—the new young doctor and his bookish wife and little boy attending the smelt fry.

But what I noticed and remember mostly vividly was a peek behind the scene. As we walked past the kitchen, I glanced in to see two men sitting on stools, surrounded by silvery mounds of smelt. They were gutting them with their bare hands, running broad, bloody thumbnails up each belly. They must have already "processed" thousands and had thousands more to go. Each had a beer at hand, and perhaps a cigarette. It looked like a fine time.

As OUR FIRST YEAR in Ashland, and Tom's contract, drew to a close, Tom received from the clinic the terms for buying into the practice. The year had gone well, everyone thought, and I believe it was expected Tom would join the group as a partner. But Tom had not been very busy in clinic, sometimes seeing as few as five patients a day; a normal workload is twenty and often more. The buy-in was steep. Tom would need a reliable patient base to make his practice profitable.

The lack of patients was not a solvable problem. The physician who had thought he would retire had not given up any patients. Indeed, he would live another thirty years and practice medicine well into his seventies.

Tom quietly began looking at practices in Minnesota, where he had many medical connections. A compatriot in his residency program, now practicing in the Chisago Lakes area, called to entice him back home. The practice and the community were attractive. I was most keen to make a decision, since I was pregnant and due in November. Tom signed a contract with Chisago Lakes, and we began looking at houses.

Within hours of announcing we were leaving, Tom had a second job offer, this one from the Chequamegon Clinic in Ashland. A third clinic offered him a job soon after. Tom knew he would be busy in those clinics. In truth, they were clinics that he had often eyed wistfully.

Now we had a wretched decision to make, something we do not do well. We both felt we were not ready to leave Ashland, but we were not sure we wanted to stay permanently. Our parents were eager to see us back in Minnesota. Tom felt he needed to honor the contract he had signed with Chisago Lakes before the Ashland offers were extended. I tossed and turned at night, heavy with the coming baby, unable to think, really, of anything but that. Unable to influence Tom in his tortuous dilemma.

In the end, and for reasons neither of us can yet articulate thirty-five years later, we left. We left the shining inland sea, the top of the world, the wonderful life, where we resonated with the north and its moods. We moved back to where our roots were planted, Minnesota.

Our second child arrived, a healthy baby girl, three weeks after we moved. The new clinic was two doors away from our new house, and Tom was frantically busy from the first day he walked through its doors. The North Branch community was thrilled to once again have a physician living in its midst and proved warmly loyal to Tom and fully embraced us.

But the change was wrenching. Each day I bundled the children in snowsuits, and we walked to the post office for the mail—for now, in North Branch, while the *Minneapolis Tribune* was delivered to our door, we had to fetch the mail from a post office box. Stepping outside, I would look expectantly to the north, anticipating a lightened sky, as happens to the clouds when a vast, shining body of water reflects the sun back to the heavens. I would try to orient myself to the top of the world.

But we weren't at the top of the world. We had severed our tie to Lake Superior. It was never light to the north. It was only dark and somber.

THE PLACE FOR US

The years that followed our move to North Branch were filled with diapers and strained food, toddlers and ride-'em cars. The intensity of our ties to Ashland waned, but the lure of Superior's South Shore did not. We discovered a family resort south of Ontonagon, Michigan, with modest cabins on a broad, sandy beach, and returned several years running, first with two toddlers, then with preschoolers and a newborn, then with a kindergartner, a preschooler, and a toddler. As beleaguered parents who just wanted a little sleep, our beach vacations offered respite from demanding schedules.

Small children and sand are a good combination. We bought our kids implements labeled "Busy Beach Set," and they labored for hours, transferring sand from one location to another, molding forms, digging moats. We languidly supervised from our low-slung sand chairs, gazing out over Superior's horizon and wondering if all the blueness was a decent representation of eternity, appreciating how the long view soothed us.

We explored farther up the Keweenaw Peninsula, coming upon a classic inn, the Lake Breeze Hotel at Eagle Harbor, run by an elderly couple. Our children were a fresh and noisy addition to the largely geriatric crowd that had been vacationing at the hotel for decades. They enjoyed a Superior view from the porch or lawn, lounging in Adirondack chairs or swings, while we frantically watched little ones crawl on the basalt outcrops in front of the hotel, intermittently yelling, "Andy, that's far enough! That's far enough!"

We had stumbled on the Lake Breeze in the summer of 1987, when four-year-old Andy went on a maniacal lighthouse tear, and we visited as many as we could on our trip to the Upper Peninsula. These were often situated at scenic spots on the Keweenaw: Ontonagon's lighthouse, built of creamy-yellow brick at the mouth of the Ontonagon River; Eagle Harbor's red brick lighthouse on a promontory adjacent to the Lake Breeze; the Mendota lighthouse at Bete Grise, on the white sand beach of the natural harbor. We took a Michigan state parks boat to the lighthouse at Copper Harbor, on the outer arm of that harbor. The life of a nineteenth-century lighthouse keeper was one of austere beauty and isolation, and it seemed to encapsulate the Keweenaw as a whole: wind, water, remoteness.

Wild blackberries were ripe and abundant on one of our visits. Tom and Andy, sharing a common purpose, picked as though possessed. Katie, age three, was given her own bucket but, like the little girl in Robert McCloskey's *Blueberries for Sal,* ate most of them. Tom reported to me that she even whispered, "Kaplink! Kaplank! Kaplunk!" as she dropped the berries into her pail.

The summers of 1987 and 1988 were memorable for unusual heat and drought. The year 1987 went down as one of the warmest in state history, and we experienced what I remember as the first of the "superstorms": eleven inches of rain fell in one night during an eight-hour period, though much of the early summer had seen drought.

In 1988, a year with forty-four days above ninety degrees, we lived through prolonged drought, our North Branch lawn bleached and straw-like by mid-June. The heat was hard on the small bodies in our house. We spent hours every day in the yellowed backyard near the wading pool. From my spot under the crab apple, I could count five dead or dying trees—trees stressed from drought that were succumbing to invasive fungi like Dutch elm disease and oak wilt. The living world that we woke to each day suddenly seemed fragile, vulnerable in a way we hadn't imagined before.

That was the same summer that NASA scientist James Hansen testified before a Senate committee that the extremely hot weather was most likely due to global warming—something Tom and I had feared, a niggling thought in the back of our minds, never taken out and examined because we seemed to be the only ones thinking those thoughts. We were aware of the possibility of global warming; there had been a brief reference to it in our college ecology textbook by Eugene Odum. But in 1973, the average temperature of the Earth seemed to be cooling slightly, not warming; scientists' understanding of global warming had not yet been fleshed out. Now, in the heat of the late 1980s, we thought once again with horror about the scenario. With our backgrounds in biology, we understood that plants and animals lived within a very delineated temperature range. We knew that global warming would be bad for the biosphere.

Tom and I viewed our vacation to the Upper Peninsula as a fleeing from the oppressive heat, a cool refuge in a suddenly warming world. I recall so vividly a picnic lunch in the city park of Wakefield, Michigan, barely over the state line in the U.P. but well within the influence of Lake Superior. Stepping outside the car, I felt the air, fresh and tolerable on my skin. The children ran about and laughed, like tender flowers that had been watered. They flourished.

THE KEWEENAW PENINSULA is idyllic in large part because it is remote, far from large urban areas, and from our home, too. The sand beach at Ontonagon was a five-hour drive away, an eternity for small children. We wanted to be cabin owners, not renters, and after looking for a few months, we found a place to buy on the South Shore west of Port Wing, Wisconsin, just a three-hour drive from Chisago Lakes.

Sometimes people fall in love after steady, warm friendship, and sometimes they tumble headlong into passion that bypasses rational thought. The latter is what happened to me as we first trudged up the driveway to the cabin at Port Wing, a sparse November snow on the ground, and three children in tow. The place was, frankly, a hovel—not squalid but small and simply constructed. It hugged the ground but was anchored by a huge fieldstone fireplace that was puffing out wood smoke as we approached.

The realtor and the adult son of the owner greeted us as we stepped inside. We could see that there was a central core to the place that had been the original cabin, built, we were told, in the 1930s from wood pilfered from the Herbster, Wisconsin, lumberyard. The current owner, with five children to house, then added a larger living area and two bedrooms. The cabin seemed to go on and on as we ventured into the back rooms. I later wrote in my journal that it was "quite large for a cabin," but in truth, it was less than nine hundred square feet.

Large mullioned windows overlooked the lake, and knotty pine paneling in every room gave the place a golden light. Scrutinizing the central cabin, which had morphed into the kitchen, we saw that everywhere screws had been used in lieu of nails to hold things together, testifying that the wood pilferer had been eccentric as well as a thief. This is one of my defining features of a true cabin: quirkiness. My childhood cabin, for example, had bar cabinets from a demolished Little Falls saloon serving as kitchen cupboards.

I tried not to look too starry-eyed, squinting, instead, as the realtor discussed with us the asking price. Tom, a better poker player than I, said little.

We walked out to survey the property. The cabin was set on five acres of second-growth mixed woods with large aspen and balsam fir growing beneath the mature trees, planted spruce, and speckled alder in some low areas. There were also a few large white pine that had escaped the ax. The original owner had dug what the realtor termed "frog ponds" in two low spots—again, quirky—which then filled with water and which were now, in November, covered with ice.

Out at the cliff overlooking the lake, we could see Minnesota, twenty-two miles away. The town of Two Harbors was barely visible, just its water tower and a plume from a smokestack. We would later learn that the Two Harbors lighthouse beacon with a characteristic flash pattern could be detected on clear nights when the water was not hung with haze.

The cliff was composed of red clay that looked raw and oozy. It rose twenty feet over the beach, and we looked down on a large red sandstone boulder, which the owner told us had only recently become exposed—for the cliff was receding at a noticeable rate. Lake Superior was becoming wider, on average one foot per year. Erosion was natural, we were told, a fact of life. The cabin was well over a hundred feet from the cliff's edge. We, and our children, would not see the cabin endangered in our lifetimes.

Tom and I, with our biology training, were skeptical that the erosion was natural. It seemed to us that erosion was a transitional process. After erosion had reduced the incline of the cliff, there would be an equilibrium reached, the angle of repose. We suspected that the clear-cutting that had ravaged the South Shore (including our land) at the turn of the century had hastened, perhaps even caused, the erosion: when the land was devoid of trees, the water ran off instead of being taken up by root systems after rainfalls and during snowmelts.

The lake was heaving below us as we stood. Water, stained with clay, appeared turbid and rosy. "The water clears," the owner told us. "And we have always had a sand beach in the twenty-five years that we've owned it. The lake moves the sand around but always gives us plenty. In fact," he added, "it is shallow and sandy far, far, out there. You can swim a hundred feet out, because the lake deposits a sandbar parallel to the shore."

The property bordered a ravine with a small creek trickling at its bottom that emptied into the lake. It often dried up, leaving a solid bar across its mouth. The chief benefit of the creek, in our eyes, was that it enabled a path down to the water without having to deal with a twenty-foot cliff that oozed wet clay.

We picked our way down to the water's edge. Waves rolled in, and the wind off the water was brisk. We had dressed the kids appropriately in snowsuits and boots, so while Tom carried John, who was toddling, we inspected the beach for the first time. The lake had tossed up an abundance of driftwood, and sizable boulders protruded from the water. From below, we could see big aspens and birch rising behind the cliff's edge. An old, mature white pine spread its furry arms over the ravine opposite the cabin, and a less-common red pine could be seen farther west.

Privately, the realtor told us that she thought the asking price was too high, and friends from Ashland agreed. We offered 20 percent less than what the owner wanted and were amazed a few days later when the offer was accepted. We were the dogs who caught the car—at age thirty-five, we were about to own a cabin on Lake Superior.

WE RETURNED TO THE CABIN next in May 1989, this time as owners, on my thirty-sixth birthday. The trees in our yard at home had boasted of tiny green leaves. Traveling north, we watched the spring recede. When we reached Lake Superior, the branches were bare, and snow from a late storm had fallen just the day before.

Still, in our reintroduction to Superior's paradoxes, the spring day was balmy. Temperatures were warm enough to picnic outside on the lawn overlooking the lake. There was scarcely a ripple on the water's surface, and a haze hung over it. We would learn that this was entirely due to the direction of the wind. Had the wind swept across the full length of Superior from the northeast that day, we would have needed winter jackets. But a southern breeze brings warmth and flat water.

Minnesota, our home, was now indistinct. I felt this was somehow emblematic. With this cabin, we were embarking on a new way of experiencing the world, and the past was blurred, a distant shoreline whose features were made indeterminate by the lake becoming something new, spring coming out of winter.

A few years before, I had had the opportunity to buy into my childhood cabin on a sandy-bottomed central Minnesota lake where I had spent my girlhood summer vacations. I had turned my father down. I knew I didn't want to share a cabin with my siblings; I had not known then that I was saving myself for something bigger.

That first day, we began to meet our neighbors. Spring peepers and western chorus frogs were calling from the human-made ponds. The peepers were so intense, so shrill, and so near that their calls hurt my ears when I was outside at dusk. But at bedtime, four-year-old Katie sighed, "I love the frogs. I love their pretty sound."

On the water near the red rock, we noticed a dozen Common Mergansers, two bright, green-headed drakes, and the others either hens or first-years with rusty, messy crests. These are birds that get their start in the small streams that run into the lake but as teenagers hang out on Superior.

We had a resident Belted Kingfisher on the creek, patrolling the ravine with a loud, confident rattle. Sometimes we had two: a lady friend and perhaps a nest.

A skein of cormorants flew low over the water, a silent black V. This was a species that we would notice dwindling in the coming years at about the same time that thousands of cormorants were targeted by the Minnesota Department of Natural Resources on Leech Lake, a large walleye lake 170 miles to the west. Since 2005, twenty-eight thousand cormorants have been killed on Leech Lake in an effort to boost walleye production for sport fishing. No one I have talked to has been able to connect the decline of Lake Superior cormorants with the slaughter on Leech Lake, but it is plausible that nonbreeding young birds might while away the summer on Lake Superior before returning to their colony to breed. We have come to see that the immensity of Lake Superior is a big palette on which even phenomena occurring far away might be observed.

In three decades since assuming stewardship of this particular patch of earth, we have received unexpected gifts from Lake Superior. We added a fourth child to our family before our second year of ownership. She spent her first summer on the beach, grabbing tiny fistfuls of sand while her siblings learned the structural support of driftwood, how to craft "forts" with substantial lengths of wood from trees that had toppled into the lake up and down the shore.

The abundance of cobbles on the beach became teaching tools, with a dad who asked, "What's this rock? And this?" holding granite, basalt, chert, gabbro, and limestone for his children to identify. That might not have been the sole factor, but we did produce two college geology majors.

Everyone learned how to swim—on Lake Superior, this is a survival skill—and on calm days, with crystalline water and a sandy lake bed with no weeds, they swam until they flirted with hypothermia. Truth be told, though, no one commands the big lake like Tom, who has been a competitive swimmer since childhood. With strong, bold strokes, he sweeps for half a mile parallel to the shore, front crawl, backstroke, breaststroke when the waves are up. Down and back, down and back, while the dog and I stand as lifeguards. The danger is slight. The water is not over his head.

Everyone learned how to canoe. Early on, we put the two oldest in a canoe when the creek had water in it but a sandbar blocked its mouth. The kids could paddle all about the creek, even out of parental sight, without fear of being pulled into big water.

In our years on the South Shore, we have learned an intimacy with Lake Superior that we couldn't have developed in weeklong vacations to Ontonagon or to the North Shore. We have seen it stormy and worry about the freighters that steam by in shipping lanes ten miles from us. We have seen it restless, bestowing on us a sense that change is imminent. We have seen it placid as a small pond, shimmering with summer heat and making us drowsy as we lounge on its shore, or beckoning to us to launch a canoe and inspect the shoreline, since paddling would seem effortless.

But there have also been more subtle and unexpected gifts from the big lake. Even though summer days at the cabin are, more often than not, cold, cloudy, or rainy (even when a mere five miles inland, the weather is sunny and warm), we cannot imagine life in a cabin on a smaller inland lake. We have become imbued with the magnificence of a great lake, the expanse of water and the yawning horizon. When we do entertain the notion of a cabin not quite so wild, we immediately reject it. We would always be wondering what we were missing on Superior.

In large part this is because of our affinity for the open view, our resonance with a horizon. In his essay "Horizontal Grandeur," Minnesota writer Bill Holm distinguishes between two different kinds of human eyes. There's the "eye of mystery, and the eye of harsh truth—the hidden and the open—the woods eye and the prairie eye." Holm, a native of Minnesota's tall-grass prairie, admitted to feeling claustrophobic in the north woods: "too damn many trees." He might allow me to propose a third eye, one that rests on open water and is satisfied. Holm claims for the prairie "magnitude and delicacy," and I would also claim this for Lake Superior. Magnitude, for sure, and delicacy not in the hidden beauty of prairie flowers but in the subtle shift of light on water, breaking into myriad blues and violets, or glinting back from surface to sun, a million tiny stars. No instant gratification here. We might think we know this lover, but time and again we are proven wrong. After thirty years, we still can't predict its weather.

That first visit to our cabin, on my thirty-sixth birthday, I wandered about inside the place we had bought, trying out the views. From the window overlooking the yard, sunshine streamed in; next to it was a view to the west, overlooking the ravine. We had a regal view of young spruce and older birch. From the kitchen, looking north, I could see the far shore; looking east, a big balsam fir with a Ruby-crowned Kinglet flitting through the branches. The fit was right all over. "I'm in love with this place," I said to myself. "It is the place for us."

RED CLAY CLIFF, SANDY BEACH

As we settled into what we hoped would be idyllic summers on Lake Superior, we soon found out that impermanence was built into the big lake's relationship with its southern shore. Impermanence, of course, is part of life. Nothing lasts forever. When one is young, one tries to minimize that fact, but Superior reinforced it in a way that commanded our attention.

As our first several summers unfolded, we discovered that we did indeed have a sandy beach, but from visit to visit we never knew what it would look like. Sometimes it was broad and open, a *Chariots of Fire* beach in miniature; sometimes it was narrow and hugged the cliff, studded with cobbles. Some years, the waves would push the bulk of the sand toward our western property line, too far away to lug sand chairs and small children, and sometimes most of the sand would land near the mouth of the creek, close to the beach path.

The sand moved beneath several feet of water under the force of the waves, roughly parallel to the shore. These movements were most pronounced during late-fall storms that we were likely not to witness. Ice piling up on the shore in winter could also shift sand. We just couldn't predict anything. Each May, when our minivan pulled up to the cabin for the opening weekend, we would rush down the path to see what Superior had given us. This was so foreign to our experience on the lake's North Shore.

Underneath the seasonal shifting of the beach was a daily rear-ranging. A summer thunderstorm with momentary fierce winds from the northeast could give us an extra foot here or retract a foot there. We learned to accommodate the constant relandscaping.

In fact, Lake Superior's currents had more influence on our lake life than we ever knew. The fact that the lake's water generally circulates counterclockwise is not commonly known among most people. But National Oceanic and Atmospheric Administration scientists have monitored currents long term and discovered they change patterns seasonally. In the fall (think November) they run swiftly, swirling from the north shore around St. Louis Bay at Duluth, then northeast along our shoreline, through the Apostle Islands, and into Chequamegon Bay. Through the languid summer months, the currents slow down and flow clockwise along our shore, northeast to southwest. If we could radio-tag a single grain of sand from our shore, it might well turn up on the beach at Park Point in Duluth, wedged between little Piping Plover toes. But then again, it might head up to Meyer's Beach and be picked up by kayakers' water shoes as they launch to paddle to the sea caves. The process is called "littoral drift," and it plays a role, often major, in forming sandbars and spits like Park Point.

Meanwhile, on the far eastern half of the big lake, there is a separate cell with a current running along the eastern shore of the Keweenaw Peninsula that also changes from month to month. I tend to think of Lake Superior in the same way I think of smaller inland lakes, only bigger, but the dynamics of the immense inland sea are different and more dramatic.

A more unsettling reconstruction of the landscape involved the red clay cliff that fronted our property everywhere but the mouth of the creek. The red clay proved a nuisance, leaving its indelible presence everywhere. I quickly learned, as a mother of four young children, that it could not be washed out of T-shirts and swimsuits. Everything that it came in contact with it—beach towels, diapers, sweatshirts, shorts—carried a signature pinkish stain.

As the clay eroded from the bluff, it stained the water a terra-cotta, with the turbidity of a rosy latte. If you swam in it, which we tried, the tiny particles infiltrated hair, skin, fabrics. The plumes of runoff from the cliffs and from rivers, like the Nemadji and the Brule, that cut through red clay on their way to the lake, are so extensive that they appear on satellite photos as earthy red stains marring a deep-blue lake.

You would think such pollution would deter us, but not always. Even today, immediately after storms, when runoff is particularly intense and waves whip the latte into frothy towers, we still venture out in the murk to bodysurf in old swimsuits, deeming the trade-off worth it to experience the thrill of crashing waves.

We had been told the cliff was eroding at a rate of about a foot a year, sometimes more, sometimes less. That can't be true, we had arrogantly thought, as erosion is a transitional process, and at some point, the cliff would reach equilibrium, the so-called angle of repose. Our error turned out to be twofold.

THE SOUTH SHORE'S EROSION is a geological story. Lake Superior's bed is volcanic in origin. About a billion years ago a rift opened where the lake is now, and molten rock from the Earth's interior spewed forth and cooled, forming igneous rocks like basalt and granite. These rocks can be seen on Superior's north shore and form the lake's edge. Rocks originating from the rift also appear on the Keweenaw Peninsula and farther into the Upper Peninsula of Michigan. These contain copper and iron deposits, as they do in Minnesota.

Fast-forward now, through a billion years, to the (relatively recent) Ice Age of only thousands of years ago. During the most recent glaciation, the ice mass crept southwest, following the rift valley that preceded Superior. When it receded, meltwater pooled at its melting edge, forming Glacial Lake Duluth. Sediment that had been ground up and carried by the glacier settled in that lake as the meltwater ran off. Some of the sediment was very finely ground, exceptionally small particles—clay, in fact. The glacier had also picked up iron deposits, grinding them, too, so the clay had a red color. When the big glacial lake finally drained through an outlet on its eastern end, it assumed the familiar shape of present-day Lake Superior.

Our red clay cliffs are the revealed lake bed of Glacial Lake Duluth, and the lake is slowly reclaiming its past as it eats into the cliffs with each lick of a wave.

While it is true that erosion should eventually come to rest when the cliff assumes an angle of equilibrium to the shoreline, that point is never reached if waves keep chewing at the base of the cliff, quaintly called the "toe." The cliff toe continually loses material, so the angle of cliff to beach remains acute. Obviously, the rate of erosion is affected by the level of the lake. If the lake is high, water continuously laps at the cliff toe; if low, there is a strip of sand that protects it. As I write this, Lake Superior is at record highs, and the erosion of our cliff has been shocking, as much as fourteen feet last year.

Undoubtedly, the level of Lake Superior hastens the demise of our cliff. Lake level is complex, and many factors contribute to it. It helps to think about the lake in terms of input and outflow. Precipitation (rain and snow) amounts oscillate over five to ten years, and presently they are at a high point. Climate change likely plays a role in the recent "deluge" storms that have contributed to the lake level. On the other hand, climate change also has affected ice-over in winter. Less ice means a greater evaporation from the exposed surface. That is an "outflow." Lake Superior's water level is also controlled, at least somewhat, at the locks at Sault Ste. Marie, Michigan, where the lake empties into the St. Marys River.

Another factor raising the lake level is more subtle: isostatic rebound. During the Ice Age, the weight of the ice, which was sometimes a mile or more thick, depressed the Earth's crust into the moderately malleable upper mantle. It, in turn, moved under the pressure—think of pressing down on a marshmallow. Following the retreat of the ice, the Earth's crust is gradually recovering to reclaim its form. In other words, the land is rising, and it is rising faster on the north and east side of Lake Superior than it is on the south shore—so, like a tilting bathtub, the south shore is sinking, seeing a measurable rise in lake level, about a foot a century. So even if Superior's level was not up due to increased precipitation, south shore lake levels would still be rising because of rebound. Truth be told, the level of the lake is not a simple story, and even the experts don't fully understand it.

ALTHOUGH IT IS LIKELY that clear-cutting of the pine forests that once grew on the South Shore hastened the erosion of the red clay, at least in some areas, clear-cutting is not the fundamental cause of it. The process of erosion is built into the geography. Lake Superior is getting naturally wider year by year.

It has been heartbreaking to witness this widening. When we first took ownership of the cabin, the lake was at a low point in the meteorological cycle, and we didn't think much about it. We first took notice when a particular old pine, one with craggy branches and a commanding crown, became threatened. It was near the cliff's edge, about two hundred yards west of the creek, and Bald Eagles maintained an impressive nest in its boughs.

We watched the nest for years and became intimate with the domestic life of Bald Eagles. Through binoculars, we spied on the parents sitting on first eggs and then nestlings. We knew that a couple of the angular branches were favorite perches for the female. We watched one mate fly in to feed the other, clutching a hapless herring in its talons.

Then the nestlings grew louder, and we could hear them beg for food early in the morning, all day, and into the evening. We commiserated with their first clumsy efforts to fly, coming in for graceless landings atop an aspen tree. Sometimes they would miss altogether and circle around for another try; other times, they would grasp the branch with one talon and not the other, teetering precariously, powerful wings flapping.

Through several years, the cliff lost material, exposing major roots of the pine. The tree began to tilt, ever so slightly. When the tilt was still subtle, the eagles abandoned the nest that they had used for a decade and moved fifty feet away to a mature aspen tree. The birds still rested in the pine's boughs but apparently deemed it not appropriate for eaglets.

The denouement was leisurely. The mature pine slowly made its way down the cliff over a period of two years. Then it leaned briefly on the sand over the water, and at some point when we weren't there, it toppled into Superior, where it remains today.

I had regarded that tree as a friend, so the lake's claim on it seemed violent. Last year, we lost another "friend" to erosion, the stately white spruce that shaded our picnic table during August lunches by the lake. We looked out on the spruce every time we glanced out a window toward the lake. Since it tumbled last winter, our view to the north has been shockingly exposed. My heart sinks when I see how much closer to the lake the cabin is than when we first bought it, thirty years ago. Tom assures me that we have eighty-eight feet remaining, more than Lake Superior will eat away in our lifetimes. That isn't consoling. We can no longer play horseshoes in our front yard.

Long ago, our neighbors to the west sought to shore up their cliff using material to stabilize the bluff and mitigate the impact of the waves at the toe. They called in heavy equipment to reduce the angle of the bluff—their bluff was perhaps ten to twenty feet lower than ours—and they planted grasses to stabilize the clay. They also hired a dump truck to deposit sizable boulders, rolling these rocks atop a tough type of cloth that has not deteriorated in twenty years.

However, the cliff has. Over time, we have watched as clay on the upper part of the cliff periodically detaches and begins its slide into Superior. The cloth, firmly anchored by the deposited boulders, ripples in the water several feet from the beach. It will never disintegrate.

I view the scene of our neighbor's beach with an unpleasant sense of schadenfreude. Superficially, I am disappointed that it didn't work because we could then go and do likewise. But I am also (nastily) pleased because it somehow justifies our inaction in addressing the problem. Beyond that, I am distressed that the erosion seems unconquerable, and I am also sickened that the shifting sand beach of Lake Superior's South Shore has, in this small stretch, been marred permanently by a family's short-term efforts.

COASTAL EROSION, of course, is a much bigger problem than what summer cabins are experiencing on Superior's South Shore. Wisconsin, in fact, faces coastal erosion on two fronts, to its north, with Lake Superior, and to its east, with Lake Michigan. Although Lake Michigan's erosion issues are chiefly related to sand and glacial till, not clay, the process and its possible fixes are the same. Recently, a college north of Milwaukee undertook a massive project to save its campus from erosion.

Concordia University sits on 192 acres of land along the western shore of Lake Michigan. The bluff fronting the lake is nearly 130 feet high and eroded rapidly in the two decades between 1982 and 2005. The college estimated that it lost twenty thousand tons of sediment each year, or about five acres of land, in that time period. As the bluff edge inched ever closer to its campus, officials decided to act.

Consulting with the U.S. Army Corps of Engineers and the Wisconsin Department of Natural Resources, Concordia hired an engineering firm and launched a campaign to stabilize the bluff. The project was multipronged. Engineers laid nearly a half mile of drains designed to collect water and stabilize soils atop the bluff. They built artificial wetlands along the coast and atop to act as sponges. They bulldozed the bluff, reducing the angle to one deemed stable, planted vegetation on exposed surfaces, and most significantly, perhaps, laid down one hundred thousand tons of stone along the half mile of shoreline to protect the bluff toe.

It was a twelve-million-dollar project, evolving over eight years of planning, funding, and execution. When launched, it received national and international attention and was named one of the top five finalists in the Outstanding Civil Engineering Achievement (OCEA) competition of 2010.

Was the massive project successful? It depends on whom you ask. Concordia University is pleased. The engineers significantly slowed the rate of erosion of the bluff, not to zero but sufficiently that the college no longer feels it will end up in Lake Michigan.

But the project had unintended consequences. The line of rocks laid parallel to the shore blocked the natural movement of sand that "nourished" the beach. Starved of material, the beach has quickly disappeared. The neighbors directly south of the campus have lost the sand beach they once enjoyed. The lake now laps directly at the toe of their bluff, and erosion is accelerating. One neighbor fears for her house. Property owners predicted this would happen, but the agencies that permitted the project apparently did not foresee this amount of damage. The neighbors brought a lawsuit against Concordia, and in 2014, a jury found the wall, termed a "revetment," to be a nuisance but declined to award damages, since the college was deemed not to be negligent.

Seven years after the completion of Concordia University's project, the effects of the rock wall seem to be moving sequentially down shore in a type of chain reaction. A coastal engineer from the University of Wisconsin, Chin Wu, has weighed in. He believes that several factors play into the erosion, a significant one being the water level of Lake Michigan, at near-record highs. But he and even the lead engineer who designed the wall agree that the revetment has played a major role in accelerating other bluff erosion. Their solution is for property owners to build their own revetments. Wu observes, "You will not see beaches anymore."

When I read about Concordia University's massive project, I realized that any kind of redress to our bluff erosion is beyond our reach. Modest cabin owners do not have the means for an eight-year, twelve-million-dollar fix to their problem. Drains, wetland creation, revetment—these are possible solutions only for the wealthy.

But a larger question remains: who does, in truth, own the beach? Who is responsible for protecting it? In a moral universe, is the beach privately owned or part of a communal trust? What would happen if, as Dr. Chu predicts, beaches disappear? People would lose the solace that water, sand, and wind afford, the wide stretch of horizon that offers the long view, something that is sorely needed these days. I have found that a long view on a beach encourages a long view in my life.

Beach is also habitat for wildlife—access to the water for beavers and mink, to food for migrating shorebirds. Endangered Piping Plovers nest on exactly those kinds of sand beaches that are disappearing north of Milwaukee. The rare little bird with its rounded head and black neckband has responded well to protection under the Endangered Species Act and had a record number of breeding pairs in 2017. If Lake Michigan's west-coast beach disappears, that is habitat lost to a recovering species.

We did not expect to confront the tension between individual property rights and the commons in 1988 when we first stood on the red clay cliff and gazed out over the water. Writ large, like Concordia's effort, or writ small, like our neighbor's, we should all be wrestling with where the line is drawn.

As I age, I find myself in odd harmony with the ever-changing beach and the receding red clay cliff. When I was younger, I was aware in a theoretical way that life was constantly changing. I accepted that, but took comfort that even though I, myself, was temporary, the wider world would remain, for my children and my grandchildren. There would be white pines and chickadees, the Boundary Waters, and the Grand Canyon in all their majesty.

What thinking person really believes that today? In my sixties, I am all too acutely aware of how transient our pleasures are. Technology increases in complexity, and the number of people using it grows exponentially. Global warming casts its pall. I can barely acquiesce to my own death, much less that of our cherished cabin site, much less that of the natural world.

But time at the lake should be sacred time, and so I am intent on making peace with this unsettled existence. I cultivate serenity, looking to the horizon as the sun rises and scanning the water to see what eternity looks like. I gaze across at Minnesota's shore, its distant hills bluish and hazy. It is my native land. It tells me where I've been. It is silent on where I'm going.

PART II

What Was Found and Then Was Lost

THE LINCHPIN

Sault Ste. Marie, Michigan

On a hot, sunny July afternoon, I ease myself into a dapple of shade on Portage Avenue, in downtown Sault Ste. Marie, Michigan. The internationally famous Soo Locks are a few blocks to the west. They are what puts this town of thirteen thousand on the map, and yet I'm thinking more of bedrock than water on this summer day. Across the street is the Palace bar and restaurant, built at the turn of the past century. The Palace is a survivor. It has changed hands several times in the past hundred years, but the beautiful carved mahogany of its bar has survived. It now offers Mexican food and boasts its chili con queso is "world-famous," a big claim. But the face it shines on the city, one of a pale, finely wrought sandstone is arresting, "world-class" in my estimation.

The pale building stone is one example of Jacobsville Sandstone, the bedrock of Sault Ste. Marie. This sandstone layer is the foundational linchpin to Lake Superior. A linchpin by definition is something vital to an enterprise. Geologically, Jacobsville Sandstone controls the outflow of Lake Superior. It is the literal linchpin. But the location along the St. Marys River has been a figurative linchpin to varied human endeavors over time. On a bicycle outing through the streets of present-day Sault Ste. Marie, I ferreted out these past lives of the site.

The Precambrian Rock

As the last glacier retreated north and east, about ten thousand years ago, water pooled from its melting ice, forming several glacial lakes, including a proto–Lake Superior. In the western end of proto-Superior's lake bed, several outlets drained the water, a notable one being the Brule River, which flowed south at the time, into the St. Croix River, rather than north as it does today. At the eastern end of the glacial lake, toward what is now the Sault, the meltwater drained through the channel of the incipient St. Marys River, gradually eroding soft rock layers. When it reached the hard level of Jacobsville Sandstone, erosion and water flow slowed. Released from the heavy weight of glacial ice, the south shore began rebounding in elevation, and Lake Superior gradually assumed the outline familiar to us today.

Initially, Lakes Superior, Huron, and Michigan were at the same elevation, but as the lake bed of proto–Lake Superior rose farther, rapids formed between the two. This was but a short time ago, geologically speaking—only 2,200 years ago. The land to the south of the retreating ice mass continued to rise. The other outlets closed— the Brule River reversed and became a north-flowing river. The St. Marys River was now the sole outlet of the big lake.

Jacobsville Sandstone is the result of an ancient seabed laid down over 400 million years ago, long before the most recent Ice Age. It is a variegated stone, some levels very pale, an ash gray, and others, a deep iron red. Sometimes, the quarried rock reveals the two colors alternating, yielding a gaily striped stone, the result of cross-bedding, where streams flowed one way, laying down one type of sand, and then another, laying down another type, to create the pattern.

Sault Ste. Marie has many fine examples of structures built of this striking stone: churches, civic buildings, the courthouse, and an incredible power plant that yawns across a wide canal running through the city. Much of the stone was excavated from this canal, dug to form a channel to produce hydroelectricity. The excavation was completed by 1902, and most of the buildings went up in that era. Like other Lake Superior cities, including Marquette, Hough-ton, Calumet, Ironwood, and Ashland, the sandstone buildings are silent testimony to bygone glory.

Before parking myself on the bench on Portage Avenue, Tom and I had cycled along the St. Marys River (tradition omits the apostrophe). Recently, frequent heavy downpours have raised the levels of the Great Lakes and that of the St. Marys, too. Nicely kept suburban yards edge the historic river, but high water is creeping onto the lawns. For some, there is little room to retreat. The placid river was blue and broad. I kept reminding myself that every single freighter calling at Duluth, Two Harbors, or Taconite Harbor passes by this rendition of suburbia. Somehow, it seemed too domestic for ore boats.

We followed the road around a bend and encountered a cause-way heading across a channel and on to massive Sugar Island, which divides the river. Largely undeveloped, this land was dis-puted territory between England and the United States, but when the dust settled, it became American soil, part of Michigan. Two Ojibwe tribes, the Bay Mills Community and the Sault Ste. Marie tribe, own the land and exercise treaty rights on the island.

Their ancestors were drawn to the area by a specific resource: whitefish. What, exactly, was the attraction?

The Whitefish

Lake whitefish, *Coregonus clupeaformis,* is the defining species of Lake Superior's fish population. Sleek and silvery with a greenish back and deeply forked tail, whitefish weigh on average four to five pounds and are about a foot and a half long. Distributed from Alaska to Maine and north of Labrador, they are a cool-water fish, eating mainly bottom-dwelling invertebrates like snails and insect larvae. Like their cousins, trout and salmon, they seek highly oxy-genated waters. The air-enriched spray of a swiftly flowing rapids like the St. Marys attracted whitefish by the thousands, which could at one time be seen wriggling in the froth, as the roar of the rushing water filled the air.

The narrowing of Lake Superior as it enters the river, the one outlet, is also a good place for fish to spawn. Whitefish breed from September to November in Lake Superior. Females swim into shallow water to lay their eggs on rubble and gravel. The larvae hatch the following spring, feeding first on plankton and later, as they grow bigger, on adult fare.

So historically, the St. Marys rapids, a place where the whitefish gathered, was also a place where Native Americans gathered. The Ojibwe call it *Bahweting*, "the gathering place."

The Algonquin Allies

The various Algonquin tribes were united by a common language. They inhabited the western Great Lakes region but were pressured to migrate westward when harassed by the Iroquois, who themselves had been forced to assimilate with the arrival of the Europeans.

When the French assumed a presence on Superior's South Shore in the 1600s and developed the fur trade, Algonquin-speaking tribes were living around Mackinac Island, on the Keweenaw Peninsula, in Chequamegon Bay, and near the rapids of the St. Marys River (Sault Ste. Marie). The French termed the latter *Saultiers*, "the Sault dwellers."

Sault Ste. Marie had been an original homesite for the other groups that had dispersed from it. The people that had remained at the Sault "had not been able to resign themselves to leaving their ancient territory," as trader Nicholas Perrot observed in his memoir. Those people and all the diaspora inhabiting the other areas relied heavily on the delicious and abundant whitefish. They termed the fish *adikameg*, and smoked them, or dried them and made a protein-rich powder that they used in soups or stews or mixed with fresh blueberries.

The scattered bands met near the rapids a couple times a year to fish, socialize, and renew friendships and familial bonds. I imagine such gatherings were joyous affairs, full of feasting, laughing, good conversation, music, and dancing.

Early French Jesuit missionaries were eyewitnesses to the feat of landing a five-pound fish into a canoe in the midst of a roiling rapids. Father Claude Dablon wrote in 1660:

> Dexterity and strength are needed for this kind of fishing; for one must stand upright in a bark canoe, and there, among the whirlpools with muscles tense, thrust deep into the water a rod, at the end of which is fastened a net made in the form of a pocket, into which the fish is made to enter. One must look for them as they glide between the rocks, pursue them when they are seen; and, when they have been made to enter the net, raise them with a sudden strong pull into the canoe.

To get a further idea of the skill involved, consider this Jesuit account of the nature of the rapids:

> [The Sault] is not, properly speaking, a descent or fall of water from a considerable height; but it is an exceedingly violent current of the waters of Lake Superior, which being checked by a great number of rocks that dispute their passage, form a dangerous cascade, half a league broad—all those waters, descending and precipitating themselves upon one another, as if on a staircase, over the great rocks that obstruct the river.

Lake Superior's whitefish population plummeted in the latter half of the twentieth century due to overfishing and the introduction of the invasive parasitic sea lamprey. With careful study and protective measures, the population has since rebounded, and the fish is on the menu at Karl's Cuisine, Sault Ste. Marie's wonderful restaurant across from the locks on Portage Avenue. It is served smoked on flatbread, or in a skillet with a lemon-pepper sauce. Somehow, it seems right that Lake Superior whitefish is served with gourmet flair.

The Portage

The Ojibwe living near Lake Superior did not confine themselves to the big lake. They regularly went down the river to Lakes Huron and Michigan and to a large community on "Michilimackinac," or Mackinac Island. A well-trod path ran on the south side of the river from the top of the rapids to the foot, both ends within today's city limits. This circumvention of the rapids, a "portage," became a fixture for travel, used by natives, explorers, missionaries, and traders. John Johnston, an early fur trader, reckoned the St. Marys portage as half a mile long. Visitor Charles Whittlesley described it in his journal as "a flat, wet, marshy piece of land, about three-quarters of a mile across."

The Jesuit Missionaries

The exploration of Lake Superior by the French went hand in glove with the arrival of men of the cloth, intent on converting the Native peoples to Christianity. Initially, the fathers had been invited by Samuel de Champlain, who founded Quebec in the early 1600s. Most missionary work was carried out by the Society of Jesus, known as Jesuits, who stressed living lives of chastity and poverty and were well educated. Indeed, twenty years after the order's founding in 1534, the society was operating seventy-four colleges on three continents. The Jesuits emphasized the mastery of language, and one mark of their efforts was that of highlighting Native American languages.

The first missionary to arrive at the rapids of the St. Marys River was Father Jacques Marquette. A tough outdoorsman, fluent in six different Algonquin dialects, Marquette established a small mission on the south bank of the St. Marys River in 1668, just below the rapids and adjacent to the Saultier settlement. It consisted of a chapel and a hut for his dwelling, surrounded by a twelve-foot-high stockade. Marquette was replaced the next year by Father Claude Dablon, the priest who observed and recorded the fishing technique of the Saultiers. The mission gave the French a toehold in the Lake Superior region. Michiganders today recognize Sault Ste. Marie as the site of the first European settlement in their state.

The mission was three years old when Sault Ste. Marie hosted a gaudy pageant to flaunt the French claim to the entire interior of North America. Seventeen Native tribes attended the show, dressed in festive clothes, and all the priests from the missionary, garbed in black. Because of his fluency in languages, Father Claude Jean Allouez, who had lived at Chequamegon Bay with the Ojibwe, served as the principal speaker. (Father Allouez was despondent over his lack of success in converting the residents of Chequamegon Bay, but to his credit, he produced a very accurate map of Lake Superior sometime after 1668, after traveling around the region from 1667 until 1669.)

Daniel Greysolon, Sieur du Lhut, spent the winter of 1678–79 in Sault Ste. Marie, as he prepared to travel west to broker peace deals with tribes that were in conflict. His chief objective was to secure peace so that the French could conduct their lucrative fur trade with the Ojibwe unimpeded. Sometime after that, the mission closed, and Jesuit activity ceased for a time.

The Voyageurs

Although the missionaries were unsuccessful in converting the Ojibwe to Christianity, the French succeeded in creating a lucrative trade with the Lake Superior bands to exchange furs for durable goods, especially items like blankets, cooking pots, and guns. French traders established posts at various points around the lake. Historian Grace Lee Nute claimed that there was a post on nearly every cove or river outlet on the lake. The most significant was a large post on the northern shore at Fort Kaministiquia (later Fort William).

A hardy class of men, voyageurs were responsible for transporting the goods in and out of Lake Superior. There were voyageurs on all the Great Lakes, but they were iconic to Superior. Notoriously easy-going, hard-working, and ready with a song, voyageurs were skilled and strong paddlers, carrying double packs of ninety pounds each on a portage, sometimes at a trot, since time was money, then as now.

As the voyageurs packed furs out to Montreal for shipping to France, Sault Ste. Marie became an economic linchpin. Canoes laden with furs were taken over the rapids by the skilled paddlers. Or in low water levels, if the rapids were deemed too risky to shoot, the canoes were unloaded, furs trundled over the portage to the foot of the rapids, and reloaded into other canoes to be sent downriver. The French built huge, thirty-foot canoes, termed "Montreals," to paddle across the big lake and down various rivers to the St. Lawrence and on to Montreal. They held four tons of cargo and were manned by up to fourteen paddlers. Montreal canoes were troublesome to portage, and the voyageurs avoided doing so when possible.

In 1789, British trader and chronicler Alexander Mackenzie came through the Sault and recorded thirty Ojibwe families living near the rapids, and ten to twelve French Canadian voyageur families, often consisting of voyageurs who had married Ojibwe women and settled in the town. When they grew too old for the rough life of a voyageur, the men sometimes settled in Montreal, but long accustomed to an unfettered life, they often chose frontier settlements like the Sault.

The Johnstons

British fur traders were also working in the Lake Superior region. One of these, John Johnston, an Irishman, arrived in 1791 and spent the winter at La Pointe, Madeline Island—after being deserted by his voyageurs. Johnston was well liked by many of the Ojibwe living in the large community, particularly the chief, Waubojeeg, as Johnston had mediated a dispute for Waubojeeg's father. In his time spent there, Johnston, then age thirty, fell in love with the chief's teenage daughter. He wanted to marry her, but Waubojeeg, having seen European traders abandon their Native wives, was skeptical. He knew Johnson would spend the coming winter in Montreal— if he wished to marry upon his return, the chief would grant his permission.

For her part, the daughter, Ozhahguscodaywayquay, was also less than thrilled. When Johnson reappeared the next spring, still interested in marriage, she was forced into the union but ran away within days of the ceremony. Her father brought her back, and eventually the couple settled in Sault Ste. Marie.

From a rocky start began a dynasty with historical implications. The marriage proved a loving and productive one in several ways. The Johnstons were a prominent family in town. Living in a spacious house located near the river, they were known for their hospitality. Visitors to the Soo raved in their journals about the fine wines that were served, and the expertly prepared specialty of the house, beaver tail, with Ozhahguscodaywayquay and her daughters presiding in the kitchen. Johnston was still a British citizen when the border between the United States and the British colony of Canada was established. Hence, in the War of 1812, he found himself on the wrong side, both literally and figuratively. He took part in the capture of the American fort at Mackinac Island in that war; in retaliation, the Americans burned down his fine house, forcing Ozhahguscodaywayquay with her children—there were by that time, six or seven in number—to flee into the woods. (The house was rebuilt.)

AFTER THE WAR OF 1812, when Michigan's territorial governor Lewis Cass appeared with a retinue and declared the U.S. Army would place a fort on the most strategic spot—the Indian burial grounds—it is widely thought that it was Ozhahguscodaywayquay who stepped in and negotiated an acceptable compromise, avoiding bloodshed. Cass later gave credit to her.

It was inevitable that the gracious Johnstons hosted a young Indian agent sent from Detroit to the Sault in 1822. It was fortuitous that the young Henry Schoolcraft, scholarly and intensely interested in Ojibwe culture, would be taken in by this family bridging two worlds. And it was perhaps fated that he would fall in love with their oldest daughter, Jane. The eight Johnston children were trilingual (in English, Ojibwe, and French), taught Ojibwe ways by their mother, and educated in Montreal. Jane, also known as Bamewawagezhikaquay, was a poet (as was her grandfather Waubojeeg) and today is considered the first woman Native American literary writer.

In the 1820s, the military community was the social determinant of Sault Ste. Marie, and during the long snowy winters when the river froze and the town was cut off from the rest of Michigan, society balls were the chief means of entertainment. Schoolcraft had zero interest in balls and instead launched a modest handwritten publication, *The Literary Voyageur,* issued bimonthly. He and Jane collaborated on content, and he frequently published her poetry. In one issue, he interviewed his mother-in-law as a source of Ojibwe history; in others, he wrote on folklore and biographies of tribal leaders. John Johnston is also thought to have contributed, under a pseudonym.

The Literary Voyageur ran only sixteen issues, one winter's worth, from December 1826 until April 1827. The Schoolcrafts lost a young son to croup in March 1827, a tragedy that devastated the parents. Though of short duration and narrow circulation, issues of *The Literary Voyageur* did eventually find their way to Detroit and New York, and Schoolcraft would build on its writings in producing his later work on Ojibwe culture.

Most of the large Johnston clan remained in the Sault Ste. Marie area. The men became fur traders; one, William, established himself at Red Lake in Minnesota. Another, John McDouall, became a U.S. Indian commissioner. Because of their command of three crucial languages, the Johnstons were linchpins in brokering agreements. Their mother, the resourceful Ozhahguscodaywayquay, became a widow in 1828. She continued to run the family fur trade business with her son, as well as a maple sugar operation on nearby Sugar Island, land that she received under the 1826 Treaty of Fond du Lac.

TIME IS LAYERED in Sault Ste. Marie. There are so many different past lives lived there to meditate on: the Ojibwe settlement, the Jesuit mission, the Johnstons and Schoolcrafts. An active historical society maintains informational kiosks around town. Traveling by bicycle, Tom and I stopped for every sign, and on Water Street—nearest the river—we came upon three houses. The Johnstons' white frame house, at least part of it, was one of them. The other two, Elmwood (Henry and Jane Schoolcraft's house) and Father Baraga's home, had been moved onto the site, but the Johnston house stands where they built it—and rebuilt it after the American torching.

We had planned to arrive at the Johnston house at noon. The historical society's website claimed it would be open then. But this was summer 2020, the year of the pandemic, and nothing could be relied on. We peered into the windows—it was apparent that we would gain nothing from a tour. The house is much reduced from when the family lived there, but it is one story, perhaps with sleeping areas under the eaves. A sign informed us that what remains was built in 1822 to house the newly wed Schoolcrafts until they moved into Elmwood. 1822! The only human-built structure anywhere near that old in Minnesota is the round tower at Fort Snelling.

Commercial Fishing

As an extractive economy developed on Lake Superior, business owners employed bigger and bigger boats to carry goods to market. The first schooners, boats with sails, were used during the fur trade.

These boats were sometimes designed below the Sault, then taken in pieces over the portage and reassembled on the lakeshore. The *John Jacob Astor,* the first American schooner on Lake Superior, was launched in 1835 in that manner.

The *John Jacob Astor* had great capacity just at a time when furs were dwindling in number. The American Fur Company, for whom John Johnston had been the agent in 1816 or 1817, reorganized a year before the launching of the *Astor.* The schooner's greater cargo capacity allowed the company to transition to commercial fishing. The American Fur Company established commercial fishing posts first on Isle Royale, then at La Pointe on Madeline Island, which became the hub of the company's fishing operation, and also at L'Anse, Grand Island, and Whitefish Point. Fish were netted, salted, packed in barrels, and sold in Detroit. The abundance of Superior's fish and the efficiency with which the company plucked them from the waters created a glut, and attempts to broaden the market failed. Commercial fishing ended in the 1840s, temporarily, amid a national economic depression.

There were consequences to this capitalistic venture. George Catlin, the artist, passed through the Sault in the 1830s and reported "money making men" dominating the fertile rapids. White commercial fishermen directly competed with the Ojibwe for a limited resource, and the rapids would be disputed territory for decades.

Copper

Nautical activity on Lake Superior grew in lockstep with the exploration for and discovery of copper ore on the Keweenaw Peninsula. Some boats were being built at a shipyard on Lake Superior's shores. Across the St. Marys in Canada is a peninsula, Pointe aux Pins, known historically for its virgin red and white pines. These tall trees were ideal for shipbuilding, and the region's first yard was sited there in 1727. It produced its first vessel in 1735, and the three fur trading companies, the North West Company, the Hudson's Bay

Company, and the American Fur Company, all specified boats out of the Pointe aux Pins shipyard. Other boats were designed and built on the lower Great Lakes, as in Cleveland, and then hauled over the portage on rollers, a laborious undertaking.

The growth of copper mining on the Keweenaw strained the limits of portaging. The heavy ore, in canisters, was off-loaded above the rapids and transported through downtown Sault Ste. Marie on a wooden track, in carts pulled by horses. The ore was then reloaded on a different boat below the rapids. The original portage made by the Ojibwe and followed by voyageurs had become an industrial track, now called "Portage Avenue."

There had been talk of a canal and lock system that could transport boats around the rapids, cargo intact. Such a system would be costly but far more efficient. In 1797, the North West Company built a lock big enough to accommodate a Montreal canoe on the Canadian side of the river. The lock functioned to lift only the upbound canoes. Downbound canoes had to shoot the rapids. A marauding American unit destroyed the lock in the War of 1812. The state of Michigan made another attempt in 1837, but it never materialized, since the lock crossed federally owned land, and U.S. soldiers prevented its building.

But in 1855, a scant decade after the discovery of profitable ore on the Keweenaw, two 350-foot locks had been opened, and ships were free to travel up the lake and down with ease. The linchpin, the historic barrier, had been permanently breached.

As I sit admiring the Jacobsville Sandstone of the Palace Bar, I am acutely aware of the tourist activity off to my left, on the western end of Portage Avenue. Amid learning the area's history, I had forgotten that the "Soo" is a modern tourist attraction, replete with fudge and curio shops. We weren't sure how many tourists this little out-of-the-way burg would draw in a pandemic—and Sault Ste. Marie, Michigan, this summer is a destination unto itself, since the Canadian border is closed to Americans. I am sad about this.

It means Pointe aux Pins is off-limits. The tourists cluster around the entrance to the observation platforms for the locks, going through security, anticipating the arrival of a freighter.

But even with all the bustle in town, the air is oddly quiet. That is, I think, because the chief attraction, the massive Soo Locks, conducts a silent operation. There's no drone of a motor, clunks and clanks of moving parts. It's run by the U.S. Army Corps of Engineers, and they are brisk and perfunctory. This is not a Disney show. This is the linchpin. There is work to be done.

COPPER, PART I

The Abundance

It was the purest, most bountiful copper the world had ever known. Protruding from rock ledges, emerging from rivers, even lying on the ground. The story of Lake Superior's copper is so big, it seems to have more than one beginning.

We could start at the metal's beginning and tell how the conditions on the Earth laid down vast deposits of pure, unalloyed copper. In this beginning, elemental copper originated in what is now the basin of Lake Superior. A rift formed in the Earth's crust, and the continent cleaved. This occurred about 1.1 billion years ago, the rift known today as the Midcontinent, or Keweenawan, Rift. Magma beneath the Earth's crust welled up and spilled over numerous times as lava flows, creating what today are basaltic rocks.

There were cracks in these rocks—fissures and gas cavities. Hot water from deep in the Earth rose, with copper and silver dissolved in it. This water permeated the fissures, and when it cooled, the metals came out of solution and in pure form remained in the cracks. Metal could also come out in the gas bubbles, forming little pockets of ore. The copper-rich water permeated a layer of mixed rock types, a conglomerate, that had settled atop the basalt, and left copper deposits there, too. Several different types of copper deposits remained when the Earth settled down.

The basalt was heavy and began to sink. At the same time, tectonic forces east and west put pressure on the rift area, and the layers sagged in the middle, so that they resembled stacked bowls, what geologists call a *syncline*. The lip of the eastern edge became the rock ridge of the Keweenaw Peninsula; the western lip, Isle Royale. The rocks of the two formations, separated today by the waters of Lake Superior, have an affinity.

This is one beginning, but is it really a story if we lack a storyteller? Or, for that matter, a listener?

For that, we need people. So here is another beginning: human beings native to the Lake Superior area discovered on Isle Royale, that large island of the big lake, a metal they could manipulate. It is hard enough to bear stress and be put to work. It is soft enough to be malleable with a stone hammer. It was found in workable amounts in long, narrow deposits, fissures, up and down the island. With their hands and with stone tools, they dug pits and extracted the metal.

They dug many shallow pits. Their mining left traces that are detectable even today. In McCargoe Cove, a narrow bay on the northwestern edge of the island, archaeologists have discovered elevated levels of lead and copper in the sediment, remnants of widespread mining activity dating to approximately six thousand years ago. Even this limited wresting of metal from the Earth created a pollution that has lingered in the water for thousands of years.

We don't know much about these early miners—who they were, who their descendants were. They do not seem to be connected to the Ojibwe or the Cree. One early geologist termed them "the ancients."

The ancients worked the copper to fashion items that made their lives easier: functional fish hooks; effective spear tips to penetrate a caribou's hide. They used the copper to their advantage in trade with people on the Pacific Coast. Aztecs in Mexico had Lake Superior copper. But there's more to the copper story than functionality, and so the beginning that truly opens the story is one that began with a big, pure hunk of copper in the middle of a river, and a man who thought: "I could make money off that."

WHEN EUROPEANS first arrived in the Lake Superior region, they had already heard stories of an immense chunk of copper in what would be called the Ontonagon River. Situated thirty miles from the river's mouth, the boulder was on fur trader Alexander Henry's must-see list in 1766. The ancients who had mined pure copper had disappeared, and the Native people in the vicinity were the Ojibwe.

The Ojibwe did not mine, but they considered the metal sacred and kept sizable chunks in their possession, which they wrapped and handed down through generations. They were protective of the resource, sometimes refusing to guide outsiders to the sacred boulder in the Ontonagon River.

Alexander Henry located the boulder, chiseled off a hundred-pound piece and departed. He later returned and attempted to mine the pure copper in the Ontonagon area, but his effort fizzled.

Fifty years later, Michigan was poised to become a territory of the United States, and a group of Americans visited the boulder. Their names would echo in other ways through Lake Superior history: Lewis Cass, Michigan Territory's governor; Henry Rowe Schoolcraft, the Indian agent at Mackinac Island, who had married a well-connected Ojibwe woman; and Douglass Houghton, a trained M.D. with more interest in geology than medicine. Their party was on official government business, and they noted that "an unknown quantity" of copper had already been chiseled off the boulder. They took a portion themselves. The Americans pondered how to take the entire boulder, but it was too big and heavy. They tried but succeeded in moving it only a few feet. That it might belong to the Ojibwe apparently did not cross their minds.

Ownership of the boulder was transferred to the United States in the Treaty of La Pointe, which was extracted from the Ojibwe by the Americans on Madeline Island and went into effect in 1843. It was a monumental land grab, extending from present-day Marquette,

Michigan, to Duluth, Minnesota, and including the copper and iron
ranges of the Upper Peninsula. A successive number of claims on
the boulder by white men ensued, and not all involved selling the
copper, which wasn't nearly as prized as gold or silver. One character thought he could put the big hunk on display and sell tickets,
à la Barnum and Bailey. In the end, the Ontonagon boulder was
transferred by improvised rail, raft, schooner, and cutter through
the Erie Canal and down the coast to Washington, D.C. Today it is
housed at the Smithsonian National Museum of Natural History.
There are various estimates of its weight, in its diminished dimensions, but it is generally agreed to weigh around 3,708 pounds.

The excitement and strife over the Ontonagon Boulder introduced a new factor into the story of Keweenawan copper: money.
After the boulder departed to be viewed by the wider world, investors began in earnest to secure the riches of the copper deposits.
Whether one labels their efforts as industrious or greedy, the driver
was capitalism, and the first major copper boom in the United
States commenced.

DOUGLASS HOUGHTON was appointed Michigan's state geologist in
1837 at the age of twenty-eight. He had arrived in Detroit intend-
ing to deliver lectures on various topics—he had a geology degree
and had also trained in medicine. He was a small man, only five
feet, four inches, but with a formidable intellect and boundless
energy. People tended to underestimate him but not for long. He
had accompanied Henry Schoolcraft on the expedition to the head-
waters of the Mississippi River, and the experience had given him
an affinity for the wilderness.

It was not until 1840 that Houghton led a survey crew to the
South Shore of Lake Superior. They embarked June 1 from Sault
Ste. Marie, which was then and still is the gateway to the great lake,
and spent the first month rowing along the shore, remarking on the
sudden changes in weather, the icy water, and the abundance of
fish. One day, they caught more than fifty trout per hour.

On July 3, the survey entered the inlet that would become Copper Harbor, a perfect natural harbor at the northern head of the Keweenaw Peninsula, and within hours, Houghton came upon a vein of copper that had potential to be commercially profitable. The next day, he blasted the vein and produced perhaps one ton of pure copper ore. This confirmed the rumors that there was mining opportunity in Michigan's remote northern reaches.

Later that summer, the survey reached Madeline Island, which was included in Michigan Territory. The heart of the Lake Superior Ojibwe was centered on Madeline, in the community of La Pointe. In 1840, there was a sizable white population also, employed by the American Fur Company, which headquartered a commercial fishing operation there.

Houghton had heard tales of ancient copper mines on Isle Royale and hopped a schooner bound for the distant island. The American Fur Company maintained a fishing post on Isle Royale, and it lent Houghton a boat to circumnavigate the island. Ever the close observer, Houghton noted the striking similarity between Isle Royale's rocky ridge and that of the Keweenaw Peninsula.

Houghton informed the state legislature of his discovery of copper in Michigan's remote north. The ore was nearly impossible to reach by land because of the rugged terrain and thick vegetation and an arduous journey via water. He cautioned against "unfounded expectations" and "wild schemes with a view to gain sudden wealth."

The report was filed in February 1841. In 1842, the Ojibwe were forced to part with their land; the treaty was announced in March 1843, and by June 20 prospectors entered Copper Harbor, eager to become rich.

ALTHOUGH INITIAL MINING SHAFTS were sunk around Copper Harbor, where Houghton had first identified ore-bearing veins, lasting success came farther west, at Eagle River. The precise discovery of the lode is disputed, but in late 1844 or 1845, speculators found a vein atop the two-hundred-foot cliff rising above a branch of the Eagle River. The vein was narrow, two inches, but farther down the cliff, it widened to two feet. A shaft was sunk, and an adit—a horizontal tunnel off the shaft—was driven into the cliff. Seventy feet in, the adit encountered a mass of pure copper, the first deposit found on the Keweenaw. Other boulders of pure copper, like the Ontonagon boulder, had been carried to their position by glaciers, but this Eagle River copper was in place where it had formed. It gave an early inkling of the wealth to be uncovered.

Pure copper ore is very rare and does not need much processing. Miners exploded the rock surrounding the masses, then using sledge and chisel, broke them into smaller pieces, each weighing a couple pounds. They separated it from the pure silver that also occurred in the vein and packed the copper into barrels to ship. Pure copper is also called "native copper," and journalist Horace Greeley described it as it lay around the mine opening in "great piles of shining Native Metal." The year that Greeley visited, 1847, the Cliff mine at Eagle River shipped one and a half million pounds of copper.

The investors in the prosperous Cliff mine had Pittsburgh and Quaker connections. The miners were from Cornwall, England, with generations of experience in copper mining. Yet even they had never seen the pure copper masses encountered in the Keweenaw mines. Cornish and Welsh copper magnates in England (Wales was world-famous for its smelting capabilities) did not believe the American claims and were uncooperative when Cliff mine owners visited, hoping to study English methods. The Cliff mine owners were anxious to find a solution to the problem of dealing with the huge masses. Their chief smelter, the Revere Copper Works in Boston, couldn't handle the masses coming out of Copper Harbor.

To counter English skepticism, the Cliff mine owners sent a four-thousand-pound copper mass to Liverpool to display. It excited comment in local newspapers, readers were urged to go see it, and the charge of "Yankee invention" was dispelled.

The town of Eagle River quickly expanded. Miners, particularly from Cornwall, flooded the Keweenaw, bringing with them expertise in copper and tin mining; their social structure, which centered around mining; and their affinity for the pasty, a self-contained pastry pocket filled with meat and vegetables that provided lunch during a day spent in the mine.

Log houses sprung up, mining structures also, including in 1851 a five-story engine house that sheltered the newly designed engine that drove thirty-six stamp heads, crushing copper ore and readying it to be shipped. In 1852, when an arsonist torched this structure, mining officials estimated that three hundred tons of copper awaited shipment out of town.

The Cliff was the predominant mine in the area. The Minesota mine of Ontonagon was second: in 1850, the Cliff produced 1,082 tons of copper; the Minesota, 257 tons. (And yes, the name of the mine was actually Minesota.) Another early mass mine, the Copper Falls, to the east of Eagle River, shipped out of Eagle Harbor, a natural inlet offering protection from the big lake. The Central mine, another mass mine, began operations later but, like the Copper Falls mine, eventually petered out.

All these mines shipped their ore out via the lake; there was no connecting railroad to such a remote area. Superior's outlet to the wider world involved the St. Marys rapids at Sault Ste. Marie, a twenty-foot drop to Lake Huron. These rapids had not hindered the previous fur trade and its thirty-to-forty-foot Montreal canoes. For the voyageurs, the rapids posed just one more portage to traverse.

But the presence of the rapids posed an impediment when Douglass Houghton came through in 1840. There were few boats and no steamships on Lake Superior. Notable boats were the *John Jacob Astor*, owned by the American Fur Company, and the *Algonquin*, a competitor, owned by the Cleveland North West Lake Company. Boats bearing copper ore somehow had to unload. The ore was transported through downtown Sault Ste. Marie on horse-powered tracks to bypass the rapids. It was then loaded on a different vessel.

Early Michiganders had spoken hopefully about a canal to circumvent the falls. Houghton, in fact, had opined that such a canal was feasible, but it was not until big industry—the booming copper mines and iron mines at Marquette—demanded it that a canal was seriously considered.

In 1852, Congress offered a land grant to builders of a canal. The following year, the Michigan legislature authorized an investment group with eastern and Detroit backers to build it, and work began that summer. It was an arduous job, hewing two 350-foot-long locks out of bedrock, but the task was completed in 1855. These two locks were used until 1887. They have since been lengthened, and additional locks have been built. The system is constantly in use even today.

With the opening of the locks, a natural barrier had been permanently breeched, and Lake Superior became accessible to the world.

But the St. Marys rapids were not the only component to what one historian termed "a shipping nightmare." The rocky coast of the lake, the changeable weather that produced sudden, deadly storms, and the paucity of natural harbors meant that it was costly and risky to ship the valuable ore east. To reduce the toll of Lake Superior's capriciousness, a necklace of lighthouses soon adorned the exposed north shore of the Keweenaw: Copper Harbor in 1849, Eagle Harbor in 1851, and Eagle River in 1858. These still stand, a testament to their sturdy construction and the rigors that necessitated them.

What was the copper produced in this early boom used for?

A major early firm was owned by Paul Revere's family. It produced copper sheeting, for example, for the Massachusetts State House dome, and copper-clad ship bottoms. By the 1830s, the demand for copper was rising, to be used additionally in bolts, rods, and spikes. An amalgam of copper and zinc, brass, was also in demand for buttons, hinges, and cabinet hardware, as well as for use in the kitchen.

The mass copper mining boom that began in the 1840s continued for several decades, and the Cliff mine produced prolifically. The start of the Civil War changed the circumstances of copper mining in several ways. The advanced technology used in war produced higher demand for copper, not only for mundane items like brass buttons and copper canteens, but also for bronze cannons and for more telegraph wires to enhance communication.

At the same time, the mines lost workers as they enlisted in the army. Miners were enthusiastic recruits, healthy, able young men, perfectly fit to be soldiers. In 1862, fifteen hundred men in tiny Eagle Harbor organized a march to nearby Eagle River, urging miners to enlist, and dozens did. Keweenaw County produced a higher percentage of recruits per population than any county in Michigan. Mine production flagged.

Around this time, the nature of copper mining also changed. Speculators were eyeing an amygdaloid lode of copper ore farther south, not part of the productive Keweenaw ridge with its pure copper ore. Interest centered on the hill above Portage Lake, in what would become the Quincy mine outside of Hancock, Michigan. Amygdules are small pockets of former gas bubbles that fill with metallic ore, embedded in non-useful rock. The amygdaloid zones under scrutiny were in the upper portions of the basaltic rock that had cooled after being spewed from the rift. This amygdaloid copper ore was still plenty rich—6 percent copper—but it needed more processing and produced more waste (tailings). It needed to be crushed up in a stamp mill, the copper ore separated from the waste rock, which was considerable, and then smelted and made into ingots, before shipping.

The processing was an expense that would have been unprofitable had the pure copper mines enjoyed the vigorous production of their prime, but the Cliff and the Minesota were running out. Shafts were sunk ever deeper, adits pushed out ever farther. Miners traveled one thousand feet down a shaft via dubious ladders. Their return trip up could take an hour. This is what mining

is: a depletion of the resource, if not in absolute terms, then in economic ones. So attention turned to the amygdaloid deposits and
also to a conglomerate rock interspersed among the amygdaloid
rock, familiarly known as "pudding stone."

It seems counterintuitive, but it was these less concentrated
lodes that became the real cash cow of Keweenaw copper mining.
Two mines in particular were long lasting: the Quincy mine, above
the hill at Hancock, Michigan, and the Calumet and Hecla mine
around Calumet. Each produced prolifically well into the twentieth
century. The Calumet and Hecla Mining Company, with numerous
locations and shafts, was the leading copper producer in the United
States from 1868 until 1886; in its early years, 1869–76, it produced
more copper ore than anywhere in the world. By 1897, it had a vertical shaft nearly a mile long (4,900 feet), the deepest mine in the
world at that time. Under the guidance of Alexander Agassiz, son
of the naturalist Louis Agassiz, who served as president of the company for nearly forty years, the Calumet and Hecla mine invested in
cutting-edge technology, expanded processing operations beyond
the Keweenaw, and provided arguably the best living conditions
for its laborers.

In the years when the Calumet and Hecla mine shone on the
international stage, the population around what would become
Calumet skyrocketed. There were multiple shafts, and immigrants
poured into Calumet to work them. Between 1870 and 1880, the
population exploded by 160 percent. Rows of clapboard houses
sprouted overnight, and within a decade, massive sandstone civic
buildings: an opera house, a fire hall, numerous Catholic churches
(one for each ethnic group: French, Italian, Croatian, and Polish),
and several Lutheran and Protestant churches. The Calumet and
Hecla Mining Company subsidized much of the building and provided a community library, as well. Subsidies often took the form of
land donation; thus, these buildings were concentrated in a com-
pact downtown.

The Quincy mine expanded laterally along the original amygdaloid lode, buying up other mines as it grew. It produced copper for nearly one hundred years, from 1846 until 1945, and was called "Old Reliable" for giving dividends to its shareholders for decades. When it closed at the end of World War II, it boasted the longest shaft (but not the deepest, for it penetrated at an angle, following the dip of the rock) in the world, at 9,260 feet. Hancock, Michigan, on the north side of the Keweenaw Waterway attracted Finns, who came to work in the mine or, more often, to work as loggers, the Quincy mine needing wood to fuel its steam engines.

The Quincy mine owners recruited Scandinavians in the 1860s, hoping to replace miners who were agitating in the labor movement or had left to join the war. They built neighborhoods, quickly labeled "Swedetowns," to house the incoming Scandinavians and the Finns, who were experiencing famine and subjugation by their neighbors and came by the tens of thousands. Although the first destination was Hancock, the booming Calumet and Hecla mine proved a greater lure for many. In the 1880s in Calumet, the Finns had a Finnish-language newspaper, two churches, a literary society, a mutual aid society, a lending library, several businesses, and nine public saunas. Quincy boasted of Suomi College, first instituted to train Finnish Lutheran pastors and later adopting the name Finlandia University. The college closed in 2023.

Today, a visitor to the Keweenaw Peninsula can tour a former copper mine (the Quincy) and visit the historic town of Calumet, which has been designated a National Historic District. The two attractions, in fact, are units of the Keweenaw National Historic Park—on par with Valley Forge and Harpers Ferry, two better-known national historic parks. The elegant red sandstone structures of nineteenth-century Calumet still stand, but many are boarded up; some have been repurposed, and others remain hollow shells no longer needed in a post-mining community.

A few of the many mines produced copper to fuel America through several wars, including the Civil, the Spanish-American, and World War I, the "war to end all wars." The Great Depression forced their closing. Some, including the Quincy and the Calumet and Hecla, reopened during World War II. The value of copper soared in wartime, and copper was traded on a world market, but after the war the mines closed permanently. The sprawling Calumet and Hecla Mining Company remained open longer than the rest, since it had invested broadly in the Keweenaw and elsewhere and had diversified into mineral mining, but it, too, closed for good in 1970. Most of its shafts are permanently capped.

Any mining venture is a story. It has a beginning, a middle, and an end. Some historians wax philosophic. Donald Chaput, while recounting the rise and fall of the Central mine, which worked mass copper, writes: "The nature of mining is constant change." That is to say, mining is an extractive business. If the lode is a good one, miners start out with a lot of ore, and prospects are rosy. At peak production, prospects are golden, as in, highly profitable. And then, rather quickly, even by short-term thinking, production slows as the ore is harder to reach, harder to extract, and more costly to dig out, until the mine dies.

Most writers, and most readers, are not interested in this uncomfortable truth. This is the case today, with 150 years of boom-and-bust cycles of copper, gold, iron, nickel—you name it, any kind of mining—behind us. The glory days of expanding jobs, domination of world markets, and imposing architecture are more compelling to dwell on than what comes next.

"If there is a lesson to be learned from the Cliff mine, and historic mining districts in general," Sean Gohman, a historian, observes in an addendum to Chaput's book, "it is that their impacts, both upon the landscape and in our collective memory, survive long after the capping of their shafts."

So let us explore what came next. What was the reckoning of the copper boom?

COPPER, PART II

The Reckoning

The hulking forms of downtown Calumet were shrouded in darkness as Tom and I trudged along the freshly plowed street. It was snowing, and the streetlights were dimmed, creating gray, ghostly shadows on the road and the snow piles that loomed over our heads. There was no one on the street, no walkers, no cars, just the two of us slogging uphill, through the snow and into the wind.

Tom and I were staying in Calumet's one hotel, an AmericInn, four blocks from the heart of town. We thought we would walk the four blocks to supper. With the heavy snow, it might be hard to park a car. We had left a hearty group of snowmobilers behind at the hotel, drinking rum and cokes and shouting at the TV. They were watching the Super Bowl, and though they had no geographic allegiance to either team, they were captivated enough (possibly by the commercials) to stay in and avoid the weather.

Tom and I, on the other hand, were here for the weather. Tomorrow we would ski the Swedetown Nordic Ski Trails, a mere mile south of the hotel. We had no idea that we were actually in the original Swedetown neighborhood, nor that it had been an enclave of Scandinavians who once worked the mines and logged the woods in the area.

We were also here for the bygone glory of Calumet, and its fabulous snow, on average more than two hundred inches a year. A walk to a restaurant seemed to incorporate all of that, so we stepped out into the night, into the weather.

Within a block, a large stone structure emerged from the dark. A church, I thought, but its arched window openings were boarded up, and snow drifted over the front steps. A church building, but no longer a church. How sad, I thought, such an immense building.

It faded into the night, and I saw that its neighbor was also huge and of sandstone, but unlike the abandoned church, it seemed to be still in use, still an Elks Lodge. It was looking a little seedy, an elephant that couldn't be properly cared for in such a climate, and so its caretakers made do with what was possible under the circumstances.

The scale and sophistication of these buildings felt at odds with the bleakness of the night, the paucity of life on the streets. We passed another intersection. We passed small frame houses that struggled under the wealth of snow. Residents had burrowed paths from their doors to the street, paths that resembled tunnels. We passed empty lots, gaps in the neighborhood, looking like an imperfect smile. We passed a pizza place, or was it a bar, with warm neon brightening the night.

At the one stoplight—a "blinker"—where the signal was suspended above the intersection on wires, we reached our destination, a three-story dark brick building, the Michigan House, home to a craft brewery, only to discover that it was closed for the Super Bowl. It seemed odd by Minnesota standards to close a bar during the Super Bowl, but we were hardly experts on professional football etiquette. We went on to plan B, a Mexican place, as far as we could tell, the only restaurant open downtown.

A snowy Sunday evening in February is not the best time to assess the legacy of copper mining on a community. In the daylight, when the sun is out, the aspect of Calumet becomes cheerier. The desolation of the place, though, haunted me. The life of Calumet, the beating heart, that night, was internal and not visible to the eye. But let's say the inheritance was not prosperity.

ONE HAS TO DIG to uncover what remains of the copper boom on the Keweenaw. In a story with an unhappy ending, people like to recall the beginning and the middle. No one wants to dwell on the tragic end, the distressing denouement, where despite it all, the hero dies, the war is lost, the fortune unrecoverable. But it's there, if you type the right search words into Google. If you read the wording carefully. If you infer.

The first casualty of copper mining was the woods. The thick forest was no match for the axes and saws of the mining companies. The Keweenaw Peninsula was largely deforested around the numerous mines. It was cleared for mining operations, cut to provide timber to support the mining shafts, and denuded to fuel the steam engines that drove the stamps and the hoists. It was sawn into planks for housing. Today, a state government website lists the remaining primeval forest remnants in the Keweenaw. There's one: the Estivant Pines, a small tatter of magnificent white pines soaring to the sky. This is not to say that the Keweenaw was entirely white pines. It was more likely a mosaic of pine stands and northern hardwood forests, which have been cut repeatedly since the arrival of the industrialists, the first to make big money off the peninsula that extends into Lake Superior.

Forests grow back but never the same forest as the virgin forest that was destroyed. The species composition changes, some are lost, new species come in. If it is cut repeatedly, as this forest was, the biological community is disturbed beyond repair, and we will never know what was lost. On my last visit to the Estivant Pines, I called in a variety of warblers, unlike any I had been hearing elsewhere on the Keweenaw.

One could argue that the forests were doomed anyway, if not devoured for mining activity, then for use in other ways. The forests in the Lower Peninsula were decimated without copper mining.

So let's focus on a degradation unique to mining: the shocking legacy of contamination from mines closed nearly a century ago.

In 1986, numerous areas of the Keweenaw Peninsula were declared a Superfund site. The sites, twenty-one in all, included all the bodies of water where stamp mills had operated, crushing unprocessed ore into small particles, from which copper was sorted and removed, and areas where smelters had spewed noxious plumes, processing the ore at high temperatures.

The ores from the Calumet and Hecla mine, which ran stamp mills on Lake Linden, and the Quincy mine, with stamp mills on Torch Lake, had copper dispersed widely in unusable rock and produced a lot of tailings, called "stamp sands." Before moving their stamp mills to Torch Lake, the Quincy had dumped tailings in Portage Lake, the Portage Lake canal—which became filled in the 1880s—and the Keweenaw Waterway. Other bodies of water receiving tailings and included in the Superfund site were the north entry to Lake Superior, Calumet Lake, and Boston Pond.

When the mines were at their peak production, the methods to remove copper from crushed ore were crude. In the twentieth century, new procedures involving cupric ammonium carbonate enabled more copper to be reclaimed from the waste, so both the Quincy and Calumet and Hecla employed dredges to bring up the stamp sands from the lake beds and recapture more copper. Eventually, these efforts became unprofitable, and the companies, in their last days, abandoned them; in fact, in 1967, the Quincy mine walked away from a dredge that became mired in Torch Lake, where it remains to this day. Barrels of cupric ammonium carbonate also found their way to the lake.

At the time of Superfund designation, federal officials estimated that Torch Lake contained two hundred million tons of stamp sands, 20 percent of the lake's volume, which was seventy feet deep in some places.

Torch Lake was named by the voyageurs, who had seen Indians spearing fish by night holding flaming flares aloft. But by the end of the twentieth century, the lake was notable for many tons of metal-rich contaminants, like copper and mercury. Onshore, the soil was loaded with lead, arsenic, chromium, and zinc, waste from ore processing. Copper on the lake bottom is toxic to bottom-dwelling invertebrates, like freshwater snails and mussels, and the aquatic ecosystem has been disrupted. After cleanup, the benthic organisms have not returned.

Additionally, mining operations released polychlorinated biphenyls (PCBs) into the lake. PCBs were used in transformers and capacitors in electrical transmission; the mines used a lot of electricity. The chemicals are notorious because, like DDT, they bioaccumulate, becoming more concentrated in organisms high on the food chain, so even a low concentration in the environment can have a disastrous effect. As recently as 2013, PCBs were traced directly to the Calumet and Hecla dock area and smelter. Fish in Torch Lake contained harmful amounts of PCBs, and people are advised to limit consumption of fish from Torch Lake to six to twelve servings of walleye *per year*.

Cleanup is ongoing. In some areas, the Environmental Protection Agency (EPA) has covered up aboveground toxic stamp sands with clean soil and has introduced vegetation. But much more remains undone, and after reclamation is complete, ongoing maintenance and monitoring will continue far into the future. Meanwhile, newly deposited sediments in Torch Lake continue to have high levels of copper, and no one knows where the copper is coming from.

Torch Lake also has high levels of mercury in its water, sediments, and fish. Mercury is known to enter lakes around Superior and the great lake itself through atmospheric deposition, but Torch Lake has more mercury than nearby lakes that did not have ore processing on their shores. The copper ores of the region all contain mercury, and drainage into Torch Lake is a continued source of the toxic metal.

The story of mercury contamination is complicated and still not completely known. Under certain conditions, mercury in wetlands is converted to methylmercury, a form that is readily taken up and bioaccumulated in living systems, like fish and human beings. The Keweenaw Peninsula has numerous wetlands, and they are expanding, as ditching, which was once widespread, is curtailed. Concern over mercury follows on the tail of the Superfund site designation. It was not recognized as significant a problem as it now appears to be. Appreciation and understanding of its scope have grown.

THE LEGACIES of copper mining resemble a hydra with multiple heads. As some of the toxic sites are capped by Superfund money, other disasters arise. A new concern is developing on the eastern shore of the Keweenaw involving stamp sands from the Mohawk mine near Gay, Michigan, which closed in 1932. The sands were deposited on the beach adjacent to the stamp mill. Over time, Superior's waves and wind have eroded a 23-million-metric-ton pile to just 2.4 metric tons, and those tailings have been carried by current southward near Grand Traverse Bay. Now they threaten the spawning beds of Buffalo Reef, a productive nursery for whitefish and lake trout, whose populations that were decimated for years are only now recovering.

In 2016, a survey of the 2,200-acre reef done by the U.S. Army Corps of Engineers and Michigan Technological University estimated that 35 percent of it was already smothered in stamp sands. Fisheries experts have not yet decided on a course of action—if any.

Finally, consider the Cliff mine at Eagle River, the first successful mass copper mine on the Keweenaw Peninsula. Although not operating on the scale of either the Quincy or the Calumet and Hecla, the mine significantly altered the landscape in numerous ways, including changing the flow pattern of the Eagle River, which ran near the mine site. Tailings polluted the groundwater, and since that water integrates with the riverbed, it poisons the benthic freshwater organisms in the river.

The Eagle River had once been a vibrant cold-water trout stream, and recently there was much interest to restore its health.

Various government agencies sought state and federal funding to begin the restoration process. Not a penny was gleaned from the private company that profited from the rich ore—this is also true for the other cleanup endeavors. The mines are gone. There's a saying that you can't get blood from a turnip. Well, in this case, there's not even a turnip. We, the people, are responsible for financing the cleanup of the copper boom through federal, state, and local taxes.

The plan was to remove the remaining tailings, cart them off to a place where they would not leach into the river, rechannel the river's course (it had been altered when the Cliff was active), and revegetate its banks. Today, the Eagle River is listed as a trout stream on Michigan Department of Natural Resources websites.

Oddly, the anthropologist relating this story in an addendum to *The Cliff: America's First Great Copper Mine,* approaches the progression from Native Americans using copper to industrial mining to decline and abandonment to reclamation as the natural state of business: "We dig in the earth. We leave behind that which we do not need . . . mines may hold finite mineral resources, but the changes they make to the landscape are ongoing. Addressing the environmental effects of mining is simply a continuation of that transformative process."

Somehow, the questions of who becomes wealthy, who pays for the mop-up, what are the benefits, and what is the value of what is permanently lost are not explored. "We dig in the earth. We leave behind that which we do not need."

What is the story of copper mining on the Keweenaw Peninsula really about? The question is worth raising, since as I write this, the people of Minnesota are poised to sanction a new copper mine within the watershed of Lake Superior. All the aspects of Keweenaw mining are present in the proposal: the dispersed ore will result in large amounts of tailings; there are abundant wetlands, lakes, and rivers connected to groundwater, ripe for contamination; there are promises by the companies of wealth for investors, jobs for the local communities, and money all around.

This—money—seems to be the prime value, esteemed above all else. The promoters of Minnesota's proposed mine would hoot at the suggestion that fresh water, or extensive wetlands, or an unbroken forest might be of greater worth. We seem unable to even have the conversation on a hierarchy of values, since as a society, we won't ponder how mining stories end.

The proposed Minnesota mine differs from the Keweenaw mines in some ways, too. As a society, we have learned something about how to contain pollution caused by mining. We will need that knowledge in spades, because unlike Keweenaw copper, the ore in northeastern Minnesota is embedded in rock containing sulfur. The tailings when wet will produce sulfuric acid. Every single copper mine in North America processing sulfide rock has contaminated the groundwater—water that will in this case eventually find its way to Lake Superior. It also differs from the Keweenaw mines in that unlike the nineteenth-century mines that seemed limitless (at least at first), Minnesota copper mining comes with an estimated end date: twenty years.

It is too glib to conclude that this story is only about greed, for it is also about creativity, ingenuity, and perseverance. Perhaps the copper mining story can be filed under the category of "Claiming a Nonrenewable Resource," and viewed in this way, it becomes part of an American parade of profligacy. We cut the pines until they were gone; we plowed the prairies until they were gone; we drained the marshes until they were gone; we shot Passenger Pigeons until they were gone. When faced with a bountiful continent brimming with resources, Americans have been unable to exercise moderation. We can't seem to pace ourselves. We show no interest in restoring as we go, repairing what is wounded. "We dig in the earth. We leave behind that which we do not need."

The entire story of copper mining, or any mining, from start to finish becomes a mirror that we hold up to ourselves reflecting who we are. So undeservedly blessed with abundance, we gobble it up with no eye to the future. We buoyantly see the beginning, we imagine the middle, we turn a blind eye to the end. At a funeral, no mourners dwell on the last days of the deceased. That would go against the grain of American optimism.

The copper mining story also says something about our relationship with Lake Superior. It has all the earmarks of a tragedy. One of the aspects we most cherish about this greatest lake is its rocks: the basalt of the North Shore, the Greenstone Ridge of Isle Royale, the Keweenaw cliff, the spine of the peninsula.

Yet even while we thrill to their rugged beauty, those very rocks contain ores that are seeds to Superior's destruction. If we take the ore to make something, something pristine is broken. Recall that even from the most limited mining six thousand years ago, the water of McCargoe Bay is polluted to this day. Calumet's sandstone church is abandoned. Tailings fill a lake once lit by torches.

YOU CAN'T SEE THE FOREST

When we bought our shoreline property in the late 1980s, the forest cover was chiefly quaking aspen. My dad used the folksy term "popple." Some of the aspen were really big, perhaps a foot in diameter. Others were more slender but still substantial. Young saplings prospered near bigger trees. It was hard to know where one tree left off and another started, though. Aspens produce suckers, shoots that sprout from their roots, so these saplings were doubtless genetically identical to what seemed to be the parent tree. In the 1980s, it was not common to think of aspen forests as one huge superorganism, but that's what it was. Quite possibly all the aspen contiguous to each other were one genetic individual.

The aspens bestowed dappled sunlight on us. The leaves clattered in the breeze, and in the fall, when they yellowed and fell to the forest floor, they gave off a delightful spicy scent. Their catkins in the spring attracted warblers, which were interested either in the pollen itself or in the small insects that buzzed around the aspen version of a flower.

The woods that we walked through or gazed upon from the cabin reminded me of Sweden, of Carl Larsson watercolors of leafy picnics at a country home. The sense was reinforced by the fact that we, too, had fair-haired children running about, picking berries, looking for wildflowers, or treading the path to the beach. Like our woods, Sweden has been clear-cut, leaving a legacy of aspen and birch that come in after deforestation.

Here and there in our woods were mature white pine, not many, maybe half a dozen, and one lone Norway pine. A few were perfect specimens, and a perfect white pine is the crowning glory of the plant kingdom. The Norway pine was also unblemished. But more often, the pines were marred—often by a missing top. These are frequently snapped in high winds, the lush, furry boughs providing enough torque when pushed by wind to break wood. Some pines were disfigured by dead limbs, killed by a non-native fungal disease that ravaged white pines in the twentieth century. Blister rust came to the United States around 1906. Our pines with denuded limbs probably contracted the disease after their cohorts had been cut. Loggers may have deliberately left these pines standing—the trees would have been much smaller—to act as seed sources to regenerate the land after a massive cut. We will never know why they escaped the ax.

Because they were so few, we cherished every pine and kept an eye on each. There was the crazy looped individual that had lost its leader—the growing top of the tree—early, and a second leader had taken over, rising heavenward and creating an S-shaped trunk. There was a genuine matriarch that grew alongside the creek, and the trio that marked the entrance of our drive at the highway. There was the eagle tree, visible from our beach path, that in our early years held a nest, and later, after the birds had built in a nearby aspen, was still the preferred perch. The Norway red pine was behind it, away from the cliff and only revealed in the fall with the leaves down.

Our land was damaged goods. I often think of it that way, with an underlying resentment that persists. That's all that past generations have left to my generation, and to my children's and grandchildren's generations. All the pines were cut, almost every one, leaving none to give us a sense of the majesty and grandeur that once was North America. We didn't know the history when we bought the property, but we could see that at some point loggers had come through and chopped down nearly every tree. Then the ruined forest had been left to heal itself. It bound up its wounds with sun-loving aspen and birch and had not been cut a second time, since the aspen were estimated at about eighty years old. One forester disparaged them as "overmature," a term one never hears in ecology. It's an odd concept. What exactly is an overmature tree? Are people in nursing homes overmature? Are old dogs?

Nonetheless, I love these damaged goods. I may in truth think of them more tenderly because they are not perfect, because the ax that ravaged them revealed the forest's vulnerability, a vulnerability that is masked and unseen when a forest is unblemished. Ever the optimist, I choose to focus on what our marred forest has to offer: Blackburnian Warblers singing high in the treetops, Mourning Warblers nesting hidden on the forest floor, a Bald Eagle pair that has nested in the damaged woods for thirty-three years, and Merlins that drop in to visit. Perfection doesn't exist this side of Eden. You have to appreciate the hand you were dealt.

THE FIRST DATE OF SALE on the title to our land is 1884. It was sold by the U.S. government to a James Bardon. All of northern Wisconsin was Ojibwe land prior to 1842. In that treaty, negotiated at La Pointe, the Ojibwe ceded the land for copper mining, but it gave the Americans access to the trees. Deforestation in what would become the Port Wing area didn't begin in earnest until the early 1890s, though. This was decades after deforestation in central Wisconsin was proceeding apace, a process so rapid and heedless that one book on the era was titled *Come and Get It!*

In the remote northern part of the state there was no good way to get trees to market. Central Wisconsin operations used dammed rivers to float the logs to sawmills. Later, railroads carried logs away. But on the South Shore of Lake Superior, the rivers run north into a vast lake. There was no harbor in the area—Port Wing's harbor was yet to be "improved"— and hence, no way to corral and transport the timber.

The first white settlers arriving in 1891 found the lake "in front," a quarry that was "little worked," and a "wealth" of timber. That same year, a vigorous entrepreneur, T. N. Okerstrom, opened a logging camp, then a sawmill, and a harbor made useful by piers and dredging. The logging camp and mill employed the newly arrived settlers in the winter, when they were not occupied with the laborious effort of clearing farmland and cultivating crops. The virgin timber was white and red pine, cedar, and oak. Less favorable for logging were sugar and soft maples, and white and yellow birch. The pines were cut first. When they were exhausted, loggers turned their attention to the hardwoods and hemlock. Cedar was cut for poles—fence posts and electric and telephone poles.

The first logging occurred along the Flagg River, which flows into Lake Superior. Then the woods that grew within a radius of six to eight miles of the mill were cut (that would encompass our cabin land), because that was the distance horses could haul logs profitably. Logging occurred in the winter, when the ground was frozen and provided a slicker surface to slide logs over.

There came a point at which the remaining trees were perched atop high hills and largely inaccessible. These were spared momentarily, awaiting a time when it would be profitable to take them down. That would happen in 1916, when the sawmill was rebuilt after a fire.

Meanwhile, the visionary Okerstrom, a surveyor by training, began laying out the town of Port Wing. Essentially a section of land, the townsite was platted, and in 1892, one year after the arrival of the settlers, they set about clearing off the site. It is possible that some of the verdant growth was spared, but early photos testify otherwise. Images of the first schoolhouse, early stores, and homesteads show a landscape eerily devoid of trees. To do battle with the forest was a badge of honor. One memoirist noted that a date was set to begin the work of deforestation. On that day, townsman Nels Johnson got up early for the distinction of cutting the first tree.

So the trees were destroyed. Then the real work of civilization could begin. Port Wing's founders built quality schools of distinction. The town is known for instituting the first school trans-portation system—horse-drawn wagons, sleighs in winter—because it consolidated its one-room schoolhouses early, so teachers could specialize in grade levels. It built churches, stores, a railroad to haul logs to Ashland. In short order, there were four blacksmiths, two hotels, two physicians, a cooperative creamery, an active stone quarry cutting red sandstone for the region's urban areas, and a national company, Booth Fisheries, which employed many during the fall herring run.

This is not a story of unusual diligence. Nearly every community in the Midwest can claim similar prosperity, fueled by the riches of virgin resources. At the time, these resources seemed inexhaustible. There were so many trees and so few axes and crosscut saws wielded by men, who appeared puny in the shadow of virgin timber. A sur-veyor of the pine-rich region of east-central Minnesota summed it up: "Seventy mills in seventy years couldn't exhaust the white pine I have seen on the Rum River."

A local historian writing in 1929 noted that the business of pro-ducing lumber brought prosperity to Port Wing. It was, he thought, the era of its greatest wealth, In this era, the town bustled. But the good times were over by the time this historian wrote in 1929. They had lasted eighteen years.

Still, it is not apparent to me, from the vantage point of the early twenty-first century, that Port Wing's prosperity sank with the waning of the trees. After the clear-cut, communities or entre-preneurs aiming at "flipping" acreage billed the land as suitable, even prime, for farming. Termed "the cutover," townsites were laid out and given names like "Cloverland" or "Cloverdale" and adver-tised to poor European would-be immigrants, or Americans eager to become landowners by hard work and perseverance.

The South Shore communities adjacent to Port Wing followed this pattern. The "town" of Clover was formed east of Port Wing and encompassed the present community of Herbster. The town of Cloverdale sprung up west of the Brule River, the sad remnants of which we pass on every trip to the cabin. All on Highway 13, there's Cloverland Bible Baptist Church and cemetery, still active and perhaps the lasting legacy of Cloverland. A store and gas station have sunk into decay, becoming nearly unrecognizable in the three decades we have driven by; and closest to the cabin, there are the weathered schoolhouse with its cupola (missing the bell) and a rusted merry-go-round, which was eventually razed just last year.

Deforestation in northern and central Wisconsin was viewed at the time as an unambiguous good. A newspaperman in Portage, Wisconsin, wrote that cutting the pines would allow for the greatest wealth in the region to be revealed: its farmland. The great undertaking to clear the forests is the stuff of family origin stories. One branch of my family was attracted to the Wisconsin cutover, lured out of Germany by the promise of productive farmland in a place called Green Valley. As a girl, I heard my cousins whisper about these initial years—of how our great-grandfather worked to grub the stumps from one farmstead, only to be displaced by his older brother, who emigrated later. Our great-grandfather was then left to start over on another parcel of land, the farm where my father's cousin still farmed. Of all the arduous activities that new immigrants engage in, that singular one—grubbing out tree stumps—is the one remembered. My grandfather, a boy in the 1890s, recalled the bonfires fueled when those tree stumps were piled and lit—the sparks rose high in the sky, he wrote. This told me that the original forest was pine, not hardwood. It is the pinaceous trees that have resin.

In Port Wing, people recalled the lush clover that appeared after the clear-cut. Clover came in naturally, and clover pastures sustained dairy cows, which historian Carl V. Dahlstedt called "one of the foundations of prosperity in this region." Hence the names of the embryonic towns. There are indications that the switch from logging to farming came earlier than the decline of the trees. By 1905, a farmers' cooperative creamery had organized in town, always the first step in commercial dairy farms: farmers can't take milk to market unless there is a place to process it, and that requires a certain number of dairy farms to support a creamery or a cheese factory.

But in the end, no amount of diligence or hard work could overcome the fact of geography. The soil of the South Shore is red clay, the lake bed of Glacial Lake Duluth. The original geologist to survey the region, David Dale Owen, thought the red clay could be plowed by the same subsoil methods that had been used on the red clay soils of Virginia and Maryland, but the soils of the South Shore didn't drain well, and there was also the cool, short growing season brought about by the nearness of the great lake. Farming eventually waned, and many farms were forfeited for want of tax payments. Today, Port Wing has hung on to its bank, and post office, and a single store, which is remarkably stocked with the essentials needed for cabin life. But there is no hint of flourishing hotels, a café, a movie theater, or two car dealers.

University of Wisconsin geographer Eric Olmanson termed the deforestation of northern Wisconsin "one of the great environmental miscalculations in U.S. history," in the same league as the Dust Bowl of the Great Plains. Forest fires periodically ravaged the slash in the years after the logging companies moved out. Port Wing experienced one such fire in 1910, a dry year. The fire started south of town around the Fourth of July. In the evening, a south wind blew the fire toward town. People collected in the streets, fearful and watchful. Some prayed. Some cried. A plan was conceived to evacuate the town to a schooner that was in the harbor to load lumber. But it never came to that: around midnight, rain began to fall and extinguished the blaze.

People divested the Great Plains of its protective, fertile sod, plowed the rich soil, and were told that "rain follows the plow." People mowed down the magnificent pine forests and were told that the true riches could be found in agriculture. Neither activity was done with careful deliberation. Neither had ecosystem science on its side—an understanding of nature that had not yet been developed. Our understanding of forest function is changing in this century. Let's look at the lost forest through new eyes.

THE OLD SAW "You can't see the forest for the trees" has special resonance in twenty-first-century forest ecology. Ecology is a science that studies the interconnectedness of living organisms and their connections to the nonliving world. Any understanding of a pine forest that dwells solely on pines would be woefully incomplete, a focus that puts blinders on those who approach a forest that way.

Readers familiar with Richard Power's novel *The Overstory* may recall the character Dr. Patricia Westerford, who studied forest ecology and the subtle communication between plants. Powers patterned his character after a real-life scientist, Dr. Suzanne Simard of the University of British Columbia, who has spent her lifetime researching how trees in a forest communicate.

Because trees are rooted in place and don't make sounds, we think of them as passive and mute, unable to respond to events around them. Simard's work has demonstrated that this is emphatically not true. Trees and other plants in the forest are connected in the soil by a fine meshwork of filaments called mycorrhizae. Mycorrhizae (singular: mycorrhiza) are fungi that are conduits connecting tree roots and rootlets of many individuals, enabling them to pass substances back and forth. Elements like carbon and nitrogen, water, and chemicals that act like alarms (warning other trees of insect pests, for example) are all passed through the mycorrhizal network. Everything is connected underground.

Simard has shown that in western forests, Douglas firs are connected to birch trees through this network. In the summer, when small Douglas firs are shaded and unable to produce many sugars through photosynthesis, carbon flows from birch to fir. In the fall, when the evergreen Douglas firs are continuing to photosynthesize, but birches are losing leaves, carbon flows from fir to birch.

Simard and her graduate students are particularly interested in the role that old individuals, what Simard calls "mother trees," play in the forest. They appear to nurture young tree seedlings growing near them, even when those seedlings are not actually their offspring. Mother trees appear to be the most interconnected trees in the forest.

European researchers are studying other means of subtle communication in trees. In some forests, hormones—chemical messengers—rather than neurons, which are animal cells, seem to be the information processing agent. Acacia trees, native to South Africa, release tannins through their leaves when grazed on by antelope. This serves to warn other trees of the predators and stimulates them to produce tannins, too. The tannins both render the leaves less tasty and put neighbors on alert.

In Switzerland, scientists have discovered that trees use an electrical signaling system to communicate alarm or distress to other individuals. These slow-pulse signals communicate drought conditions, disease, or insect attack. The trees receiving them alter their behavior. In the case of trees, this "behavior" isn't movement but a change in metabolism—what chemicals the trees put out—but it falls within the definition of behavior as being "the way in which one acts."

All of these varied means of communication suggest that an intact forest is a close-knit community whose individuals rely on each other to stay healthy. How naive it is, then, to assume that a forest clear-cut would not do inestimable harm that echoes far into the future. How naive to think that a lone "seed tree" spared the ax here and there could successfully restore what was taken.

And of course, it didn't. Our seed trees, if that was indeed what they were, did not reseed a pine forest. Some of the white pines have produced slender saplings growing nearby. The red pine remains solitary. This falls into a familiar American pattern. We destroy first and rue later.

MEANWHILE, the erosion of our cliff continues. The very substrate on which our forest grows is being reclaimed by Lake Superior. It is sadly ironic. Our land could join the rest of the biosphere in resisting the rise in carbon dioxide in the atmosphere that our species has brought about. Forests are immense carbon sinks—they take in carbon and store it in leaves and roots and woody trunks. Scientists estimate that there is more carbon stored in the world's forests than in the atmosphere. But with its mycorrhizal network disrupted, the woods on our land is fighting its greatest enemy with one arm tied behind its back.

Those so-called seed trees have taken a hit from climate change and its associated events. The eagle tree washed into the lake over a period of a decade. We still swim around it as it lies where it fell. The red pine growing directly behind it will be next, and we may see its demise in our lifetimes. The matriarchal white pine growing along the creek snapped nearly at its base during a tremendous storm last summer. We arrived the next day and saw its raw, exposed wood laid bare. That same storm took off the crown of one of the pines at the base of the drive. It was devastating to see.

Still, I have to believe that in the one hundred years since the clear-cut, some of that network has been restored. There are thick balsam fir stands in cool, shady areas. The white pine seedlings Tom planted by hand thrive, and most even escape the chomp of hungry deer, which in one bite can destroy the leader of a young tree.

At night we hear wolves howl. In the morning, we see deer and otter tracks on the beach. There are owls and vireos, phoebes and warblers nesting in the woods. Animals live here. It is an acceptable home to them. The forest is giving them what they need to survive, reproduce, and grow.

I need to balance the grudge I carry against the past with the resilience I see in the present. After all, my own generation is hardly free from blame. Thirty-five years ago, when as adults we heard the clarion call of climate change, we did nothing, for decades, and even today we largely ignore it. I need to continuously remember this truth: nothing is as simple as it seems.

THE TWO-HEARTED RIVER

On a pellucid blue morning, the river shimmered like a mirror at the base of the hill, a dune, actually, that we had driven down to reach the boat landing. There was sky streaked by stratus clouds, there was scrub anchoring the sand dunes, there was the sand itself, a delicate petal pink. But the actual emptying of the Two-Hearted River into Lake Superior was not visible. A long, high dune ran parallel to Superior's beach, forcing the river to run parallel also. I had never seen a river with an oblique approach to the mighty lake. It was the first indication that on the Two-Hearted River, not all is as it seems. We did not know what the two hearts were, but if we were to learn, the revelation would be subtle and slant.

The day's plan was to drop our bikes off at this landing and hide them in the woods, locked together. When we arrived after canoeing, we would pedal back to the put-in point where we left the car. We didn't know how long it would take us or if obstacles, like fallen trees, blocked the river at points. We knew hardly anything about this river, except that it had a lovely name and that Ernest Hemingway thought so, too.

But then, before we could do any of this, Tom pointed to a sign near the landing: this was the site of one of four Life Saving Stations dotting what has been termed "the shipwreck coast." The Two-Hearted River, an hour and a half's drive west from Sault Ste. Marie, runs parallel to a notorious stretch of shoreline. This coast, from Whitefish Point to Grand Marais, Michigan, saw more shipwrecks in the early days of navigation than any other. Strong prevailing winds caught boats broadside, pushing them toward shore to founder on shallow shoals. A constant battering by wind and waves ensued. Boats stranded like this did not readily sink, and their crews could be rescued by courageous, trained men who ventured out into the teeth of the raging storm. After the installation of the Life Saving Stations, far more sailors were rescued than drowned in storms on Lake Superior.

The station at the Two-Hearted River was located on the dune between the lake and the river, a precarious place to be, exposed to continuous erosion from wind and water. It had not been used since the 1930s, and the building was razed in 1944. We could see nothing that indicated that such a place of high drama had ever existed there. Perhaps it was the sunny day that cast aside all apprehension of doom. Still, this was a *Life* Saving Station. Desperate attempts to save lives had occurred on this site many times. A sense of daring and determination hung in the summer air. Perhaps this was one of the river's two hearts.

We were so occupied by the romance of a Life Saving Station, the dunes, the sapphire river, and the coy nonappearance of Lake Superior, that we gave little thought to what else was in plain view before us. Three weeks later, as I scrutinized photos I took that day, I realized that the banks of the river are starkly bare. Now, I think: shouldn't those banks be dressed in green, in pines and spruce, and not only scrubby growth of alder? Again, the Two-Hearted River did not readily reveal its truth.

We stashed the bikes, got in the car, and retraced our route over the sandy, hilly unpaved road to the landing at the Reed and Green Bridge, a popular put-in spot. From there we would paddle eleven miles, about a three-hour trip including a lunch stop, depending on the river's flow. From this site, the river looked unbelievably beautiful. Tannins stained the water a tea color, and it was so clear, we could gaze on its sandy bottom. The banks crowded in, creating a narrow green tunnel, and the flow was swift.

We used to bring binoculars on day trips like this but tend not to now. I never use them. By the time a bird is spotted, the current has carried me away from a good view. Instead, I identify birds by ear, and the music filling the air as we picked up our paddles was complex. The brightly plumed warblers are my favorite group, and I immediately began calling out the singers. Black-throated Green Warblers with their buzzy song ("Trees, trees, murmuring trees") predominated, but Black-and-White Warblers (very high-pitched, it won't be long before I can't hear them), Nashville Warblers, and Blackburnians were also common. It was warm, ninety degrees, but we were shaded, and water was just a splash away.

The Two-Hearted River is known as a trout stream for fly fishermen. It is clear and cold, and there are quiet pools behind downed logs in which fish can rest. Many fine writers, beginning with Izaak Walton, have reflected on the art of fly-fishing, but the Two-Hearted River is tied to one writer: Ernest Hemingway.

Hemingway was well acquainted with the Upper Peninsula. A doctor's son, he spent his boyhood summers at the family cabin in the northern Lower Peninsula. In his teens, he ventured into the wilder U.P. to fish and hunt. Perhaps his best short story, "The Big Two-Hearted River," is set in the U.P. Nick Adams, the main character and a stand-in for Hemingway, comes to the river ostensibly to fish but, more significantly, to heal after being wounded in war. He is a young man, shattered in body and soul, and there is a mute, instinctual understanding that the beauty of this river will be a balm to his brokenness. The reader isn't told this in the story, though. Like the river, the tale is subtle. Readers must take their time, surmise details from the spare, plain prose.

> Nick looked down into the clear, brown water, colored from the pebbly bottom, and watched the trout keeping themselves steady in the current with wavering fins. . . . He watched them holding themselves with their noses into the current, many trout in deep, fast-moving water.

A young Hemingway did come to this area after a war injury, but he was accompanied by two friends, and they didn't fish the Two-Hearted but the Fox River, south and west of here. The round, rich sound of the name "Two-Hearted River" appealed to him, though. He termed it "sheer poetry." Perhaps the ambiguous meaning also attracted him, for what does it mean to have two hearts? Did he see the damaged Nick Adams as having two hearts, one in the present, one in memory? In the story, Nick deliberately undertakes the tasks of setting up camp. He is aware of remembered routine—setting up a tent, starting a fire. These were the motions of his former heart, and their familiarity helped to restore his broken one. Perhaps he desired to become like the trout, able to keep his place despite the press of life's currents.

PADDLERS THINK of many things as they make their way downstream, but we did not think of Nick Adams and his possibly two hearts as we floated the Two-Hearted. Instead, we tussled with sweepers—downed trees that blocked passage of the narrow stream. The first, encountered within minutes of dropping in, needed to be portaged around. It was a solid, robust white pine admitting no throughway. We had to haul the canoe to the bank and lug it a short way through the underbrush to downstream of the horizontal pine. That was the last of dry sandals for the day. Good thing our shorts were quick-dry.

> [Nick] stepped into the stream. It was a shock. His trousers clung tight to his legs. His shoes felt the gravel. The water was a rising cold shock.

Another big jam blocked our way an hour later, and for this imped-iment, we had an audience observing us from a cabin high atop the bluff. They watched, no doubt beer in hand, while we scrambled out to balance on the logs as water flowed swiftly past us, then using brawn, pulled the canoe up and pushed it over. As I successfully got back in the canoe, I heard, "Nice job, you guys."

It was soon after that logjam that the river changed in character. We had been luxuriating in an emerald tunnel, punctuated by the dark spires of spruce, but shortly after noon, we stopped at a sandbar for a little lunch, looked around, and thought, "What has happened to this forest?" No longer shaded by verdant trees that hugged the banks, the landscape had become open, with dead trees standing vertical, forming a stark, spiky silhouette that perforated the sky.

It looked like a catastrophe. What has happened, we wondered again. Perhaps it was logged. The watershed of the Two-Hearted cuts through the Lake Superior State Forest, and state forests are frequently logged, but something was not right here. Why would loggers leave so many logs behind? The substrate was very sandy. There was a green cover to the sand, but large cuts in the banks showed the same blush-pink sand that we had observed at its mouth.

As we paddled through the afternoon, it became clearer that this lovely little river had experienced a fire, and a big one. The skeletal remains of a mature white pine were blackened to the top: this had been a crown fire, the hottest, most destructive kind of fire. No trees, even with protective bark such as pines have, can survive a crown fire.

Indeed: on May 24, 2012, a lightning strike kindled a fire that at first seemed minor. But the Upper Peninsula had experienced a dry winter, and with the sere conditions and high winds, the flames began to grow. As it raced toward Lake Superior under a stiff south wind, the fire in some places produced temperatures intense enough to burn the soil and the seed sources buried within. Pine forests depend on fires to prepare the bed for new pines. Jack pines even produce cones that are sealed with resin that needs a fire's heat to pop open the cone and release the seed. But conditions did not allow for a beneficial fire. Instead, they produced a scorched-earth landscape. From satellite photos, the fire's smoky plume could be seen stretching for eleven miles. Drone photos showed the fire pushing toward Lake Superior, and it is evident that only the cooling waters of the immense lake would staunch the wounds.

That fire, which is today known as the Duck Lake Fire, was the third largest fire in Michigan history. Twenty-one thousand acres were destroyed in two days, though the fire was not fully out until mid-June. Damage to human structures was estimated in the millions of dollars, including an esteemed resort, Rainbow Lodge, perched atop the hill that leads down to the boat landing on the river. Accounts that I read did not mention the toll on wildlife. Their destruction during the breeding season, the deer and moose, rabbits, raccoons, weasels, mice, voles and shrews, and baby birds in nests: it makes me wince. Imagine all the young animals helpless in the face of a swift, hot fire. Where were the Life Savers? The two hearts must have broken.

OUR CANOE TRIP had turned hot; air temperatures were in the nineties. The river widened as it approached the great lake, but we continued to see deadheads; the landscape continued to be dead the whole way. Temperatures in the nineties are hot for the Upper Peninsula. Not unheard of, but uncommon. Bowing our heads to the inevitable, Tom and I mutely understood the torrid heat to be another indication of climate change. The burning sun on our skin accentuated the devastation of the forest, which could also be linked to global warming. An unusually meager snowpack had led to an unusually dry spring, enhancing the likelihood that a lightning strike would spark a flame that would ignite first pine needles on the forest floor and then the trees themselves.

The scene was not pleasant, but it was beautiful in its own way. It reminded me, oddly, of the work of Canadian artist Lawren Harris. A member of the legendary Group of Seven, Harris painted Lake Superior in a stylized, geometric way. Forms are pared to their essence—the shape of a dead tree, the curve of bedrock. For Harris, it was a way of expressing the inner working of northernness. It was a spiritual endeavor for him.

But Harris did not have an intensely hot crown fire in mind when he painted spare, denuded trees. More likely, he was picturing trees in their winter form, without the gaudy dress of leaves and flowers or cones, forms without embellishment.

Hemingway opens his story with the remains of a forest fire. The bemused Nick begins his fishing trip at the town of Seney, where he "looked over at the burned-over stretch of hillside, where he had expected to find the scattered houses of the town," only to find that nothing remains—to this day. Seney is a name on the highway, nothing more. But Nick, even as he takes in the devastation, is moving to the river, to the water. The pull of the water is magnetic. Nick instinctively understands that if there is healing to be had, it will be there. That is where the trout keep themselves positioned even in the face of the strong current.

The fire of 2012, after consuming the state forest and the riverbanks, and their uncounted inhabitants, raced to the shore of Lake Superior, under the imperative of a south wind. There, it died, because there was nothing left to consume. The big water opened wide and took it all in.

In the same way, we felt our canoe now racing to the big lake, as the current pulled us swiftly to the mouth. The sky opened, and we realized we were running past the great sand dune with Lake Superior on the other side. We swiftly passed the landing where our bikes were stashed, but we didn't care. We wanted to experience the falling away of the river and the broad expanse of the lake. There it was! So blue! So eternal! Unfazed by fire and smoke and char.

Later, I would read that eight years after the fire, foresters are seeing hopeful signs of new life. Millions of jack pine seedlings have been hand-planted, have taken root, and are on their way to becoming habitat, it is hoped, for Kirtland's warblers. It would be an extensive tract of land for the rare little birds, suited to their specifications.

The Two-Hearted River appears to be healthy, as we can attest to. It has suffered minimal erosion, and the trout population flourishes. It is clear and cold. Fish hide in the deep pools. They still face into the current, pectoral fins waving.

Nick Adams, too, finds solace on the river. Stepping into its waters is a baptism for him, a promise that this act will heal him. The many little rituals of threading a fishing line, setting bait, playing a fish on the hook, will bring him into new country where he will learn to live with his wounds.

Perhaps Nick does have two hearts, as does the forest, and Tom and I in our canoe. Perhaps these are the river's two hearts: there's the battered heart caused by living, and the aspiring heart striving to be whole.

PART III

What Was Lost and Then Was Found

THE BLACK CREEK
NATURE SANCTUARY

A few miles outside of Calumet, Michigan, on the western shore of the Keweenaw Peninsula is an uncommonly lovely, small nature preserve, the Black Creek Nature Sanctuary, owned by the Michigan Nature Association. The 242-acre sanctuary protects the last stretches of two small waterways, Black Creek and Hill Creek, where they converge into a lagoon, and the lagoon's connection to Lake Superior. More than fifteen hundred feet of pristine Lake Superior shoreline is also protected in the sanctuary.

This quiet little gem is not heralded as a tourist attraction in nearby Calumet. There, visitors come for the Keweenaw National Historical Park, tours of the erstwhile Quincy copper mine, and the gleaning of fluorescent "Yooperlites," rocks with sodalite that glow orange and yellow under black light shone on them at nighttime. Frankly, vegetated sand dunes seem boring compared to glowing Yooperlites, but Tom and I were blown away by the beauty of the Black Creek Nature Sanctuary.

As I considered this place, I recognized that, like the two creeks that flow through the small tract, there are two stories embedded in the preserve, each worthy of reflection. One is the story of this ecological time capsule, the plants and animals that live there. The other is the tale of how it came to be protected, the people involved, and their motivation.

An informational brochure available at the parking lot of the site mentions a woman, Ruth Sablich, a Calumet High School graduate, as the person instrumental in donating the land and saving this little slice of heaven. Though it had been several years, with a pandemic intervening, since we had visited Black Creek, I wondered if Ruth was available to tell me the story of the preserve. Through the wonders of the internet, I found her, noting that she had been born in 1926, which meant she was ninety-five years old. I wrote to her at an address on the Lower Peninsula. Within a week, I received a reply in the mail, and the next day, I picked up the phone and called her.

The voice at the other end of the telephone was vigorous at ninety-five, with a merry laugh and thoughtful pauses while she considered my questions. Ruth's memory was keen and precise. During the course of our chat, we discovered, among other things, that the Calumet Airbnb apartment I had rented in 2019 was once the dental office that Ruth had gone to, the place where she had had her first tooth pulled. Indeed, photographs of a dental office, including the dental chair, had been hanging on the walls of the Airbnb, and my friend and I had spent time walking from room to room, surmising which was the waiting room, which the dentist's personal office, and where The Chair had been. "Well, I was in that chair," Ruth said with a laugh.

Throughout our conversation, it was evident that Ruth loved being immersed in nature, although she didn't go into the woods as a young child. Perhaps in her 1920s childhood, the woods were still pervasive and not in tattered fragments. As a young woman, she and her friends accessed Lake Superior on foot from Cedar Bay Road, northwest of Calumet, which even today dead-ends close to the shore. On the rare hot summer days, having the big lake accessible seemed a God-given right. There were other places to access the water near Calumet, but Cedar Bay was quiet and away from the crowds. Ruth had memories of picnics and swimming accompanied by the roar of the lake.

Then one summer, after she and her husband, Joe, had left Calumet, they were back in town visiting and thought they would take a beach walk. To their dismay, there was no access to the beach at Cedar Bay. Signs now clearly marked a private road. Probably it was privately owned when Ruth was young, but there was less concern about trespassing then.

"I said to Joe, 'Gee whiz, that's terrible! Nobody can come down here and go down to the water anymore!'" Joe checked the plat book and saw that land on the right-hand side of the road was owned by Universal Oil Company, formerly part of the Calumet and Hecla Mining Company. A few years later, they learned that the firm was interested in selling, and Joe and Ruth Sablich bought it. An additional purchase of two small lots gave them access to the bigger parcel.

After that, the couple had a lot of fun just hiking around on their land. "We'd go there with a compass and wander around all over," Ruth told me. "We didn't know where we were, but we did have the compass to tell us how to get [down to the lake]." They went up and down over sandy dunes, which had become carpeted with vegetation, far from the water. They crossed Black Creek on a little bridge at the start of the trail, and farther into the property, on logs.

"We thought that when we'd retire, we'd try maybe to build something there . . . never really . . . he passed away at sixty years old. . . ." Ruth's voice trails off. Then she adds that a realtor approached her with an offer from a client who was interested in her land. The client, though, would probably develop it. Ruth held strong to her original desire for people to have access to Lake Superior's beach. She cast about for ways to protect the property from future development into perpetuity. To her surprise, the realtor suggested the Nature Conservancy. They offered to take it but only as a trade for another tract of land. Again, there was no protection in that offer. "I said, 'No thanks.'"

She approached the Michigan Nature Association, based outside East Lansing. The MNA was established in 1952 with holdings on both the Upper and Lower Peninsulas. Its network of sanctuaries is now sizable: 180 to date, focused on protecting threatened and endangered species by protecting the habitat they need to thrive. It was a perfect fit for Ruth's hope for the property, and the MNA said it would take it.

The MNA thought there was a chance to add acreage to Ruth's holding and explored ways to raise the funds to do so. Ruth thought her long-ago classmates from Calumet High School might have an interest in contributing to a fund to add to the sanctuary. The MNA approached the school's alumni association, which sent out a plea, and the money came in. People remembered their hometown with warmth and generosity. "Some of the people I knew," Ruth told me, "and others were just alumni, not necessarily my class." With the additional funds, the MNA was able to add another 120 acres, doubling the size of the parcel. The scenario illustrates well how land can be brought under protection: a private donation, a willing seller, partnership with a company, and a nonprofit to identify desirable tracts, organize the proceedings, and make it happen.

I asked Ruth if she thought that the milieu of Calumet fostered a sense of giving back to the community. Ruth wasn't sure, but then she immediately described the town as a melting pot of numerous ethnicities. Most of her cohort's parents were from all over Europe: Irish, Finnish, Swedish, Italian, Polish, Croatian—all attending school together, all woven into a community that worked together, educated the young, and made a vibrant life for themselves. "It was," she said, "just amazing."

"Amazing" is how I described Black Creek Nature Sanctuary in my journal after our first visit there. Tom and I had come for the most prosaic of reasons: we were about to drive home, a five-hour trip, and we wanted to walk the dog to get the wiggles out. Clipping Lily onto her leash, we headed out.

Visitors enter the preserve on a bridge over Black Creek and then catch the 2.85-mile trail that takes hikers to the lagoon at the shore of Lake Superior. The trail wends up and down over sand dunes far from the water's edge. I had never seen a landform like those dunes. They are not as high as the famous ones along Lake Michigan at Sleeping Bear, or they would have been preserved long ago for their outsized stature, but they were much higher than dunes on the Anoka Sand Plain in Minnesota. Lake Superior has massive dunes at Grand Marais, Michigan, part of the Pictured Rocks National Lakeshore, but these Keweenaw Peninsula dunes are tucked many football fields away behind the beach, the only ones I had ever seen that far away and wonderfully vegetated.

The dunes closest to the lake are the youngest. Small, sprawling plants growing low to the surface anchor the sand. These are diverse—blueberries, wintergreen, bunchberries, and lichens. Their diminutive stature is misleading; long roots probe deep into the dunes, holding the substrate in place. In the sunny patches grow bracken fern with wild lily of the valley beneath the leafy fronds. Small white birches are pioneers on this dune. Tom, looking for it, discovered one twinflower; the genus name is *Linnaea*, his sister's name, and so a favorite with him.

Behind this first dune is an open, treeless area, with marsh grasses and alder thickets. Black Creek meanders through this swale.

Farther away from the shore, the dunes are older, and the plant community more complex. Here we found a diverse forest, with sugar maples, red oaks, and aspen, and atop the hills, white and red pines. The microclimate on this dune is cooler, and the conifers create dense shade. This is where the Lilliputian boreal plants grow: more bunchberries and wintergreen in fruit, also called "pipsissewa," a Cree name that refers to its diuretic property. This plant was in bloom the mid-August day we visited, a little late, perhaps, but the chilly presence of Superior delays the growing season for plants rooted near it. Clintonia, with its blue bead-like berries (chomped off—by a chipmunk?), grew here also. On his hands and knees taking photographs with his cell phone, Tom discovered a rare find: a trio of ghostly white Indian pipes, a freakish angiosperm plant that does not have chlorophyll. We seldom come across it and always admire it when we do.

The woods were alive with mostly residential, nonmigratory birds. These were chipping short calls, but the exciting breeding songs of summer were silenced. Making pishing sounds, I called in chickadees and Red-breasted Nuthatches (so tiny!). On the well-defined path, we watched an Ovenbird strut along, unaware that it was under observation, and content to walk and not fly. We spent a long time with it, five to ten minutes. A leashed Lily is a good birder's dog, content to sit quietly while her mistress goes after the avians. The Ovenbird's insouciance made me think that this preserve does not get a lot of human visitors.

As we hiked the trail through dappled sunshine, the roar of Lake Superior was a constant presence, whipped to whitecaps under a northwest wind. The lack of birdsong, a maple leaf turning here and there, a drop in temperature wrought by a cold front moving in the night before—all served to remind us that summer was waning.

After about an hour's hike, we arrived on the shore. The sandy beach yawned in all directions. No other people could be seen. A large expanse of Lake Superior beach on the Upper Peninsula is one of the pleasures of this patch of earth, and a common sight. The beach dune community that we had just hiked through, however, is rare. My delight in it stemmed, in large part, by my surprise that such a community existed. How beautiful Michigan's shoreline must once have been.

On writing this, I am still delighted. I am also so grateful that a woman had the instinctive attitude that Lake Superior's beauty should be accessible to everyone. Ruth Sablich was tempted twice to relinquish the land to development and resisted. The Black Creek Nature Sanctuary is her legacy.

Near the end of our conversation, I asked Ruth if she had a particularly vivid memory of being on the preserve. She said that she and Joe were always amazed at how Lake Superior sculpted the entrance of the lagoon into the lake. The mouth of the outlet changed constantly, depending on where the incoming waves shoved the sand. Sometimes the flow was shallow, and they could easily reach the shore. Sometimes the mouth of the lagoon was wide and deep, and on those visits they couldn't. Embedded in Ruth's legacy here at Black Creek is the little irony that the permanency of a sanctuary allows visitors to see its transient forms.

THE PIPING PLOVERS
OF LONG ISLAND

It has been three full weeks since I was on Long Island in Chequamegon Bay visiting the Piping Plover nests. All of July has spilled out, and part of August. From my desk I gaze out over tangled woods, subdued from the rigors of abnormal heat. Summer is growing long in the tooth. The Merlins that successfully nested fifty feet from our cabin have taken their fledglings and moved farther down lake, perhaps to where the plump birds that make the choicest meals are more abundant. This morning, bands of young warblers—Nashvilles, Black-and-Whites, and Yellow-rumps—roam the treetops. We have heard that the spongy (formerly gypsy) moth population is high. Maybe this year's young are glutting on moth caterpillars, preparing for their first migration.

I am not sure that the plovers are still around on Long Island. Shorebirds are the earliest birds to leave their breeding grounds and head south. In the thirty-five Augusts we have spent on the South Shore, shorebirds have appeared on our beach with regularity. One surreal afternoon, I spent hours in the presence of a Baird's Sandpiper, on migration south from the high Arctic. The exhausted bird tucked its head under its wing and dozed while I kept watch, ten feet away.

I have read online that the Piping Plovers nesting at Sleeping Bear Dunes of Michigan's Lower Peninsula migrate in mid-July.

I had been on Long Island in Lake Superior July 15 and was lucky enough to see a plover. Had I been more fortunate than I knew? Had its neighbors already departed?

Apparently not. It seems that Sleeping Bear Dunes on Lake Michigan warms more quickly than the beach at Long Island. Lake Superior is considerably colder than Lake Michigan. The Michigan birds at Sleeping Bear arrive earlier, begin nesting earlier, and hence, fledge young earlier than the pairs at Long Island. The last I heard, on July 26, of the six nests on Long Island this summer, three had fledged their young, and three were still awaiting the time when the fluffy chicks would leave the nest and begin skittering willy-nilly down the beach, driving their parents to distraction.

Piping Plovers are among the rarest shorebirds in North America. I had long ago recorded a Piping Plover on my life list of birds, but I had seen it on Marconi Beach at Cape Cod, Massachusetts. It had not been a Great Lakes bird.

There are three distinct populations of the species: one nesting on the Atlantic coast, one nesting on the Northern Great Plains (think Saskatchewan), and one nesting on the Great Lakes. The first two populations are considered merely "threatened," but the Great Lakes population is the smallest. It has been on the federal endangered species list since 1986 and was down to a shocking low of seventeen nesting pairs when it was listed. In later years it dropped lower still, to as few as eleven pairs. All those birds at that time nested at Sleeping Bear Dunes, and still today, over half of the Great Lakes population spends the summer on the broad, sweeping beaches of that national lakeshore in lower Michigan.

I have been a birder for most of my life. I consider all birds beautiful and interesting, but I seldom think of them as "cute." I make an exception for Piping Plovers. These birds are *winsome*. Smaller and rounder than their cousins the Killdeers, Piping Plovers have big, round heads and large, dark eyes. They scurry about the beach on bright-orange legs, poking their stubby little beaks in the sand in hopes of nabbing dinner. Other birders have labeled them "clowns" because of their jerky antics, but of course there is nothing comical in being a clown. Clowns at circuses and rodeos have serious roles to play, luring dangerous bulls or bucking broncos away from riders who have been thrown, and the beguiling little plovers are in dead earnest as they arrive on their wide-beach nesting grounds in late May and prepare to make new plovers.

There are several reasons why the Great Lakes plovers find themselves in such dire straits. What sent them tanking initially may have been habitat loss due to human activity. Piping Plovers gravitate toward the broadest, most iconic beaches—Indiana Dunes at the toe of Lake Michigan, Sleeping Bear Dunes with its abundance of sand, and the Apostle Islands. People are also drawn to these beauty spots and have erected resorts and seawalls to shore up the eroding sand. Humans, sometimes accompanied by dogs, stroll the beaches, admiring sunsets, collecting driftwood, and enjoying the horizon.

Plover nests are subtle. The birds scrape out a simple nest right on the sand and lay four speckled eggs that blend in with their surroundings. Even an observant person could stumble into a nest area and destroy it, and over the years, with human feet working their way over the sand, this has been an all-too-common scenario. Predators like skunks and raccoons are also drawn to human activity and roam the beaches at night, devouring eggs and nestlings.

In recent years, rising lake levels have played a role in reproductive failures. As climate change has settled in, high water in the Great Lakes has eaten away at the broad beaches that Piping Plovers require. The lake chews up shoreline, and trees topple, becoming driftwood. Increased wood clutters the beaches. The birds won't nest in areas with accumulated driftwood. Nest areas are also vulnerable to flooding as the severe storms of our warming world pound the shore with waves.

HAPPILY, THE PIPING PLOVER STORY is not one of despair, at least not yet. The turnaround has begun on Lake Superior's South Shore, on Long Island. For this reason, I had wanted to visit the site for two years. Unfortunately, my interest coincided with the Covid-19 pandemic. With Covid restrictions, the park service couldn't accommodate visitors. A year passed, then two. I feared I would never see where the rare little birds were recovering.

In 2022, I tried again, but this time I approached the biologists of the Bad River Natural Resources Department. I was put in contact with their nest monitoring program. The tribe hires people during the summer to live at an outpost on Long Island and monitor the nesting birds.

When I lived in Ashland in the early 1980s, Long Island was an actual island situated at the mouth of Chequamegon Bay. In the years since I lived there, Lake Superior has shoved sand around (there's always an abundance of sand on the South Shore, but it's not always evident) and formed a sandy spit, connecting the island to the mainland at the shoreline of the Bad River Indian Reservation.

The Bad River Band claims part of the spit—they may, in truth, claim *all* of it—and the National Park Service tends the tip. Together, the two entities, along with the Wisconsin Department of Natural Resources (WDNR), the U.S. Fish and Wildlife Service, the Nature Conservancy, and University of Minnesota researchers conduct a program to preserve and restore the population of this rare little bird.

In the 1950s, as the plover population approached its nadir, a young researcher from the WDNR observed five adult Piping Plovers on Long Island, so biologists knew that the plovers had historically hung out there. In 1974, the same researcher encountered plovers along the St. Louis River estuary near Duluth and Superior, but by 1983, they had disappeared—the plover population was bottoming out. But then, in 1998, the plovers reappeared at Long Island and produced three young. These successful parent birds had been banded as chicks at Sleeping Bear Dunes. Despite what was known about Piping Plovers—that they are extremely faithful to the small, sandy patch of earth where they are hatched—these birds pioneered a new beach and produced offspring that would then adhere to Long Island, in a new Great Lake, Superior.

Photographs from 1998 show Long Island with a very broad beach, something resembling Cape Cod. In the 1990s, Superior's level was low and allowed for expansive beaches. Environmental conditions were to the plovers' liking, and the population began to recover.

Since 1998, Piping Plovers have nested on Long Island every year. In the early aughts, only one pair was seen, but since 2006, there have been as many as six nesting pairs. When high lake levels eroded the beach on Long Island, the birds checked out the beaches on other islands and found them acceptable. There have been nesting plovers on Outer, Stockton, and Michigan Islands, and they have been seen on Cat Island. One hundred twenty-five chicks have been banded, 82 percent of these in the past three years.

It is on Long Island near the nests that the monitors protecting the plovers live throughout the summer. The nest monitors are usually young adults, ideally wildlife biology students or recent grads, who camp near the breeding sites from early June to mid-August. They observe the birds, take careful notes, help locate nests, build and maintain protective cages, and not insignificantly, act as plover ambassadors to the public. The National Park Service supplies some monitors. Those I accompanied on my visit were hired by the Natural Resources Department of the Bad River Band of Lake Superior Chippewa.

The allure of a remote sandy beach is strong. Visitors to the Apostle Islands National Lakeshore can take their boats to Long Island. The morning I was on-site, a sailboat had dropped anchor on the lee side of the spit and spent the night. If people do come ashore, it's the monitor's job to point out the nests, describe the protective efforts, and ask them to leave and give the rare little birds space.

On Long Island this year, there were seven defended nest sites, but one was abandoned early in the season. The youthful monitors bestow monikers on the sites. Nests identified as #2 and #3 have been nicknamed "the Duplex" since the territories share a boundary. Because of colored leg bands, the birds can be individually identified, and the two side-by-side nesting females are related—a mother and her daughter. The males select the sites and scrape out the nests, and the two males were not related.

Both nests in the duplex produced chicks: Duplex A had four chicks in the third week in June, and Duplex B, three chicks in early July. Nest 5 on Long Island is termed "Joe's Nest," and Nest 6, "Caspian Nest."

Both Piping Plover parents share incubation duties over a time period of about four weeks. When the chicks hatch, they are precocial, tiny balls of fluff running about soon after emerging from the egg, able to feed themselves. The females migrate within a week after hatching; the chicks stay with their paternal parent for another several weeks as they grow bigger and prepare to migrate.

This behavior is flexible, though. In 2019, a Long Island pair hatched four chicks, but the parental male and one chick disappeared soon after. The female stayed longer than she otherwise might have and tended the remaining three chicks until they were ready to be on their own.

Banding the birds gives researchers an accurate population count, allows them to understand how the birds move between the Great Lakes, and provides a rough estimate of how genetically diverse the population is. Great Lakes Piping Plovers sport a variety of leg bands. Every chick gets a metallic USFWS band with an identifying number soon after hatching. Records are kept by the federal government. The birds also get colored leg bands in various combinations that enable researchers to identify individuals at a distance. On the Apostle Islands, all chicks are banded on the same day.

The Piping Plover Recovery Team on the Great Lakes uses wire cage enclosures around nests to keep out predators and protect the eggs from human feet. These are extremely simple structures that can be built on-site from wide-mesh fencing material—small enough to keep out predators but just big enough to let the birds in and out. Territories are also staked out with little flags to easily identify.

On my visit, one monitor was ending a four-night stay, and we shuttled another out in our boat, dropping him off with his pack, binoculars, food, and ten gallons of water. The shady camp on the end of the sandspit had a sleeping tent, a cooking/living screen tent with a table, and a bear-proof locker. The monitors do not have access to a boat. It's a solitary life, difficult for socially inclined young people. Our monitor told me he didn't want to do the job indefinitely. He passed the time by reading a lot of books.

The monitors spend days and nights facing the blue expanse of Lake Superior. The opportunity to do fieldwork, meaningful work, for an endangered species, is excellent. I'm guessing that long after the summer ends, the scent of balsam fir and the soughing of pines will bring back rich memories.

When the federal government places a bird on the endangered species list, it includes a recovery plan that indicates when the species is considered no longer at risk of extinction. For Great Lakes Piping Plovers, which once numbered as few as 22 birds, the recovery goal is 150 breeding pairs. As of 2022, there were 74 breeding pairs on the Great Lakes—Michigan and Superior. The population adds about 2 to 3 pairs per year.

At this rate, it may take thirty more years of endangered status for a complete recovery. It seems like a gargantuan effort for a species that is sure to face continued high-water levels, disappearing beaches, and eroding sand.

Researchers like to apply the term *umbrella species* to Piping Plovers; that is, they are a charismatic species that captures human attention, but protecting them also protects a host of other associated species, like beach plants and insects. For their part, the plovers, though seemingly fussy, have proven themselves resilient in the face of constantly changing conditions.

It all passes quickly, the summer life of a Piping Plover. If I were to return to Long Island tomorrow, would any birds remain on their beach, this first week in August, or have they already migrated, winging their way to the Gulf of Mexico? The passage of the breeding season is like shifting sand, here today and gone tomorrow. The brevity of it all—the breeding season, the summer, a lifetime of summers—takes my breath away.

FROG BAY

Be Part of the Whole

We make our way through a dark, leafy tunnel, cool in September, the last days of summer. Then, a break in the canopy, and we step into the open of a sandy beach and the expanse of a shallow inlet. Oak Island, one of the twenty-two Apostle Islands, is directly across the water. Before us is Frog Bay, blue and clear, the many colors of the lake-bed stones vivid and true, seen through its crystalline water. The scene is everything we expect of Lake Superior: azure and pure, seemingly untouched, fringed with conifer greens.

Beauty is the beating, living heart of Frog Bay. My family has made a day trip here to enjoy that beauty, out of love for the lake and out of curiosity for something entirely original. At this bay, the Red Cliff Band of Lake Superior Chippewa has established the first tribal national park in the United States. When we visited in 2019, the fall before the pandemic, the national tribal park had been in existence just two years. The band set aside some of its original reservation land, reacquired another equal parcel that had traveled out of tribal ownership and been logged, and set up a Conservation Management Area (CMA) bordering the park to act as a buffer and protect the Frog Creek watershed. The CMA includes a tract of forest that had been part of the original reservation but had fallen into Bayfield County hands as forestry land.

What seems like a crazy-quilt description on paper is in truth a seamless whole. The park encloses a large tract of boreal forest the likes of which I did not know existed on Superior's South Shore. On our family's cutover land, we have mostly quaking aspen and balsam fir, with an occasional white pine that escaped the ax. But the tribal park has old, large hemlock—like those we have seen growing on the Upper Peninsula of Michigan. It is true, there are also enormous stumps, the remainder of cut hemlocks, but the culling was done in such a way that it did not destroy the integrity of the forest.

The lower branches of the hemlocks are wispy and devoid of the small, sharp needles that define the tree—not a lot of sunlight reaches into the depth of the forest. The floor is mostly bare of plants in the darkest areas, blanketed with leaves from the previous summer and sphagnum moss.

Back home, studying the photographs I snapped on my phone, I see that the forest also reveals the next-generation inhabitants: tiny, two-leaved red maple seedlings poke up through the leaf litter. There are also delicate, apricot-colored mushrooms piercing the dead leaves. Though the end of the summer has been dry, the moss and litter retain enough moisture for mushrooms to flourish.

A walk along the 1.7-mile path through the forest is also a lesson in Anishinaabemowin, the Indigenous language of the Ojibwe. At intervals, informational signs label the various plants and animals of the park. There's *baapaagimaak*, black ash, whose straight trunks are used for making lacrosse sticks. It is a species threatened by the invasive emerald ash borer, a beetle from Asia that is just now making its way into the western Lake Superior area. The prospect of its destruction is causing a great deal of anxiety. Years earlier in Lower Michigan, Tom and I had seen extensive stands of dead ash— bad for the trees but a feast for Yellow-bellied Sapsuckers drawn to the insects in the dead wood.

A sign points out the notorious *zagime* (mosquitoes)—not necessarily at that exact place, in that exact time, but guaranteed to be around most days. Another tells me that the word for "grandmother" in Anishinaabemowin is *nokomis,* easy to remember for those who grew up with the Longfellow poem *The Song of Hiawatha.* I am startled to learn that the name for the large, rangy quadruped with a big rack and pendulous schnoz is *mooz.* How many years have I spoken English and not known that the source of that word came unchanged from the Indigenous people? The term is widespread. The Eastern Abenaki called the animal *mos,* and the Narragansett, of what is now Rhode Island, *moos,* meaning "twig eater." Both tribes share a common language base, Algonquin, with the Ojibwe.

It is a good thing the Red Cliff Band is doing, holding up this precious remnant of boreal forest and cherishing it. But it occurs to me, thinking back over our visit, that all of it—the black ash, the hemlock, the moose, the tiny boreal plants of the forest floor, the cold water and its clarity—is threatened in a way that no one can easily fix. As global warming clamps down on us, it endangers all these northern inhabitants. Cold places are becoming exceedingly rare. Soon they will be very hard to find, and there will be no place for boreal dwellers to go.

BACK HOME, we talked enthusiastically about the tribal park and the nearby distillery, the Copper Crow, selling craft spirits on the reservation. It had been packed with white tourists wearing "I Love the Apostle Islands" sweatshirts when we had dropped in after our hike through the park.

"I've been there!" my sister-in-law Kirsten exclaimed—meaning the tribal park, not the distillery. "That was Lisa's cabin!" For years, Kirsten had raved about her childhood friend Lisa Melberg's family cabin, on land that had been part of the reservation. It was on a bay of Lake Superior near Bayfield. Kirsten had been a frequent guest at the cabin for almost fifty years. I was interested in what Lisa's childhood summers had been like on Frog Bay, and what she now thought about her family's cabin reverting back to tribal land. Kirsten thought Lisa would be willing to talk to me.

"The wind will keep the deerflies at bay," Lisa said on a breezy

July morning as I got into her car. I ride with her to the tribal park and the parcel of land that her family had loved since the 1930s.

Lisa Melberg is a tall, trim, outdoorswoman with a blond mane, dressed in rugged sandals and hiking wear. When I ask her how a part of the reservation came into her family's hands, she tells me the story about the Ojibwe chief Buffalo, or, his Ojibwe name, Kechewaishke.

Kechewaishke was born in the 1700s at La Pointe and led the Lake Superior Ojibwe for decades. A skilled negotiator on crucial treaties of the 1800s, he successfully prevented the removal of the Ojibwe from the Lake Superior region and won for his people reservation lands in northern Michigan (Lac Vieux Desert, Ontonagon, and L'Anse), northern Wisconsin (Lac Courte Oreilles, Lac du Flambeau, and Bad River), and northern Minnesota (Grand Portage, Fond du Lac, and Bois Forte).

At the time of negotiations, a small parcel of land was set aside for the chief and his family across from Madeline Island on the mainland at Miskwaabikong (Red Cliff). The Melberg family story goes back this far, when Buffalo sold a portion of this land to lumber barons, who logged it and then sold the stumpage to another buyer.

Lisa didn't know how many times the land changed hands, but in the Great Depression, it belonged to a friend of her grandfather. He could not pay the taxes on it—at this point, we know that Bayfield County recognized it as taxable land—and so Lisa's grandfather took over the payments, receiving the land in return. A small log cabin was on the site. Grandpa Melberg, a Norwegian immigrant, hauled in his portable sawmill and added a kitchen to the cabin and an outhouse. Surrounded on all sides by the reservation, it would serve as the Melberg vacation home for eighty years.

"How would you describe your childhood summers there?" I ask her on our drive out.

"Wonderful." She says it confidently, not needing to elaborate. "I am blessed . . . I grew up in a national park. It's beautiful, wait till you see it. Crazy beautiful."

After arriving at the tribal park car lot, we head out on foot on an abandoned road that leads down to the water. The Melberg clan accessed their cabin this way. Park personnel now travel this road on ATVs to reach this area of the park.

Lisa wants to approach the cabin and its yard by crossing Frog Creek. "The bridge is out, but we can roll up our pants. It's not deep."

The Melbergs sold their land to the Red Cliff Band in 2017. Tribal efforts to reclaim the original reservation land had been underway for some time. Funding for the buyout came in part from the National Oceanic and Atmospheric Administration's Coastal and Estuarine Land Conservation Program, which has been protecting fragile coastline since 2002. The tribe's desire to consolidate their original reservation dovetailed nicely with the federal program to prevent the degradation of this inland coast.

As we walk toward the cabin, I listen to Lisa tell me about her life with cousins, aunts, and uncles in a one-room cabin, summer days on the sandy beach, learning to water-ski on the calm waters of Frog Bay. Learning to read the fickle and sometimes dangerous weather of Lake Superior. Evenings lit by kerosene lamps and candles.

On the path, I notice diminutive boreal plants, the same plants I saw growing in the boreal forest on our previous visit: bunchberry, wintergreen, tiny wild lily of the valley. Fittingly, in the middle of the path I see small specimens of *Plantago major*, what Indigenous people have called "white man's footprint" because of its tendency to colonize hard-packed areas tamped by boots.

We are brought up short by a large white pine that has fallen over the path. It is a huge tree, impossible to scramble around. Lisa knows this tree and becomes distressed. It is like an old friend has taken ill and died. We need to retrace our steps and skirt the edge of the lake, and when we reach the boathouse, we discover another tree down—another large pine, this one fallen across the ridgeline of the erstwhile Melberg cabin, crushing it. From the looks of the boughs, this is not a recent event. I wonder if these trees didn't go down under the same high winds that took several of our white pines down a year ago. Lisa is quite sad to see the cabin so neglected. In addition to the fallen tree, brush and brambles surround the graying walls so much that it resembles Sleeping Beauty's castle. The cabin was finely crafted, a work of art by a Scandinavian immigrant who had the skill to tightly join corners.

I mull over this apt metaphor: a European immigrant craft placed on tribal lands, loved and valued in its time, and now returned to the Indigenous owners, who are shaping the land back to what they value.

Lisa and I are both surprised to see that the boathouse still stands. The family kept what she calls a "Dunphy" in there. It was a small, modest motorboat with a molded plywood hull. With the Dunphy the family explored the Apostle Islands, which hunker just off the shore. The double doors to the boathouse hang open. There's nothing of value inside, but Lisa recognizes some familial stuff that remained after the sale. By 2005, her dad had sold his portion of the cabin to his siblings, so Lisa had no hand in the sale.

Although this patch of earth was once the dearest to her heart, Lisa has made her peace with the sale. Her father was the one to sever his family's tie to the cabin. She knows that if the place had been sold to another family, she would never have been able to come back to sit on the cobbles and recall what the lake murmured to her as a girl. "Now, I can visit any time." She said this several times, reassuring herself of her claim on it, and the lake's claim on her. She is keenly aware that the Red Cliff Band's largesse, their new and unusual vision of a tribal national park open to all, gives her access to this patch of earth.

"What do you remember most poignantly about your summers here?" I ask her in closing.

Lisa pauses and then says, "It's a completely off-the-grid cabin, right? So it taught me about being in the outdoors. That whole experience of being outside, of not having a lot of shelter . . . you learn how to survive. We'd go out in the boat—this is before the weather radio—and it would be a beautiful day, and my dad would say, 'Let's go out to Devil's Island! It's glassy, it's smooth, let's check it out!' and then the wind would shift, and we'd have a horrendous ride home. When I was a little kid, I thought I was going to die in that boat. It would smash on the big waves." Lisa smacks her hands together. "I was scared when I was young. I was very afraid. I got over that. You learn survival skills."

The sun had wheeled to the west. It was time to leave. Lisa stops to appreciate the pink wild roses blooming profusely at the edge of the sand. Then, after looking around once more, we head up the path to the car.

IN A RECENT NEWSLETTER put out by the Treaty Natural Resources Division of the Red Cliff Band, I found the word *ganawenjigaade*. It means "It is taken care of, protected . . . we take care of, protect, keep it." The newsletter made clear that it is not only the tribal park at Frog Bay that they take care of but also the fish in the water of the bay, the wild rice, *manoomin*, the sacred grain that grows in the Frog Creek estuary, and indeed, all the inhabitants of this patch of earth that the Red Cliff Band nurtures. If asked, tribal members might point out the reciprocity—they take care of this land, but the land also takes care of them. It nourishes them, it connects them to the Creator.

What does it mean to own something? Freedom to use with no restrictions, no boundaries? That kind of land ownership in America has always made me wince and made me ill.

I am struck by how the Melbergs resonated with this same patch of earth, revered it, greeted the pines as friends, considered the roses with affection. It seems that Frog Bay calls to the deepest reverence embedded in humans. It asks visitors to the park to be aware, to be gentle, to be selfless. To lose the ego and be part of the whole.

THE KAKAGON SLOUGHS
OF MASHKIIZIIBII

The waters of the Kakagon Sloughs, the delta of the slow-moving Kakagon River, are luminous and reflect the sky. I can't tell where one ends and the other begins. This lovely, quiet river flowing through the Bad River Reservation of northern Wisconsin empties into the northeast corner of Chequamegon Bay. It is sheltered from the battering of Lake Superior's northwest winds by a protective peninsula that curves over the northern edge of the delta. In May, the wild rice plants that have brought me here are growing unseen beneath the water, but round, sage-green lily pads dot the surface and indicate the channels of waterways that comprise the delta.

My guide to this fabled wetland is Mike Wiggins, the tribal chairman of the Bad River Band of Lake Superior Chippewa. Mike has been acquainted with the meanderings of the Kakagon River since childhood and susses out the channel to avoid damaging the hidden plants, even if, in his enthusiasm for the beauty of the sloughs, he sometimes wanders astray. Young wild rice is particularly vulnerable to uprooting at this submergent stage, and Mike is vigilant to protect it.

We began our outing at the tribal fish hatchery upstream from the sloughs. The tribe raises walleye and yellow perch to replenish the fish taken from Lake Superior by sport anglers. In operation since 1968 and expanded in 2005, the hatchery has the capacity to produce a million walleye fingerlings when conditions are right, the most productive hatchery stocking Superior. Bad River is justifiably proud of this operation and its restorative work. It was there that I met Mike and began the trek downriver.

The spring air is chilly, and the trees have leaves the size of mouse ears as we start out for the sloughs downriver. We travel in a broad-beamed aluminum skiff, powered by a big outboard motor, which traverses the large expanses of marsh with ease. The Bad River Band has been the guardians of these bountiful wetlands for centuries.

Bad River treated with the United States for this water-rich land in 1854. It was land they already occupied and knew intimately. They knew its generosity, how it could sustain them, and they vigorously pursued guardianship of the wild rice beds. They call the grain, which is native to North America, *manoomin*, "the food that grows on water." Their relationship with the beds, with manoomin, began over a thousand years ago and is the stuff of prophetic visions, signs, and a migration. Wild rice defined them as a people. At the conclusion of the treaty negotiations, the Bad River Band successfully retained 124,459 acres of land, the largest reservation in the state of Wisconsin, with thirty-six miles of Lake Superior shoreline. The tribe calls its land *Mashkiiziibii*, "good medicine."

Numerous tributaries feed into the Kakagon, creating a network of waterways, each quiet, with wild rice beds lining the margins. As the river carries us near the big lake, the leaves on the shrubs fringing its banks get smaller and smaller, until the landscape seems more like late winter than mid-May. At this point, the river divides into four different segments, and Mike distinguishes each one in turn.

"This is Little Round River," he begins, as the skiff slows down and settles into the water. "It is primarily comprised of an island, the channel route goes right around it and joins back with Kakagon. Little Round is an old, traditional fish camp, it's a wild rice camp. There's a lot of ancient history that happened on these places."

During the ricing season in late summer, families past and present have gathered on the island to camp and harvest. High ground is scarce in the watery delta, and this island is so dry, it supports oaks. Certain families have a generational connection to this patch of dry land, with memories of stories being told around a campfire, meals shared with elders who are no longer with them, of babies once small and now grown.

"So, Little Round River," Mike says as we pass by, and then, "we'll come up on Big Round River." The skiff picks up speed and zooms onward. We pass dry cattails that have not yet greened, Red-winged Blackbirds flashing their scarlet epaulettes, and a female Northern Harrier skimming the dry surface, looking for mice.

"This is Big Round River," he says, after a few minutes have passed. "It's a bigger island and similar to Little Round. It breaks off and then circles back upon itself."

The skiff zooms along until Mike gestures and says, "This is where Bear Trap Creek goes up in there, under U.S. Highway 2, about five miles over. There's rice beds all along here. We're still on our way to the main expanse." The motor starts up, and off we go. In summer, all of these channels will be thick with the green stalks of wild rice. Kakagon Sloughs are unique in that wild rice, an annual plant, is the dominant species in this productive wetland.

As we reach the "Y" and then Snake Island, we are in the yawning expanse of wild rice that makes Kakagon Sloughs one of the largest intact natural wild rice beds in the Great Lakes region. In precolonial times, wild rice was abundant throughout Minnesota, Wisconsin, and Michigan, but the grain, *Zizania palustris*, is fussy about where it grows. Mike observes, "Wild rice needs the Goldilocks Effect: not too deep, not too shallow, not too clear, not too dark, everything's got to be just right." When these conditions are met, "Boom! Wild rice."

The wild rice plant matures through distinct stages. At one point, leaves from the main stalk rest on the surface of the water, the floating-leaf stage. Later, they will become emergent and grow toward the sun, the emergent-leaf stage. Water levels that allow this are crucial. Leaves must be able to float, and they have to be able to stand erect.

This particularity is a result of wild rice being an annual plant—one that reseeds and germinates anew every year. Other wetland plants, like cattails, have roots called rhizomes that form a mat on the riverbed. Rhizomes store energy that will be used by young growth each spring. But wild rice seeds can't store enough energy to propel a stalk upward. Instead, the plant produces leaves that photosynthesize, first underwater and later in the air, to make the energy it needs.

Wild rice is very sensitive to pollution. Any activity that encourages algal growth and increases the turbidity of the water is detrimental to the plant. The tiny seeds embedded in the lake bottom germinate in early May and begin to grow. Fueled by the sugars produced in photosynthesis, they reach upward. If particles in the water like clay silt or algal cells block the sunlight penetrating the water, the rice is affected. Hence, it is a species indicator of a high-quality wetland. When you see wild rice growing in a lake or stream, it's a sign of purity.

The environmental tinkering of the white colonists was disastrous to native wild rice beds in past generations. Lumbermen dammed waterways to create passages to float logs to sawmills. This caused water levels to fluctuate unnaturally. Cultivation of the land resulted in sediments flowing into lakes. Farm and industrial chemicals and artificial fertilizers polluted once-pristine water. Today, the Great Lakes' heritage of wild rice beds is but a shadow of its former self. Many a Rice Lake or Rice Creek is barren.

AT THE "Y," Mike and I pause and take in the day. Far off, a *migizi*, a Bald Eagle, is silhouetted on a weathered snag. A *zhashagi*, a Great Blue Heron, wings its way across the horizon with deep, slow beats. It is quiet in the slough, a light breeze barely ruffling the surface. I try to imagine a lush growth of wild rice. The loud, wild bugle of an *ajijaak*, a Sandhill Crane, carries in the air. The Ojibwe call it "the echomaker," presumably because its pronounced call can bounce off cliffs and come back to a listener. I look around at a marsh that has not yet greened up, a marsh slowed in its awakening because of its proximity to the big, cold lake. It will be leisurely in its growth toward maturity. It is perched on the edge of promise.

THE VAST WILD RICE BEDS of the Kakagon Sloughs were, long ago, the stuff of visions. Fifteen hundred years ago, the ancestors of the Anishinaabe received a vision from one of their prophets, who told them that a light-skinned race would be coming and that the people needed to migrate westward, following the waterways, and continue until they came to a place where food grows on water. This vision began the migration narrative that shapes Ojibwe understanding of who they are as a people even today, and their perception of wild rice as a sacred food.

At the time, the Anishinaabe were living along the eastern Atlantic coast in prosperous communities. Some were not inclined to heed the vision, but others were. A rich, detailed oral tradition describes the centuries-long journey, a tradition bolstered by maps drawn on birchbark scrolls and archaeological work. The people began moving westward along the southern shore of the St. Lawrence Seaway through what is now New Brunswick. At times the migration paused, sometimes for hundreds of years, but then the prophets would speak again, and the people continued westward.

The first stop was on an island in the St. Lawrence River where the St. Francis River enters, just east of the present-day site of Montreal. The initial prophet had spoken of a turtle-shaped island, which would be the first of seven stops. This earliest part of the migration is the most obscured by the mists of time. Another island might also qualify as the first stop. But the second stop is clearer: it was at the *Animikee*, the "Thunder Water," or Niagara Falls.

It is said that the people carried the Sacred Fire with them to kindle their campfires. They also received a secondary vision of the

Sacred Megis Shell, which rose from the water to confirm that they had reached the correct place.

When it came time to move again, the people were looking for a place where a narrow river connected two large bodies of water. The Anishinaabe were now in the heart of the Great Lakes region. Stop three is believed to have been the Detroit River where it connects Lake St. Claire to Lake Erie. The Sacred Megis appeared here, as well.

Moving westward across what is now the state of Michigan, some people came to what is believed to be the eastern shore of Lake Michigan. Another group moved northward along the eastern shoreline of Lake Huron, up the Bruce Peninsula and to the islands dotting the margin of Georgian Bay. They may have paused at Manitoulin Island, or it may have been Michilimackinac (Mackinac Island). Or both may have been considered the fourth stop. Both are prominent communities in the Ojibwe recent past. The migration paused here for a long time. Their society flourished. Their clan system matured and the mystics, the Midewiwin, gained followers.

Eventually, however, the people were called westward once more. The fifth stop was not far, at Bahweting, what is now called Sault Ste. Marie. Here the people found abundant fish in the rapids that ran from the immense lake to the west, Superior, into Lake Huron.

From Bahweting, the Anishinaabe split into two groups. One group went north along the shoreline of Lake Superior. They left pictographs depicting their journey, and they came to a pause when this shoreline terminated at a large river estuary, what is now St. Louis Bay. Their sixth stop was Spirit Island, at the foot of Spirit Mountain. It seemed that the prophecy was fulfilled here. In the estuary, they encountered wild rice, the food that grows on water.

The second group took a southern route along Lake Superior's shoreline, and they, too, came to the estuary and manoomin. But the elders sensed something was not quite right. One long-ago vision had told of another turtle-shaped island, and backtracking, the people came upon Mooniingwanekaaning-minis, later called Madeline Island. Then, according to Bad River tribal members, they looked across the water to the mainland and saw the Kakagon Sloughs, and they knew that they had arrived. This was their seventh stop.

The Ojibwe community at Mooniingwanekaaning-minis grew large and prosperous. The people fished and hunted, gathered food, including wild rice, and planted gardens. Later, groups spread to different sites along the South Shore, including Bad River. The Red Cliff Band retained the closest ties with the people on Mooniing-wanekaaning-minis.

AS OUR SKIFF PAUSES on the slough near where it spills into Lake Superior, Mike Wiggins takes up pen and paper to draw me a picture. He says that topographers refer to the landform of Lake Superior's western south shore as a "bowl," but the Anishinaabe see it more as a nest. To the west, the Bayfield Peninsula forms one rim. The skiff is too low in the water to see this, but were we out on the big lake, the hulking form of the peninsula would be clearly visible. To the east, the second rim is formed from Birch Hill, a topographical rise of a thousand feet. Birch Hill is notorious for its snowfalls. Storms coming off the water hit the rise and dump their snows.

To the south, the Penokee Range consists of ancient mountains forming two elevated ridges running east–west for about eighty miles. They rise 1,872 feet above sea level. The Bad River springs from this elevation.

Cradled in this bowl, this nest, is the Bad River Reservation, the sacred stones, and the bountiful Kakagon Sloughs. The nest also includes the rich fishery of Chequamegon Bay.

Chequamegon Bay, on which the communities of Ashland, Washburn, and Bayfield and the Bad River Reservation are sited, is one of the largest bays in Lake Superior. It is shallow and southerly, warm and isolated, and one of the most productive spawning beds in the lake. It is essential for native fish like lake trout, lake whitefish, and cisco, otherwise known as herring or tullibee. Cisco are a major component of the lake trout diet, and the smaller cisco come from all over Lake Superior to spawn in Chequamegon Bay. The bay contains the largest spawning aggregation in the big lake.

Lake Superior is a premier example of an oligotrophic lake. It is a body of water that is clear and cold with low production. The base of the food chain, green plants and algae, is sparse, so every other trophic level above the base—herbivores, carnivores—is sparser.

Zooplankton are the tiny grazers that consume the phytoplankton, the tiny plants. There are fewer zooplankton in the waters of Lake Superior than there are in the other Great Lakes. In the Chequamegon Bay area, the density of zooplankton is four times greater than elsewhere in the lake. There are also large, shrimp-like invertebrates living there that are no longer found in the other Great Lakes; these are crucial energy sources for growing young fish.

Other species give testimony to the richness of the Kakagon and Bad River Sloughs, a complex that encompasses sixteen thousand acres. It is one of only two wetlands of Lake Superior where the ancient fish, the lake sturgeon, can be found. The Ojibwe call the sturgeon *name* and rely on it for food. The pristine sloughs are also home to a mussel bed nurturing rare species of these freshwater shell bearers. A small insectivorous terrestrial plant, the English sundew, is found only in the sloughs.

Lake Superior is so big that it is subjected to seiches—changes in lake levels somewhat like tides in the oceans, only caused by changes in barometric pressure rather than the gravitational pull of the moon. The atmosphere bears down on the lake surface and pushes water toward shore, raising the level on one side and lowering it on the other. This is why the sloughs are considered an estuary. There is a mingling of river and lake water—the river flows outward, the seiche pushes the lake water inward, and at one point there is a pause as the flow reverses. The effect is measurable away from the shoreline and into the sloughs.

Sometimes seiche activity can be dramatic—there are photos showing entire dock areas momentarily devoid of water. But usually seiche effects are more subtle but measurable, with regular ebbs and flows, about six maximum highs in a twenty-four-hour period. These can be as high as forty centimeters (sixteen inches—noticeable!) but are more commonly from twenty to twenty-five centimeters (eight inches).

Researchers believe this subtle change in flow has a beneficial effect on wild rice. During the momentary pause, water neither moving outward nor inward, the sediment it carries drops to the riverbed, where rice seeds lie, always hungry for nourishment.

Researchers also suspect that larval fish are swept into the big lake in the ebbing of the seiche, along with other organic matter, such as carbon, nitrogen, and phosphorus. Thus the seiche, a dynamic but delicate phenomenon, recharges the ecosystem. What seems on the surface unchanging is actually maintained by continuous flow.

All of this bounty supports Mike Wiggins's contention that the concavity of land features that form a bowl are actually more properly seen as a nest, a rich nursery renewing the world.

"Wendell Berry writes that all land is sacred," Mike observes. "I'm not saying it's not. But not all land is functional." The Bad River Reservation, snug in the nest, enjoys the largess of the land's production.

WHEN WE FIRST started down the Kakagon River, Mike carefully contrasted it with the other major river flowing through the reservation, the Bad. Where the Kakagon is quiet and meandering, the Bad River is tumultuous and serpentine, roaring into Superior with a load of red clay. It meets its major tributary, the White, south of the reservation boundary, and the enhanced waterway is a force. The voyageurs, it is thought, labeled it "Bad" because it gave them trouble in navigating. Taking a more benign view, the Ojibwe call it *Mashkiiziibii*, or "Medicine," and named their reservation after it.

The watersheds of the two rivers are in proximity. Only two hundred yards separate the streams. There was a time in tribal memory when the White River flowed into the Kakagon, creating a channel with a current that didn't support wild rice. But the White River eventually abandoned that channel—which is visible today. When we passed it while on the water, Mike pointed it out. "That is the shed snakeskin of the old White River bed. The White doesn't come into the Kakagon anymore. About seven hundred years ago, it breached through the banks and was captured by the Bad, and the Bad takes that spirit by the hand and says, 'Hey, man. These Anishinaabe want wild rice, we can't be messing with the sloughs, let's go this way.'" With the turbulent White now running with the Bad River, the quietude of the Kakagon was restored, and wild rice beds were established and protected.

Mike told me an Ojibwe story of this epic event, with the rivers as serpents under attack by the thunderbirds. The commanding thunderbirds arrive in the spring with the other birds; they boom with thunder and flash with lightning. They were created by Nanabozho to fight the underwater spirits, in this case, a waterway that had ruined a vital food source. The thunderbirds pounded those river serpents, and everywhere was blood (red clay.) In the aftermath, the Kakagon Sloughs came back into balance, and the wild rice returned.

But just to be sure it stays that way, each fall at the beginning of ricing, the band's drummers return to the narrow height of land that separates the two rivers and pound the drums. They thank the Creator for taking care of the wild rice.

THERE WAS A TIME in the recent past, less than ten years ago, that the Bad River Band was called on to defend against permanent destruction of the Kakagon Sloughs, the wild rice beds, their reservation, and the Anishinaabe way of life.

In 2011, Gogebic Taconite, an international mining company based in Florida, proposed mining the Penokee Hills for taconite, thirty miles from the Bad River Reservation. Taconite is an iron-containing rock. It is not a pure ore; it needs refining to concentrate the iron and make it profitable to ship to a foundry. Upon exploration, it was found that the taconite was 25 to 30 percent iron, a fairly concentrated ore. Furthermore, there were large amounts of taconite in the Penokees, including a huge volume near Mellen, Wisconsin, a tiny town directly south of Ashland. Mining interests estimated that there were sixty-six years of domestic supply of iron in the deposit, based on American usage between 1995 and 2008. Gogebic Taconite promised hundreds, even thousands, of jobs to an area of Wisconsin that had been perpetually poor.

Of course, there was a catch. Taconite is soft and reached through open-pit mines. In the Penokees, taconite is buried deep in the roots of the hills. The open pit to mine the taconite, as estimated by Gogebic, would need to be four miles long, a mile and a half wide, and six hundred to nine hundred feet deep. The gash in the earth would run from Hurley to Mellen through what is at present a bucolic, wooded landscape.

An open-pit mine is a permanent scar on the earth. It cannot be filled in and remediated. In fact, the material that must be scooped out and removed to get to the taconite, labeled "overburden," must be carted away and stored permanently somewhere else. So there are a hole and a pile, both of massive proportions, that are left behind in the area when a mining company leaves after the mine is exhausted, as mines always are. Gogebic's mine would destroy the majestic Penokee Hills for all time.

High in the Penokee Hills, a pristine little river springs out of the depths and rushes north toward Lake Superior. It joins with the Bad River at Copper Falls State Park, and thus, Mashkiiziibii has its origins in the hills threatened with a taconite mine.

Exploration also found that the taconite deposit contained asbestos-containing rock. When rock is mined and crushed during processing, the asbestos fibers enter the air and water, contaminating both. In addition, the rock was determined to contain sulfur compounds. These form sulfate and sulfuric acid when exposed to air and water. Sulfate can be converted to hydrogen sulfide, which is toxic to wild rice. In the water-rich environment of northern Wisconsin, all water flows north, through the Bad River Reservation, to the big lake.

Wisconsin's governor at the time, Republican Scott Walker, was keen to promote economic expansion through the relaxation of environmental regulation that he saw as a hindrance. Together he and the Republican-dominated state legislature pushed through a bill that expedited taconite mining and modified permitting standards for it that exempted the proposed mine from state laws that were already on the books. The Wisconsin DNR's hands were tied. Later, it came out that Gogebic Taconite helped write this legislation enabling their mine, and that the corporation donated sixteen million dollars to Governor Walker and other key legislators to help them fight a recall attempt.

The bill was devastating to democracy. It marginalized the ability of the Bad River Band to speak for the reservation, the water, and the wild rice. Representatives of the Bad River and Red Cliff Bands were invited to attend a hearing, held three hundred miles away in Milwaukee, and were given fifteen minutes to make their case. The issue was so broad, the stakes were so high, that no one could lay out a rational legal case against the mine in fifteen minutes. Instead, the tribal leaders attended the meeting accompanied by drummers, who pounded out the heartbeat that connected them to the earth, to the water, to the wild rice.

Bad River Tribal Chairman Mike Wiggins has been described as being the best weapon the tribe had in fighting the mine. He skillfully used the news media and social media and spoke directly to Wisconsin residents with this message: if the state legislature can wipe out laws that protect us in northern Wisconsin, they can do it to you in your part of the state.

Mike told me that rational argumentation wouldn't be sufficient to stop a mining project pushed by a corporation hell-bent on making money. What is needed is an epiphany, an awakening, a sudden tectonic shift—when one morning we wake up and see the world differently. We see that clean water is more valuable than iron ore. That protecting the Earth is more important than making money.

Up to this point, the Kakagon Sloughs had been tucked away in the Bad River Reservation, a sacred place for the tribe. Few non-tribal members had seen them. Mike offered whites a tour of the sloughs, to let them see firsthand its loveliness, to see for themselves what would be lost if the mine became a reality. It was an appeal to a common humanity, a common sense of beauty and of justice. People in the northland, he believed, had hearts that would understand.

Mike also appealed, as one head of state to another, to President Obama, and to Obama's Department of the Interior to intervene, and to the Environmental Protection Agency to deny Gogebic Taconite the necessary mining permits.

Before this could happen, however, the company suddenly withdrew its application for the mine. Iron trades on a global market, and the price had been falling, reducing anticipated profits. The federal wetland regulations would also be costly. The company would need to mitigate one and a half acres of wetlands for every acre destroyed. Gogebic Taconite estimated it might cost as much as $60,000 an acre.

So the prospect of a mine was abandoned, on the basis of dwindling profits. But the fight may not be over.

"Until our tribe has ownership or at least part ownership of the metallic mineral up there, we haven't stopped the mine," Mike said. "The spirit of greed is often defined as a Windigo. Rather than characterizing it as 'we stopped the mine,' I would say that the Windigo is sleeping. We put it to sleep. And how did we do that? By celebrating the actual landscape that is here. To remind [people] why these waterways are special in real time—not to destroy something, [only] to wake up to the fact that it was really beautiful."

Everything is bound together in a complete whole: the big lake, the sloughs, the rivers, the wild rice, the people who had a vision and were drawn here by it, and the people who live at Mashkiiziibii today, its present and future caretakers.

"Protecting our waterways is rooted in a seventh-generation ethic," Mike observes. "While we're here, we're temporary. Part of our responsibility as Anishinaabe is to send the things we're blessed with here, that we've inherited, upon our arrival on this planet, to send that stuff into the future for all those babies that are still on the way. Look seven generations forward. How will things we do affect that seventh generation? We want them to have that *mino-bimaadiziwin*, that 'good life,' just like we do. It's important to take the long lens."

THE SACRED ACT OF RICING

April Stone bustles into the Black Cat Coffeehouse in downtown Ashland, Wisconsin, finds me without delay, grabs some refreshment, and settles in to talk with me about wild rice and her experience with the sacred grain. She's a woman in her prime, dark haired, smooth skinned, confident, relaxed, ready to unwind at the end of a workday. She's a mother of four; all her children work at the Black Cat, she tells me. In fact, the smiling young woman who waited on me is her oldest, Isabella.

April is a member of the Bad River Band of Lake Superior Chippewa. She corrects my pronunciation of *manoomin*—it's ma-noo-min, not ma-noe-min, like we Minnesotans pronounce the town.

I begin by asking her when she first became aware as a child that manoomin was not just a dish on the supper table, but a foodstuff set apart and foundational to an Ojibwe sense of being.

A flicker of emotion crosses her face, and she replies, "I was not aware of that because I was brought up . . . ," April pauses momentarily, then resumes, "I wasn't connected to my culture at all." This is not an answer I expected, and I ask her to tell me more.

"My family from my dad's side is from the reservation. I didn't grow up with any culture because my father didn't grow up with it, because of history, because of St. Mary's school, a mission school. You weren't allowed to speak your language, you weren't allowed to carry on any customs, your hair was cut. It was all about taking the

Indian out of the person. That was my father's generation. If children went there and they spoke their language, tried to grow their hair out, tried to put on their buckskin, tried to carry their medicine bundles or whatever, they were beaten. That was his generation. It blows my mind." April's dad was six years older than I.

In a move to protect their child, April's grandparents did not speak the language, Anishinaabemowin, in the home, at least when her dad was present. Quickly, the ability to speak the language, that interface by which an individual interprets the world, was lost. April's mother was white, and the family lived off the reservation. As a girl, April felt adrift, not really white, not really Indian. "I went through my own trauma trying to fit in," she tells me.

After graduation, April enrolled in Northland College. She has had in her life a series of small but significant epiphanies, and it was at this time, on the cusp of adulthood, that she experienced her first one. She began learning the history of her own tribe. It startled her that a rich cultural legacy had somehow been hidden in her childhood. "I was like, *Are you kidding me?!*" She began asking her dad questions, she took every Native American studies course she could, she studied Anishinaabemowin, and she began to reframe American history in terms of colonialism.

As a young woman, she fell in love with a white man who, like her, was an artisan who appreciated finely crafted useful objects. They married and had a child. Now a young parent, she faced the question: how do you want to raise this daughter? The Ojibwe have a naming ceremony for their children. The parents ask a medicine man to discern a name through prayer, meditation, and dreaming. The name is important: it will be how the Great Spirit recognizes you when you pass from this world into the next. The name is a mark. April had already received her name, and she made sure her children did also.

She also started ricing, an act both sacred and practical. While wild rice might be the envisioned "food that grows on water," the act of harvest is a social event of food and storytelling, laughing and sharing. She had a pair of "knocking sticks," with which to harvest the rice, made especially for her hands, carved out of cedar.

April and her husband began to go annually to rice camps with other families. They learned how to process rice. They built machines—not fancy machines but rough-and-ready, functional equipment that could be relied on. In that early time of parenting, April took her one-year-old in the canoe when ricing. But one-year-olds aren't enchanted by long hours in a canoe. In later years, the couple shared childcare with other families.

As she discovered her place in the world and her identity as an Ojibwe woman, April and her husband traveled with their three small children to the East Coast, all the way to the mouth of the St. Lawrence Seaway to retrace the route of the migration that the Anishinaabe people had taken more than a thousand years ago.

The route identifies the seven places that the Anishinaabe stopped while making their way following a prophecy. "I was on a physical journey," April tells me, "to see . . . ," she pauses to articulate her thoughts, "part of those prophecies." As they traveled, the ancient migrators had been told to look beside the path, to see what was left there, bundles of some sort, to pick up the bundles and carry them. "I took the physical journey out, wondering what are these physical bundles that are left beside the path, not realizing that they're not actually physical bundles anymore. They're spiritual bundles"—and here's another epiphany—"They're in here" (she points to her heart). "It's more like a mindset or a lifestyle. What I took away was that it's about living in balance. It took me two thousand miles to go out there to realize that the answers were really within myself. I needed that physical journey to understand that."

A physical journey with three small children (a four-year-old, a two-year-old, and a three-month-old) is an act of optimism and courage. There came a point on the trip when the family realized that April needed to take the children home. Her husband remained on the whole journey, and April and crew rejoined the reenactors on

Madeline Island, the seventh and final stop of the original migration. "It's a pretty powerful story that exists upon the Anishinaabe today," she observes.

THESE DAYS, as August turns golden, or in September, when it becomes undeniable that summer is waning, April heads to her favorite wild rice bed for a day of harvesting. She has not ever riced in the famous Kakagon Sloughs, which the Bad River Band has cared for over centuries. As a non-native, her husband's presence might have offended some ricers, although she said he would have been welcomed by most people. Still, he didn't want to intrude in any way on the sacred rice beds. "So we just stuck to ceded territory," she says, "ceded territory" being land that the Ojibwe relinquished under pressure in treaties. Her favorite lake is Island Lake in Vilas County, northeastern Wisconsin.

It is of benefit to know a rice lake intimately by ricing on it year after year. Rice beds tend to grow in a pattern, and after long acquaintance with a lake, a ricer knows how to best enter the water or knows beds that are tucked away, unseen by a casual eye.

That is not to say that wild rice can be counted on to grow in exactly the same way every year. "You could go to Chequamegon Waters down by Medford one year, and the rice would be on the edges on both the north and the south end of the lake, and the next year, it's no longer there. It's on the east and west sides. Or it's only a quarter on this side, and a quarter on that side, but it was half on both sides. It changes. It doesn't always stay the same."

April also notes that some people aren't as appreciative of wild rice as the Ojibwe are. "Because it's weedy or it's wrecking the hunting—it *attracts* what you're hunting—waterfowl." Indeed, migrating ducks, both dabblers like Mallards and teals, and divers, like ring-necked and scaups, feast on wild rice in the fall. The grain is a high-energy food source and fuels their migration.

Nonetheless, people have been known to take their boats and motor through the rice beds, trying to uproot the plants.

WILD RICE MATURES at different rates from year to year, depending on environmental conditions. Wind and rain impact the ripening seed heads. Consequently, April hedges her bets when she finally decides to head to the marsh. "I'm very, very particular when I go ricing. I don't say, 'I'm going on this day.' No, the weather will determine when I go out at all. And I usually only know the day before, or the morning of." The weather will tell her that the time is right.

When the children were young, she and her husband riced with other young parents. The children stayed back at the rice camp, and the adults partnered up in different combinations. One adult remained in camp to see that the children were fed, gathered firewood for the evening fire, and started dinner to feed the hungry ricers at the end of a long day in the marsh. Ricers are out the entire day, taking a lunch and water along.

At the start of a day on the water, there is always a giving of thanks to the Creator, gratitude for being out in the marsh again, asking for safety in the canoe and for the safety of others on the water. Tobacco is offered up as another gesture of thankfulness.

Ricing always involves a canoe. April lines hers with a clean sheet to eliminate excess debris and dirt at the start. It's a two-person job, traditionally one tasked to women, but today involving men and women, sometimes couples, other times friends. One person propels the canoe along, using a pole; the other person sits in the bow and uses a pair of carved wooden sticks, knocking sticks, first to bend the laden seed heads over the sheet, and second, with the other hand, to knock off the heads. When grain is truly ripe, the seeds fall readily into the canoe. Ricers get into a rhythm, one hand, then the other hand, with the sound of a "shoo, shoo" as the rice rains down. "It sounds like it's literally raining into your canoe," she says.

April observes that some people may brag about how much rice they have collected or will claim that they won't go ricing unless they know they are going to harvest two hundred pounds that day.

But when it comes to taking in the food that grows on water, the grain of prophecy, quantity is not the point. "The lesson and the teaching is in how much you receive and to be thankful for what you get," she says.

After the harvest, wild rice must be processed before it can be eaten. First, it needs to be scorched, or parched. The parching dries out the kernel and renders it incapable of sprouting. Traditionally this was done over a fire, spreading the grain out on tightly woven mats suspended by scaffolding. The kernels change color under high heat, going from brownish yellow to a glossy black.

Then the grain is threshed to remove the hull from around the kernels. The Ojibwe call this "dancing the grain," and often in the past, the first round of hulling was done by children with their feet. A pit, called a *bootaagan*, was dug and lined with wood. The "dancers" wore special moccasins to protect their feet, since the kernels of the rice are encased in hulls with sharp little barbs.

Lastly, the rice is winnowed, meaning the chaff is blown off. The Ojibwe were accustomed to using a birchbark tray for this, placing the wild rice on the surface and lofting it high, letting the wind remove the last bits of hulls, the chaff. Then the rice is picked clean and stored.

April built machines for this several-step processing. "You make your own scorchers, you make your own threshers, you make your own winnowers. Well, maybe these things are for sale, but I've never actually purchased them. I've never seen any purchased. Any rice processor I've known of made their own things. They make them out of whatever they can, just so long as they're efficient and they work. And do a good job with everything." She stores her harvest in five-gallon pails in her pantry.

If ricers choose not to process their harvest themselves, most take it to a professional processor. There are rice processors in Odanah, the village on the Bad River Reservation, and some in Minnesota. Some processors have machines with enough capacity to prepare the grain while you wait. The wild rice harvest can be big business. "But," April cautions, "sometimes you don't actually know if you're getting the rice you actually gave them."

There is no specific amount that a Bad River family might collect. A family might harvest enough for an entire year, or just for a day's outing. They may sell it, or they may give it away.

There is no stigma attached to selling. If they do sell, the wild rice may be sold "green" or "done." Green wild rice comes right off the water and is left unprocessed. Harvesters sell to the Great Lakes Indian Fish and Wildlife Commission (GLIFWC). The selling price is low, two to three dollars a pound, and GLIFWC uses it to reseed lakes.

Others will fully process the rice and sell it in one-pound bags. The Ojibwe hold that wild rice growing naturally and hand-harvested is the only "true wild rice." The commercially cultivated variety growing in paddies and harvested by machine, what I can buy at my local grocery store, is a poor imposter.

Participating in the yearly wild rice harvest is one way April repairs the severed ties to her Indigenous past. She communes with her grandmothers when she holds her knocking sticks in her hands and begins the process of providing food, the sacred food, for her family. "I've always been somebody who has done a lot for my family, for my husband, for my home, for my community," she tells me. "Learning crafts, learning how to do this, to make that, keeping the tradition alive. Doing this because we don't have a lot of makers. Not just making a home, but bringing back mat making, bringing back basket making . . ."

April Stone has become a distinguished basket maker, crafting fine pieces by hand in the Ojibwe manner. She taught herself. There were no basket makers alive in the Bad River Band when she became interested in the craft. She learned from books, from museum collections, and by studying pictures. Among the Ojibwe, the tree of choice in basket making is the black ash. It likes a wet substrate and grows abundantly in the wet areas of the water-rich

Bad River Reservation. The tree's bark has a quirk of not producing filaments that connect its annual growth rings. The soft, spongy spring wood can be compressed into the denser summer wood when pounded by a mallet. Then the bark is easily peeled off into strips and woven into sturdy, hardworking baskets.

Sadly, even tragically, foresters consider the black ash a doomed tree. A non-native beetle, the emerald ash borer, is sweeping across the North American continent, decimating black ash, as well as its close cousins, the white ash and green ash. Whole swaths of dead ash stands have been left in its wake. There is little, it seems, to be done. When it is gone, what April has found will be lost again.

But April is nothing if not resourceful and resilient. I suspect she will find another source for her functional, beautiful baskets. The lesson she learned as a young woman was this: it is essential to live in balance. "The answers are in yourself." Being in balance is not staying still. It is moving forward in harmony, in a rhythm with the earth. It is what leads her one morning in late summer to say, "Today is a perfect ricing day!"

PART IV

Immersed in the Bracing Cold

SWIMMING TO LA POINTE

The sun rises out of a pool of molten metal on this August morning. Lake Superior is quiescent, flat water at dawn. The sky is clear but hazy from morning mist and distant western wildfires. In the haze, the rising sun becomes smudged and assumes an apricot hue. Basswood Island and the tail end of Madeline Island are dark and serene as they loom above the shimmering water.

I am in Bayfield, Wisconsin, near the ferry dock, where hundreds of people scurry about in the golden morning light. Some clutch duffle bags; some stand in small groups, chatting; some wait in long lines for the restrooms. Kayaks are lined up at the water's edge, their paddlers bent over them, inspecting knots and paddles.

Soon, those gathered don wet suits, garments of neoprene, a black synthetic rubber that swimmers and surfers wear to protect from the cold. They wiggle and ease into the form-fitting suits, adjusting tight legs, encasing the hips, the belly, the chest. Lastly, the back is zipped with a long dangling tab, so the encased can work it herself. The suits come in a variety of styles: long-sleeved, sleeveless, short-legged, capris, a few with straps like suspenders, a few two-piecers. They bear fierce names such as "Vortex" and "Viper" and, my favorite, "Hurricane Cat." Offsetting the funereal black are brightly colored swim caps, which some have already pulled over their heads. These are color coded. Men wear orange, women wear pink, and the noncompetitive swimmers wear neon green, colors chosen for visibility over a long distance.

It is the morning of the annual Point to La Pointe open-water swim race, and all swimmers are required to wear wet suits to brave the chilly waters of Superior. In August, Lake Superior is the warmest it will ever be. Generally, the water temperature peaks August 10 at about seventy degrees near shore. (By comparison, a competitive swimming pool maintains temperatures between seventy-seven and eighty-two degrees.) Offshore surface water remains in the sixties. The National Center for Cold Water Safety admonishes: "treat any water temperature below 70 degrees with caution," adding that even water temps between sixty and seventy degrees are dangerous.

The swimmers love their wet suits. They're expensive, yes, hundreds of dollars. They feel constrictive at first. But everyone I talk to effuses over their suits and wishes they had gotten one years before so they could have swum earlier in the season, like May or June, and into the fall. An added bonus is that the rubber suits make swimmers faster and more buoyant. One man told me that with the wet suit he doesn't worry about drowning at all.

The race begins near the Bayfield dock, and participants swim across the channel to the town of La Pointe on Madeline Island, two miles away. The race has become so popular in its thirteen years of existence that it fills all 550 slots. The event raises money, forty thousand dollars on average, to fund the Bayfield Rec Center, supporting everything from aquatic swim groups to Red Cross lessons, programs the small community of Bayfield would have trouble funding on its own.

Dozens of highly trained volunteers in kayaks accompany the racers like aqueous border collies, corralling them if they stray from the course, always just a few strokes away if someone needs assistance. The U.S. Coast Guard is also on hand to provide help. There are a medical boat and EMTs and other medical personnel on both sides of the course. Multiple meetings held prior to the race ensure that everybody knows the plan.

Big neon-orange floats mark the course every third of a mile. At the water's edge, they seem to string out like a giant necklace, disappearing into the rising morning mist. The floats are useful as guides. Every swimmer on the course has undoubtedly used lane markers and bottom lines in a swimming pool. This race, the guidelines are gone, the bottom hidden in the dark depths. Some swimmers will orient by the floats. By necessity, the 550 swimmers spread out for elbow room. The floats become obscured by waves and distance.

Down at the surface of the water, it is hard to see Madeline's shoreline, much less the finish line. To give swimmers something to align to, people at the finish build a huge bonfire, and the smoke rising can be seen by every lonely swimmer, low on the water. This is the true guide, reeling swimmers in. Even as starting time approaches, the bonfire is being lit, tendrils of smoke reaching upward.

My husband, Tom, a competitive swimmer for more than fifty years, will be in the water this morning. It will be the fourth time he has swum from Bayfield to Madeline, and he is ecstatic with anticipation, ebullient in his own restrained, Swedish way. The morning is glorious. The water, sublime. He says he will use the profile of Madeline Island for his initial signpost. There is a notch in its upper silhouette that provides the first coarse-grained sign. Later, he will fine-tune to the smoke.

Tom discovered open-water swim races in midlife and has fallen in love with the sport. He swam breaststroke in high school and college and was accustomed to one-hundred- and two-hundred-yard intervals, begun with a dive, punctuated by flip turns, and ending with a precise, decisive touch. Swimming in a pool is like running on a track. There are diving blocks, a gun, lanes, and a stopwatch.

Open-water swimming is like running cross-country. The race starts with everyone in the water; everyone swims the front crawl, the most efficient stroke; and swimmers wind up their race in a kind of chute, climbing up a ladder onto a dock to touch a timing pad. In this race, the finish is festive, not with colorful flags but with a huge yellow rubber ducky bobbing in the water. That never happens in a cross-country race.

I have other friends swimming this morning. Two, Ben and Therese, are also former competitive swimmers. A third, Ben's wife, Shanda, has never swum in competition and for years could hardly imagine doing so. But she began swimming because Ben and his entire family were competitive swimmers and found the activity mesmerizing—the pulling of the arms, the rhythmic breathing, not unlike meditating. Initially, she pushed herself: one lap, two laps, and then "at some magical point, I just passed a barrier at which time I could just keep doing freestyle." She and Ben train for this race by swimming every morning across the much-smaller lake that their cabin is on, one mile across and one mile return. No watch, no pace clock—just swimming.

Everyone races for personal reasons. Most involve a goal of achieving something difficult. Interestingly, nobody that I talked to feared that they couldn't swim the two miles across. But the big lake provides a psych-out factor. "I was irrationally afraid of the depths, of big water," Shanda confessed. "It's 150 feet deep, right? So it was almost like that little kid feeling of the monsters under the bed."

For Therese, it was simpler: "I'd just like to see if I could do it." For Ben, family members—cousin, niece, son—were swimming and coaxed him along. The challenge of a destination swim, going from point A to point B appealed to Tom. It was a bit like an English Channel swim in miniature. And there was the draw of Lake Superior, the big lake: so clear, so pure, so cold, so almost godlike in its indifference to the struggles of human beings. A lesser lake lacks the mystical pull. Tom swims other open-water races during the summer, circular courses following the shoreline of small lakes, but they are just run-ups to the encounter with the Superior god.

The swimmers are alerted to the imminent start of the race by an announcement from a bullhorn. They wade into the water in three waves: the men, the women, and the noncompetitive third wavers, who are allowed to use flippers and other floating devices, to be accompanied by a friend in a kayak, and to swim simply for fun. Therese opted for this third wave, despite years of competitive swimming, because this would be her first time across. To her surprise, the swarm at the start of the noncompetitive race was, in fact, very competitive. At the starting horn, there was a mad scramble, she got kicked twice in the head by sets of flippers, and one hellbent swimmer ran over her. Shaken, she was thrown off her game and became nauseous—but still swam two miles in the cold water and rolling waves. Her anticipated fear of having two hundred feet of water underneath her was obliterated by her focused determination not to vomit en route.

Being run over by a fellow swimmer with flippers is not a common concern at the start. The swimmers wade in, lake water invades the wet suit, and they feel cool but not cold, because the wet suit provides insulation. As swimmers adjust their goggles, aiming for a tight seal, they chat amiably or nervously. Shanda has learned that she needs to withdraw and focus, to remain calm. During her first solo race, she felt anxiety sweep over her, to the point of not being able to breathe through a stroke. She flipped on her back and fell into her meditation routine, centering on her breath. She had to do this twice, asking herself, "OK, what am I supposed to be learning from this? A beautiful sunny day with a flat lake calling to me. I had to overcome my frustrations." Then, something just clicked, and she swam a good race.

Year after year, the Point to La Pointe offers swimmers an endless banquet of possible conditions. The water temperature may be especially cold or tolerably warm. The waves may be high or nonexistent—and the start may be flat with a chop arising midchannel. Swimmers need to be flexible and adjust their strokes or their breathing to changing conditions.

During one memorable race, Lake Superior presented Ben and Shanda with big, rolling two-foot swells, which buoyantly delivered them to the island. Shanda called it "magical. . . . It was: OK, I'm way up, [I see] people, OK, I'm on my way down, can't see anybody but water when I breathe on this one." It was as if the lake were inhaling and exhaling, carrying them along on its breath.

A third, more subtle factor affecting the race is the current that runs between the mainland and Madeline Island. Few people notice Lake Superior's currents, but they are ever present and can be strong. In general, the dominant current runs counterclockwise around the lake's perimeter, but near the Apostle Islands, wind direction, uneven water temperatures, and all sorts of environmental factors play into their strength and direction. The current running between Madeline Island and the mainland often changes direction and can be in favor of the swimmers or working against them.

On her most recent race, Shanda felt the frown of opposing current from the start. Family commitments had kept her from training for the race as thoroughly as she had before, but she could still swim two miles at her lake cabin, so she had every reason to think she could swim that channel.

The karma was bad from the start. In the days leading up to the race, the weather had been unfavorable, stormy and unsettled. The morning of the race, thunderclouds blued the horizon, and there was already a chop on the water. Once the race began, she had trouble breathing, and meditation didn't help as it had in past races. She could feel the current impeding her progress. It was strong and running to the northwest along the shoreline of Madeline. "I kept trying and trying and the current was really . . . ," her voice trails off as she tries to describe the feeling. "I started [to tire] after an hour and a half."

In frustration, Shanda asked herself, "What can I get positive out of this if I'm having so much trouble? Then I could see how beautiful the day was, with these dark thunderclouds way off, rain coming down, light rain, busy water. It was still beautiful in a different way."

After the start, as the race matures, swimmers find themselves in big water with no land in sight. They have left the mainland behind them; they may have left fellow swimmers behind. Therese, on her first race, swam in a straight line with the buoys in sight all the time. But Tom only catches glimpses of them. The biggest surprise of his first race "was being all alone in the middle of Lake Superior, not seeing anyone around, buoys, other swimmers, boats. It just seems like you're out there on your own." He was instead surrounded by blues, multiple hues of aqua and azure and aquamarine in the sky and water.

Ben agrees. On his first race, he swam with his twenty-something son, but of course, the son was faster, and so "it was amazing. Just being by yourself and occasionally seeing other people so you didn't feel lonely. You could sort of see legs or arms but you weren't near anybody . . ."

Shanda adds: "Fun. It was just fun, and we got to the middle, and I stopped swimming, and I did 360 degrees, and I just looked around, and I said to Ben, 'I love this. I'm not afraid.'"

Ben appreciated the sense of being suspended in the water, an entirely novel way of experiencing the planet. "Suspended. You're floating between the sky and . . . ," he struggles to express the sensation, "I don't know, it's so different from standing. It's hard to explain."

Midway through the race, the swimmers face different conditions than they had at the start. Close in, early in the day, the water is usually pretty calm, but away from shore and as midmorning approaches, a breeze may arise. "The lake tosses you about," Tom observes. "You just have to deal with what you get . . . the waves come in and sometimes I have to roll more when I get a breath so I get my face up a bit higher, sometimes if a wave is coming in, your breath gets shut off so you can't breathe in, and sometimes you feel the wave pushing you a bit." He adds, "It's cool to be out there. You're just sort of on your own, the lake and the sky and swimming. I love to swim outdoors. I read a book once about swimmers over the years. For example, Lord Byron was a big swimmer. He would do crazy swims all over Greece and England and other places in Europe . . . the Brits called it 'bathing.'"

After an hour, or two or three, swimmers approach the shore of Madeline Island. The finish line is at the dock of a private home owned by a generous family who every year welcomes the invasion of 550 swimmers and their fans who have come over on the ferry to cheer them on. The hosts build the bonfire, set up chairs for spectators, and allow changing tents, timing pad, and everything that goes with a race event to dominate this particular August morning at the lake. Truly, one of the sweetest aspects of the Point to La Pointe is this family's integral role in the race.

Sometimes the race ends unexpectedly, as it did for Shanda in the year of bad karma, rain, and strong currents. She struggled from the start and never felt good. "I was getting nosefuls and mouthfuls [of water], and that's hard for me," she explains. Yet, she told a kayaker who paddled over to her, "I want to do this race! I'm confident my breath will come." And yet it didn't.

The kayaker stayed with her, and they chatted. They found out they both were elementary school teachers. The kayaker sang songs to her and reassured her that she wouldn't leave her.

But the race has a time limit of three hours. And so, the kayaker eventually told Shanda (who was fighting the current with a breaststroke) "It's time. We all have to get out of the water."

The kayaker radioed, and the Coast Guard boat came over. Two beefy Coast Guard seamen bent over Shanda, each one taking hold of an arm, and yanked her aboard, and her race was over.

She thanked them and promptly burst into tears. She felt so guilty for needing rescuing. "I was supposed to swim to the other side!" She was the first one that they picked up, but there were others. Some were grateful and marveled at how far they had swum, and others crabbed at the Coast Guard for yanking them in so close to shore.

The next day, her son asked her if she would ever swim the Point to La Pointe again. "Absolutely!" Shanda replied, not missing a beat. "I did not feel like it was Lake Superior's fault," she explained. "I had to face the fact that I had not been prepared."

But the vast majority of races end happily. For kicked-in-the-head Therese, her nausea had passed, and she was just beginning to enjoy herself when the finish line loomed. She focused on trying to maintain a straight line in, since now, feeling well, she had begun to think about her time and ranking in her age group. The next day, she signed up for next year's race.

Ben looks for the bottom of the lake as he nears the end. Superior is so clear, swimmers can see through thirty feet or more of water to the lake bed. At the completion of each race, he has noticed the sand on the bottom. The shoreline is fairly close, and the water is still thirty feet deep. "That's when I feel I've done it. It's like 'Yeah! I've made it!' Seeing the sand."

The splendor of being suspended in blueness, the otherworldliness of the middle of the channel, cannot be replicated away from Superior's watery expanse. Swimmers cannot relive their experience except in memory. Tom concludes, "I felt sorry it was coming to an end. You know it wasn't going to happen again for another year, and it's glorious to be out there."

MAKING A NATIONAL LAKESHORE

The Clumps of Mud

Rising out of Lake Superior off the tip of the Bayfield Peninsula, the Apostle Islands at first appear mounded and dark. They might be called the "crown jewels" of western Lake Superior, so rich in emerald hue and intricate facets are they. The Ojibwe, long familiar with the channels of the many islands, refer to them in their sacred stories. One story explains how the islands came into being: Winabojo (sometimes called Nanabojo), a *manido* spirit who is intimately involved in human life, had seen a giant beaver living in Chequamegon Bay and wanted to capture it. He built a dam at the neck of the bay, thinking to trap it, but the beaver escaped and swam away. This angered Winabojo, and he picked up great handfuls of muck and threw them at the beaver. Where every handful fell, it formed an island.

A close look at the islands reveals an archipelago that surprises in its diversity. There are twenty-two, twenty-one of them protected as a national lakeshore (the largest, Madeline Island, is not). There are golden beaches and terra-cotta sandstone outcrops terraced into ledges or hollowed into caves. Their blue water shimmers to jade along some shorelines.

The island forests are mostly boreal, white spruce and balsam fir, fragrant conifers with spires pointing skyward. Some is old-growth, and other patches are second-growth, a recovery from clear-cuts. On Sand and Basswood Islands, trees edge cleared land that once was cultivated. Because the various islands experienced different land uses, the forests that have grown back have different compositions of tree species, making them a kind of inadvertent experiment. But casting a casual eye over it all, the islands appear pristine, with few traces of human activity.

The sandstone that forms the lowest rock layer of each island is old. Laid down between a billion and 660 million years ago, the Bayfield Group sandstone has three layers, deposited at different times, in different ways. The middle layer, the Devil's Island formation, is particularly susceptible to erosion by wave action. The famed sea caves of both the mainland and two islands occur in this middle layer.

The rosy-red stone was quarried on Basswood, Hermit, and Stockton Islands and shipped to Chicago to rebuild after the fire of 1871. Visitors to the islands can still spot the quarries, hidden behind veils of forest regrowth. The nature of a quarry—a permanent change in a rock layer achieved by cutting the stone into blocks with ninety-degree angles—meant that when the Apostle Islands were brought under federal protection in the late twentieth century, they were hardly pristine wilderness, even though some folks considered them that.

Scattered beyond the thumb of the Bayfield Peninsula that juts into western Lake Superior, the islands front the open lake. Historically, their outer margins have been dangerous to mariners, and nine stunning lighthouses, placed on six of the islands, have been preserved as national treasures. All occur on the national lakeshore, and concessionaires run tours to the Michigan Island and Raspberry Island lights. This concentration of lighthouses is the greatest in the National Park Service (NPS).

The lighthouses are no longer tended and have been replaced by automated lights. Originally meant to safely guide commercial traffic, they now are beacons for pleasure craft in and about the islands. These nine lights are working lights. The original nineteenth-century structures still stand and are destinations for tourists, who take private watercraft or hop a boat tour for day visits. From Raspberry Island's central square light tower with domiciles flanking each side, to Devil's Island's singular cylinder rising high over the island's red cliffs, the lighthouses speak to the remote loneliness of island life.

The Apostle Islands became a national lakeshore, a unit of the National Park Service, in 1970. The path to such revered status for an American patch of earth was not smooth. For much of the twentieth century, the NPS attempted to address an imbalance, where the preponderance of national parks was in the West, but the large population centers were on the East Coast. The park service searched for opportunities to add to its holdings east of the Mississippi. By the mid-twentieth century, most of the open space, especially the beauty spots, was in private ownership and had been subjected to human activity. This was true for the Apostle Islands. The conundrum of establishing a worthy park under such conditions begs to be pondered.

The First Attempt

The push to achieve national park status for the Apostle Islands began in 1930. Interest in a national park for northern Wisconsin came from two somewhat incompatible sources: those who saw in park status a way to protect the natural environment; and those who hoped for economic benefit and development by attracting tourists to the region, creating more restaurants, tours to the islands, boating, gas stations, and jobs.

In 1930, a local newspaper editor, John Chapple, called for a national park to protect the Apostle Islands. He perceived a land grab by wealthy outsiders and fretted that local folks would be shut out of using the islands. His chief concern wasn't a loss of beauty; it was a loss of local access. A Wisconsin congressman attracted the attention of the NPS, which sent a representative, Harlan Kelsey, a landscape architect, to the islands to evaluate them for park status.

On the same trip, Kelsey also visited the similar landscapes of the Superior National Forest in northern Minnesota and Michigan's Isle Royale in Lake Superior. He flew over the islands and was taken out to some of them by private yacht. Local leaders escorted him to a logging camp on Outer Island.

Kelsey was not impressed by the islands and was blunt in his critique: the Apostles might once have been stunning, but clear-cut logging and subsequent fires had ruined them. Top brass at the NPS worried about acquiring what they deemed "inferior" parks, resulting in an agency that no longer preserved only America's most spectacular landscapes. They passed over the Apostle Islands and gave Isle Royale, a large island off Minnesota's north shore, national park status instead, chiefly because, Kelsey said, it had not been logged.

Kelsey concluded that there was a lot of untapped recreational opportunity in the islands and that they might be a better fit as a state park.

A Second Chance

Thirty-five years later, however, nature had healed many of the wounds that human exploitation had made. Forests had grown back—growth that was verdant and lush. Clear-cuts had matured into woodlands with sizable trees. Encroaching vegetation had nibbled away at roads. To an undiscerning observer, it might have seemed as if the earlier human activities that had so altered the islands had never happened. Twenty-first-century land managers have termed the process of land returning to wild nature as "rewilding."

In 1959, Wisconsin's young, environmentally minded governor, Gaylord Nelson, took up the cause of creating a national park in northern Wisconsin. By 1963, Nelson was in the U.S. Senate. He was able to coax President Kennedy into visiting the islands, and Kennedy was properly impressed. Legislation to give the Apostle Islands national lakeshore status was introduced soon after.

In the late 1960s, there was a growing consciousness of environmental damage everywhere on the continent. Significant legislation passed in 1971 to protect air and water quality and species that were sliding toward extinction. Nelson, who is remembered today for instituting Earth Day, was at the forefront of this movement, and the Apostle Islands became part of it.

Nelson shepherded legislation for the national lakeshore to fruition. Deciding what to include in the lakeshore was a complicated process because there were so many moving parts. There were publicly owned lands and privately owned parcels. There were two Indian reservations, Red Cliff and Bad River. The tribes were originally in favor of the park. But later, as the legislation became more defined, tribal governments opted out, fearing they would lose autonomy in crucial activities such as ricing, hunting, and fishing. Madeline Island was not included in the designation because of its extensive roads and permanent population. Sand Island was like Madeline, with farm fields and summer homes, but was nonetheless included in the legislation as part of the national lakeshore, despite howls of protest from the island property owners.

At congressional hearings preceding the legislation, outside groups like the Wilderness Society and the Sierra Club lobbied for designating a large share of the islands as wilderness. The NPS had used the term loosely since the 1930s, but the 1964 Wilderness Act spelled out what such a designation would look like in precise terms. The act defines wilderness "in contrast with those areas where man and his own works dominate the landscape, is hereby recognized as an area where the earth and its community are untrammeled by man, where man himself is a visitor who does not remain." Given the islands' history, they did not fit neatly into a definition like this. The local community was leery of wilderness designation.

Though the 1970 legislation establishing the national lakeshore did not have official wilderness designation, the NPS's first management plan was written to enhance the islands' wilderness qualities. The course of the nascent park was set.

What Is a Wilderness?

To Americans, wilderness has had many meanings. It was the vast, seemingly untouched landscape that European explorers first encountered when they stepped onto the North American continent—oblivious to the fact that the land was fully occupied. As white colonists turned forests and grasslands into farm fields and cities, wilderness was that yawning wildness that shrunk and fragmented, until it could be found only in pockets, about to disappear altogether.

Some define wilderness as not a place at all but a subjective state of mind, and for that reason, a cell phone tower visible from the Boundary Waters Canoe Area Wilderness in northern Minnesota, or a cell phone itself, is anathema to wild places.

Cape Cod naturalist Robert Finch relates a tale in which he got lost in the dark in a tiny patch of woods, less than two hundred feet in breadth, that was next to his house in Orleans, Massachusetts. Walking home one night without a flashlight, he was not paying attention when he entered the woods, got turned around, and lost his bearing. It was only when he thought to look up to the stars that the Big Dipper oriented him. For Finch, the wilderness was lurking in every dark, confusing night.

To stem the erosion of wildlands, in 1935 a group comprised largely of white middle-class men formed The Wilderness Society. The group rose to prominence in the 1950s to protect Dinosaur National Monument on the Colorado-Utah border as the U.S. Bureau of Reclamation, on a rampage of dam construction, threatened to submerge much of it. The society's founder, Bob Marshall, wrote of "the tyrannical ambition of civilization to conquer every niche on the whole earth." Through persistence, the society was able to push through legislation in 1964 that legally codified wilderness. Wilderness advocates finally had a tool to preserve wild spaces.

A PROTOTYPE for managing a national park for wilderness qualities emerged long before 1964 as the NPS made plans for Isle Royale in the 1930s. The island had no roads or trails, and wilderness advocates wanted to keep it that way. They thought that when foot traffic was channeled in a specific way, wilderness lost its essence. But park managers foresaw an eroding mess of unguided feet. As a compromise, Isle Royale was designed with a network of twelve-inch "man-ways" for hikers.

The Wilderness Act considers man "a visitor who does not remain." When the legislation bringing the Apostle Islands into the NPS was signed into law, 60 percent of the land was in private ownership with residents in both summer cabins and year-round homes. If the islands were to become a wilderness where "man is a visitor who does not remain," these residents would eventually have to move.

The federal government began acquiring privately held land in 1972. This was accomplished either by forced buyout or by taking the land by eminent domain. To make the buyout palatable, owners were offered twenty-five-year or lifetime leases on their former properties. Residents whose roots in the islands ran several generations deep were compelled to sacrifice their land for the common good. But many didn't sell willingly. At one point in the process, the NPS was mired in fifty condemnation cases to procure the private land.

A History of Island Use

Most of the Apostle Islands had had inhabitants at one time or another for thousands of years. When the Ojibwe arrived in the 1500s, they congregated on Mooniingwanekaaning-minis, which the French voyageurs renamed Madeline Island. This largest island of the Apostles became a spiritual and economic hub for the Lake Superior Ojibwe, but they also went out to the lesser islands to fish. It is possible they used the islands in other ways; the Ojibwe call Rocky Island Ziinsibaakwado-minis, Sugar Maple Island.

As the fur trade waned in the 1830s, the American Fur Company set up a commercial fishery based on Madeline. A financial panic in 1837 affected the market, and the endeavor went belly-up in 1842. Commercial fishing then paused in the islands.

By 1856, Bayfield, adjacent on the mainland, was founded. The town was remote until a railroad, built by logging interests, connected it to a rail network in the 1880s leading to Milwaukee, Chicago, and Minneapolis-St. Paul. The railroad meant that fishermen could get fresh fish to market, and interest in fishing the islands rekindled. The island fisheries attracted families from Quebec and Norway.

Booth Fisheries, based in Chicago, set up shop in Bayfield in 1884, establishing a national market for Lake Superior fresh fish. The company organized runs twice each week to the fish camps of individual fishermen on the islands. The runs served to pick up the catch and drop off supplies, like fresh groceries, to camp residents. Families learned to anticipate the arrival of the sturdy green-and-white *C. W. Turner* at their dock.

Over half the Apostle Islands sheltered fish camps at one time or another. The community at Rocky Island illustrates the rugged, persistent existence eked out by those who once fished Lake Superior. Two local Rocky Islanders, Bob Nelson, son of Julian Nelson, and Paula Nourse Cunningham, granddaughter of Laurie and Grace Nourse, sat down with me to talk about their relatives' lives.

Apostle Island fishermen specialized in one of two types of fishing. Deepwater fishing occurred beyond the islands, in water greater than 30 fathoms, or 200 feet. Fishing closer to shore involved fishermen setting gill nets in 12 to 30 fathoms (72 to 180 feet).

Early operations focused on deepwater fishing. Fishermen set their nets for lake trout, deepwater fish that swam between 240 and 540 feet deep. They sailed in small Mackinaw boats ten miles beyond the outer perimeters of the islands, east to the border with Michigan and north of the Sand Island lighthouse. This is the open lake, with zero protection from the brutal storms coming in from the northwest and the northeast. It was a treacherous way to make a living, and a fair number died in the attempt.

By the time Rocky Island became a locus of activity in the 1930s, fishermen plied the waters close to shore, in search of lake trout (especially in spring when the water was cold), whitefish, and in the fall, herring, also known as cisco. Rocky attracted deepwater fishermen, too. Julian Nelson of Bayfield, an independent fisherman, moved his camp to Rocky from Stockton Island in 1947 because Rocky was closer to the deepwater fishery off Devil's Island and North Twin Island. The trip out to this fishing ground was now quicker.

Fishing began in the spring as soon as the ice was out. The men set their nets, and up to six days later, lifted them mechanically. Deepwater fishing required as many as fifteen miles of nets per fisherman. Fishermen made most of their money in the spring, so it was crucial to get a good start. These mariners were early to bed and early to rise. Most of them worked alone or with a couple of hired men. Often, the crew was their sons.

The fishermen had permanent residences in Bayfield. When school was out in June, their families joined them at summer cottages on the island. The kids enjoyed a carefree summer, learning to swim, learning to row, learning to sail. For the women, island life was without the amenities to be had in town, like flush toilets or electricity. They produced copious meals on woodstoves and hauled water from the lake. A few kept a garden. The Booth Fisheries' *C. W. Turner* and, after 1938, the *Apostle Islands* tug appeared twice a week with fresh garden produce and ice for iceboxes and to chill the catch.

Fishing the Apostle Islands provided a modest, productive life. No one got wealthy, but no one starved. Most of the fishing families of Rocky Island were second- and third-generation Norwegian immigrants, born to a life on big water. What the vocation had to offer was the natural beauty of broad beaches, jutting sandstone outcrops, and dark quiet forests. And, of course, the blue expanse of an unfettered horizon.

Island Life after Fishing

By the late 1950s, commercial fishing in Lake Superior was in serious decline. The invasive sea lamprey had made its way into the upper Great Lakes by the Welland Canal. The fish resembles an eel and has a huge, sucker-like mouth that attaches to the flanks of lake trout and sucks the vitality out of them. For years, fishing had also been pursued at unsustainable levels. These two factors decimated the lake trout population, which in turn upended the aquatic ecosystem of western Lake Superior. Several decades would pass before robust commercial fishing returned.

The Rocky Islanders received the word in the early 1970s that the Apostle Islands would be designated a national lakeshore and that the National Park Service wanted their land. Acquisition began in 1972. Owners were given the option to rent their lands back from the federal government for twenty-five years or for the lifetime of the owner. Most families put their youngest child on the title, thinking it would give them the longest time span with their cottage. There were six year-round residences, twenty-two summer cabins, a few rental cabins, and seven docks on Rocky. The erstwhile fish camps were clustered along the northeastern shore. These cabins would remain, because they were leased back. The islands all together had more than one hundred summer cabins.

The islands were divided into management zones. Most of the twenty-one islands were to be managed as "primitive," that is, there was to be no development at all, no campsites, roads, or trails. In other words, they would be "wilderness." Sand, South Twin, and Rocky Islands were not designated as primitive, because of the presence of residences.

Although one might detect just a trace of anger from Rocky's summer residents at having to lease from the federal government a cabin that their grandfather built, the present-day leasers, what the NPS calls "use-occupancy tenants," harbor no ill will toward the NPS and generally support its efforts. These summer folks continue to enjoy the same clear air and crystalline water that their forebears did. The lap of waves, the wind through the trees, the glint of sunlight on pristine water—these pleasures of life at a cabin remain, regardless of ownership.

But there was one family substantially altered by the decision to manage the national lakeshore as a wilderness—Grace and Laurie Nourse Sr., owners of a quirky eatery on the island's eastern shore.

Coffee and Pie

The Nourse family is a pillar of Bayfield history. Its progenitor, J. H. Nourse, arrived in Bayfield in 1858, the second family in town. Grace Butler Nourse's family is equally rooted. Her father had a cabin on Rocky Island that he lived in year-round in the 1940s.

Laurie Nourse Sr. wore many hats in his life. He began fishing commercially in the early 1930s, using Rocky Island as his base. He set gill nets and trolled for lake trout in deep water. When his two sons reached their teens, they joined their dad.

Grace spent summers on the island. Tourists venturing the twenty-five miles to Rocky Island on the tour boat frequently remarked that a cup of coffee and perhaps some pie would be a welcome refreshment. Thus emerged a lakeside restaurant, Rocky Island Air Haven, established in 1946 and acquiring legendary fame in the late 1950s and 1960s as it attracted more and more diners. The name refers to Lake Superior's pure air, a respite from ailments like asthma and hay fever.

Grace was an excellent cook, and she enjoyed it. Her reputation grew, and the couple remodeled an old dockside net house into a dining hall. Grace decorated the walls with the accoutrements of fishing—nets and bobbers, life buoys. Laurie crafted the tables, which in a pinch could seat eight. Grace prepared all the food. On the menu was fried lake trout or boiled whitefish, scalloped potatoes, coleslaw, and rolls. Or a diner could order a sandwich on white or rye bread. Grace rose every day at five o'clock to put the dough on to rise, and to make the pies she offered as dessert—apple or lemon meringue.

Laurie's job in the endeavor was to ferry tourists out to Rocky Island in the elegant tourist boat, the *Chippewa*. He met vacationers at the Bayfield city dock and welcomed them onboard. Once underway, the entire trip was fifty miles out to Rocky and back. Captain Nourse entertained the boatload by pointing out each island in turn and rattling off information: its Ojibwe name, length, ownership, and miscellaneous fun facts. Dockhands passed out menus, and during Captain Nourse's commentary, his passengers selected their lunches.

At 11 o'clock, Laurie got on the radio and called over to Rocky, where Grace waited at *her* radio. She took all the orders down as Laurie read them off. One of the waitresses transcribed them into kitchen numbers. Then, with one hour to spare—the *Chippewa* docked at Rocky at noon—Grace heated her big, fourteen-inch skillet and began frying lake trout. In the high season, Air Haven might serve one hundred customers a day. Grace hired three local girls to help. They stayed on Rocky all summer in cabins on the Nourse compound.

The tourists disembarking knew they had one hour on the island. Big orange trays laden with fish, potatoes, coleslaw, and pies awaited them. After luncheon, the diners were free to beachcomb or sit out and admire the view. Then, it was back on the boat for a loop around Devil's Island, if the lake permitted, before heading back to Bayfield.

In the 1960s, Devil's Island still had a manned U.S. Coast Guard station, and the seamen often motored to Air Haven for their afternoon break. Grace's pie, of course, was a draw, but so too was the Hamm's beer she sold.

It was a charmed life for Laurie and Grace. Tourists remembered their Apostle Islands tour with warmth and nostalgia. Grace had a certain charisma, and people treasured their lunches at Air Haven for years.

Needless to say, it was quite a surprise when the Nourses received a letter from the NPS informing them that the islands were now national lakeshore and the NPS would be buying their land. They were unaware of such a development and were among the first to be contacted.

The Nourses were given a choice: lease their property from the NPS or have it taken by eminent domain. The first communications with NPS indicated that Air Haven would be allowed to operate as a concession, because it was so widely known and popular.

The 1965 original proposal for the national lakeshore had included a restaurant, a lodge on Sand Island, and a scenic drive along the perimeter of the Bayfield Peninsula that would have picnic areas and hiking trails. So, it was plausible that Air Haven would be allowed to continue to operate.

But then, things changed. The restaurant was found not up to public health standards, and the NPS did not want to spend its limited funds to bring it to code. At the hearings preceding the enabling legislation, Congress had received quite a bit of pushback against this kind of development from outside groups, despite local enthusiasm for it. With the first plan focused on managing the islands as a wilderness, the cards were stacked against Air Haven.

Rocky Island Air Haven shuttered its windows in 1974. It seemed that coffee and homemade apple pie were not a wilderness experience. Although there was some anger over the situation, mostly a deep, dark sadness reigned. Grace made one more trip to Rocky in 1981, during which her companions reported that she cried all the way out, all the time on the island, and all the way back. She never returned. When her granddaughter was married on Rocky Island in 1984, she missed the wedding.

The Sand Island lodge was also scuttled. Again, outside groups, like the Sierra Club and the National Parks Association, spoke out against it. And the scenic drive? Highway engineers had serious doubts that the red clay soils of the Bayfield Peninsula could support a high-volume road. There are deep ravines creasing its shoreline, and they would need to be filled or bridged were such a road to be built. The scenic beauty of the lakeshore would be permanently marred. So, it too was scuttled, and the kind of development that local residents had enthusiastically supported when the Apostle Islands received national lakeshore designation took a backseat to the wilderness ideas of national environmental groups.

Making a Worthy Park

The Nourses were unlucky. Their restaurant and their way of life were lost in part because in the 1970s the dominant expectation of an outdoor experience took place in an unblemished landscape. The most satisfying time, it was thought, was spent in a nature that bore no human imprint. People could re-create themselves in such a setting, but they couldn't live there. They could visit and then, renewed, reenter their fast-paced lives. This is succinctly expressed in the Wilderness Act of 1964: "the earth and its community of life are untrammeled by man, where man himself is a visitor who does not remain." But the deep human history of the Apostle Islands made it difficult to fit neatly into this characterization.

When the first park management plan opted for preserving the islands without human presence and with limited development, local life in the former fishing camps was irrevocably changed, even if islanders were given the opportunity to rent back their cabins. The NPS took ownership of more than two hundred structures in the great buyout. Some of the cabins were rented back to former owners, but many were burned by the NPS—summer homes, net reels, wooden docks, all the evidence of a vibrant fishing life. Eleven buildings on Rocky Island were razed in 1977; Air Haven followed in 1982.

This obliteration of an honest, dramatic way of life really stung the islanders, who had already relinquished their family cabins. To them, it seemed the past had been unnecessarily devalued and erased.

Americans lost more than just physical buildings when Rocky's cultural past was discarded. We lost an opportunity to appreciate and ponder a way of life that requires an accurate reading of nature, that wrestles with big water, and that is lived in the rhythms of our restless planet. In the twenty-first century, when we struggle to define our human role in the ecosystem, it would be helpful to meditate on an obvious existence where nature is big and humans are small.

To be fair, over time, the NPS modified some of its more severe policies. A new park superintendent and a sympathetic NPS historian have recognized the human activity on the islands. Signage at Little Sand Bay relates the history of commercial fishing. An intact fishing camp remains on Manitou Island. The Rocky Island family cabins are designated the "Rocky Island Historic District."

It seems to me that there are at least two ways of thinking about nature. In one, an old idea in Western thought, life-forms are ranked in terms of complexity, lower and higher, with people at the top. Humans can visit the community of life, but that is not "home." Home is technological human society, where we live and work. The Garden of Eden lurks in this way of thinking. We can visit this "untrammeled" wilderness, but we can't remain. We have already been cast out. And having been cast out, we are now forced to contend with an altered landscape that we pretend is pristine, but in so pretending, we lose the richness of deep time, with its many versions of what the Earth can be.

What if, instead, we saw all of nature as "home"? There is no wilderness, no civilization, there's only the Earth in all its fragility and beauty. Tourists could be encouraged to see the extensive diversity of the Apostle Islands' history as instructive. Like the Ojibwe, who have called these islands home for generations, we might see ourselves in relationship with the community of life, including the rocks and water. The park would not be sculpted into something it cannot be—an unblemished environment. Rather, we could see ourselves truly as animals that change our environment, nurture it for future life, human and nonhuman, and recognize the inherent right to life of our brother and sister animals and leave space for them.

Then there is no proscribed wilderness designation with its rules and expectations. The land is wild to varying degrees. There are only twenty-two islands, Winabojo's creation in a big blue lake, with human stories that need to be told so that we can hear their words of wisdom.

PLUMBING THE DEPTHS

Far out on the horizon you see them, small dark figures stark against the immensity of ice and sky, dwarfed by the yawn of a very big lake—a true depiction, I think, of the relationship of humans to Lake Superior.

The figures are bobbers, fishermen who venture far out from shore to where the lake runs deep. These are not the little red-and-white balls that attach to fishing lines. These are human beings who travel some distance over Superior's ice to reach waters that are a hundred to two hundred feet deep. They are fishing for lake trout, a prized cold-water fish, one that fights when hooked, and one with a succulent, buttery taste. Fish in deep waters grow large, and sport anglers respect large fish. Great size signifies great age, and big ones may not, in truth, be eaten if caught, but photographed and returned to the depths, to live and breed another day.

I was in my thirties when I first saw bobbers out on the ice; I thought they were nuts, these men out for foolish glory and the need to prove their masculinity by landing a really big fish. I don't think that any more. As I have grown older, I have seen how presenting oneself to extreme physical challenge can reveal something about oneself. How it can define a person's place in the great scheme of things.

The sheer distance needed to reach a place where one can cut a hole and drop a line a hundred feet down once limited the scope of bobbing. Old-timers recall stories of early bobbers using dogsleds to venture miles from shore, one or two dogs, sometimes a team, pulling a sled with gear and hauling a nice catch of fish on the return trip. Their stories were among those recorded in the book *Lake Superior: Blood on the Ice,* by bobber enthusiast John Esposito. Esposito interviewed scores of men (and a few women). Reading their interviews opened the world of bobbing to me.

Early bobbers, I read, often used a boat outfitted with runners— like repurposed old skis—to haul the gear, pushing the boat ahead of them. These handmade wooden boats, now a thing of the past, had a dual purpose: they would float and could be rowed, in case things turned ugly on unstable ice.

Technology soon stepped in, and bobbers, creative problem solvers, rose to the challenge of adjusting it. The Ford Model A proved very popular. They were reliable starters and built to last. Some anglers modified them to haul gear. Some added chains to the back wheels for traction. Some tied long poles to front and back bumpers: if the car broke through the ice, the poles would hold it up. Still, there was no modifying human risk. A lot of Model As went through the ice and ended up on the bottom.

Model Ts, which preceded the Model A and were smaller, were also popular. In one story, several Model Ts carried anglers out to the east side of Madeline Island. The cars were lined up offshore from the island, anglers busy at their holes, when the ice broke off. Both the cars and their anglers went for a ride. The story could have ended tragically but didn't. The ice floe wedged against the shore miles away at Saxon Harbor, whereupon the fishermen started up their reliable Model Ts and drove home.

In 1960, life changed for the art of bobbing and for life in isolated communities more generally, when Bombardier Recreational Products introduced a snow machine with a two-stroke engine called a Ski-Doo. Almost overnight, far-off fishing grounds could be reached in a matter of minutes.

Ashland resident Greg Alexander, an award-winning wildlife

artist and bobbing aficionado, spent a morning with me, discussing the art of bobbing. Alexander is also an emergency medical technician, and he noted that the choice of snow machines to take out on Superior's ice should be a prime safety consideration. He pointed out the studded belt that propels the vehicle forward. "Studs are everything," he told me. They allow the driver to increase speed quickly to provide enough momentum to jump widening ice cracks, and they aid in quick stops. His machine also sports extrawide front runners to help stabilize the vehicle when hydroplaning and to avoid being mired in slush.

Alexander also believes in carrying everything he needs for an outing on his snow machine. Pulling gear behind in a sled is too risky. A snow machine can be counted on to skip open water, but a "pull-behind" might not make the jump. Coming up short would send both into the drink.

There's a place in the "beavertail" (the compartment behind Alexander's seat) for his bait, kept in a cooler, and for his tackle. He carries a tentlike shelter to block the wind, collapsed and fastened to the machine. A coiled rope with a float hangs at the ready; a rope that sinks is of limited use. He doesn't use a stove to provide heat, unlike many other winter anglers. Also, for safety, he is adamant about ice picks, slung around the neck with two nails that can be grasped, one in each hand, to gain a hold on the ice, should he find himself struggling in the water. Alexander carries two pairs; he wears one, and he keeps the other in his tackle box, to be handed out, gratis, if he encounters other anglers without. The catch: the recipients need to buy another pair when they are back ashore, and hand them out in likewise manner.

Bobbing for lake trout and other cold-water fish is difficult to learn on one's own. Most bobbers are initiated into the sport by invitation—accompanying a father or grandfather, a neighbor or friend. Many early bobbers got their start during the Great Depression, when people fished for sustenance. Life on the South Shore has always been meager for most folk, but the Depression years hit particularly hard there. Fish fed families. In the 1930s, the Apostle Islands were not yet designated a national lakeshore (that would occur in 1970). During this time, bobbers had access to cabins on several of the islands. They made the long trek from mainland to island, stayed the week fishing, and then brought their catch back to shore to sell or to barter. Several bobbers identified Ehlers General Store in Cornucopia as an outlet for the fish. One recalled that store owner Herman Ehlers was very fair to the anglers, allowing them to barter for groceries they needed.

These early bobbers made their own fishing line from linen, at first, and, later, Dacron. It was essential that their lines could withstand twenty to thirty pounds and not stretch. The old-timers pine-tarred their lines and then stretched them out so they wouldn't give when a fish took the bait. They would wrap two hundred to three hundred feet of tarred line around an elongated piece of wood whittled to the task and called a "hoop" or a "bobbing stick." Neither term accurately conveys the device, which had H-prongs on both ends, somewhat like a weaving shuttle; the line was wrapped between the prongs.

The line had a heavy sinker and a sizable hook, baited with fresh herring, which the bobber had netted in shallower water. There was a certain art to feeling how the line behaved with the currents running beneath the ice, deep in the lake, and how the line felt in mittened hands when a fish made the move to trifle with the bait.

Hauling a fish in also was an art, much different from cranking a reel. The tarred line stiffened and would not lay flat when yanked out of the water, so bobbers developed a "hand-over-hand" technique or walked away from the hole while their fishing partner dealt with getting the fish up on the ice.

Bobbing gear has changed in the twenty-first century. Gone are the hoops and tarred line. Anglers now use heavy braided monofilament, tied to stainless steel line, and wound around a reel on a rod. Greg Alexander also uses heavy lures, something with enough weight to hold the line on the bottom so he doesn't need a sinker, about the weight of a deck of cards. Lures quaintly called "Banti Beetles" are standard, and Alexander adds fresh bait, pieces of herring, to make the hook as attractive as possible.

Early bobbers erected wind-blocking squares of canvas for respite from sharp winter winds. Today's bobber usually owns a tent. Alexander's is a heavy, dark-blue canvaslike material made by a local firm in Ironwood, Michigan. When set up, it stands about six feet tall, without windows but with a heavy zipper at the opening. Other bobbers used sturdy Winslow tents, originated in Bayfield, Wisconsin, which were truly deluxe by bobber standards—spacious, room for a heater, and with two windows.

Technology has also found its way into the fine art of bobbing. Most anglers now use a depth finder to determine the bottom. Ice holes are cut by electric augers. Underwater cameras allow anglers to look around and see what's beneath the surface. But Alexander scoffs at the suggestion that technology has made a bobber's job easier. Nothing has been invented, he says, to make a fish take the bait. That is up to the fish—and a bobber's ability to think like a fish.

Being able to hook a fish and being conversant with the equipment involved are skills any good angler acquires. But fishing on Lake Superior requires other skills, and to lack them could be deadly. One must be to be able to read the big lake and its many hazards. This is where bobbing departs from ordinary fishing and becomes something more, something mythic, an Old Man and the Lake story. How can Superior deceive a bobber? Let us count the ways.

Ice can take so many forms that bobbers have an entire lexicon for it. *Lake ice* refers to ice that forms naturally when the surface freezes over. The edge of newly formed ice where it meets open water is the *lead*. *Pack ice* forms when wind breaks up the leading edge of the ice and shoves it into a pile. Pack ice may or may not be stable. *Blue ice* is beautifully clear lake ice, frozen without air mixed in. Lake Superior's water is so clear that when blue ice forms, details on the bottom are wonderfully visible—multicolored rocks, skeletal snags. *White ice* is slush that has frozen over. *Candled ice* occurs in the later winter when the angle of the sun is high enough to melt ice even on cold days. Little vertical shards form to two-foot depths, honeycombing the ice. "You don't ever want to be on it," Alexander remarks. A rule of thumb is to be off the ice by noon, when the sun has the most impact.

Keep in mind that Lake Superior seldom freezes entirely, so ice that seems solid is subject to winds that move it about. It expands and contracts as air temperatures change, causing cracks. These might not affect the integrity of the ice, but when water seeps up through cracks, slush forms that can impede a snowmobile. A machine that mires in slush and remains overnight becomes, in the acerbic observation of Alexander, "a monument to your transportation."

A crack can also morph into a pressure ridge if the two plates expand with enough force to break up the ice at the seam. Pressure ridges are weakened areas in otherwise solid ice and can be easy to misread. It is not unusual for a pressure ridge to open up, blue water rippling between the sheets. A few inches can be easily spanned, but under a persistent wind, a gap can suddenly become many feet wide. This is not uncommon.

Experienced bobbers carry with them ice bars—rods—with which to tap the ice at intervals as they travel away from shore. They tap and listen, tap and listen, assessing the tension. Is the ice hard or soft? Trustworthy or not?

Experienced bobbers are also exquisitely attuned to the wind. Along the Wisconsin shore, north and northwest winds as well northeast winds blowing uplake are generally benign, but south or southwest winds can detach ice at a weak point like a pressure ridge and create a floe. This is the unhappiest of scenarios for bobbers because they are suddenly adrift. The Apostle Islands offer some protection from the wind, some opportunity for ice to be anchored, but in other areas along the shore, particularly Port

Wing, the "harbor" is almost nonexistent, and ice is easily swept into the wider lake.

Lake Superior also has circulating currents, which experienced bobbers keep in mind. Certain areas are notorious: in the Apostle Islands, both the North Channel and South Channel of Madeline Island agitate with currents. Points that jut out from land seem to affect currents, which eat away at the ice from underneath, making it deceptively thin. Seemingly innocuous Roy's Point, south of Red Cliff, and Houghton Point, north of Washburn, have reputations for danger, as does Little Girl's Point, near the Wisconsin–Michigan border.

Currents manifest themselves by how a line behaves when dropped down the hole. Is it drifting to one side? A strong current is taking the lure. An alarming experience frequently mentioned in Esposito's interviews involves becoming aware that the current beneath a bobber has "switched directions." This, of course, doesn't happen. It means the ice is drifting with respect to the current. At other times, water may suddenly bubble up in the hole; that is another indication that the ice one is fishing on has been set free.

Winds change throughout the day, so what is safe in the morning might not be safe at noon. Alexander related a story of a fishing trip he made with his young daughter. They were away from shore, but they knew a storm was forecast to arrive around 11 o'clock. By 10 o'clock, they had moved their tent closer to shore near Red Cliff. When the storm hit, as predicted, the wind had force enough to knock over their tent and create a whiteout. All they could do was hunker down and endure, knowing that at least they were on secure ice.

Meanwhile, a foursome of men, including two brothers, were fishing farther out by Stockton Island, perhaps fifteen miles offshore. When the snow squall arrived, they decided to pack up and leave, but visibility was terrible, and their GPS didn't work because of thick snow swirling about. They ran into bad ice, and the younger brother went into the water, along with his snow machine, which was carrying the only safety gear. He had some difficulty reaching ice that was strong enough to hold him. The shelf was so thin, it kept breaking off. His brother and a friend took off their jackets and tied the sleeves together, forming a makeshift rope, and eventually hauled him to safe ice.

This same man relates, in Esposito's book, how he had fallen in at other times, jumping cracks: "bad spot in the crack," but added, with no irony, "other than that, I've never had what'd be close calls."

Falling into open water is common enough that savvy bobbers consider that possibility before heading out to fish. Many wear "float pants" or "survival suits," clothing that will float when wet. First responders also wear this gear. Float pants won't save you, but they will enable you to expend less energy getting into position to get back on the ice. And smart bobbers carry ice picks—around their necks, not in a tool box. Alexander advocates using the buddy system—always go out with a friend. You are both responsible for seeing that the other gets back home safely. More generally, the axiom is that you, yourself, are responsible for getting back on the ice, should you fall in. Don't expect anyone to save you.

Alexander has another inflexible rule: alcohol has no place when fishing far from shore. You want to be as clearheaded as possible, to be aware of subtle changes in the environment, and to be able to act quickly and effectively to take yourself out of danger.

Area first responders are trained to make water rescues, but because of distance and the dicey ice conditions, they often cannot arrive in time to save a life. They frequently employ a wind sled, a contraption not well known beyond Wisconsin's South Shore but which figures greatly in life there, particularly for Madeline Island. A wind sled is a transport on runners that is propelled by enormous fans in the rear. Several are based on Madeline. Perhaps the most famous, the one written up in the *New York Times*, carries twenty-four passengers. It transports island school children on their daily commutes in the weeks between when a ferry can safely operate in water, and when Superior's ice is thick enough (eleven inches) between Bayfield and the island to support cars and trucks on a plowed "ice road."

For rescue operations, first responders use a smaller, more nimble wind sled. This fire-engine-red vehicle resembles a motor-boat with a huge circular fan in back. It can skim over thin ice and open water. It is based at the town of La Pointe on Madeline Island and owned and operated by a pair of brothers, Arnie and Ron Nelson (who also built, own, and operate the twenty-four-passenger wind sled). The rescue squad is all volunteer.

In his book, Esposito describes witnessing a drowning that occurred in the waters of South Channel, south and west of Madeline, where ice is often unreliable. After the 911 call went out, it was thirty-five minutes before the wind sled arrived from relatively close La Pointe, breaking ice all the way, leaving a trail of water behind it. Although Esposito recounts heroic efforts to save the man, it was far too late. This harrowing incident, witnessed by many bobbers, changed behavior. Flotation suits, ropes at hand, ice picks always worn around the neck, and a buddy system assumed a significance they never had before.

Notably, the accident did not stop bobbers from venturing on to the ice, from succumbing to the allure of the expansive ice, the great depths, the big fish.

What is the hold of the great lake on these men? For although some women do venture far from shore, it is mostly men who take the risks, endure the cold, and go to great lengths to be present.

There is, of course, the lure of the fish, the excitement of possibility, the pursuit of records in Catching the Big One. There's the camaraderie of friends, the layering of tradition, of going out with fathers and grandfathers, and then with sons and grandsons.

It's not just about catching, though. One angler commented, "I like bobbing for lake trout because of the bite. The lake trout bite on a handline is one of the best things I've ever [experienced] in fishing." Another added, "It's just that you're sittin' there fishin' one line and any time, you never know when it's gonna be, and WHAM!

It's that jerk you get!" A third added, "A rush! Bobbin' is. You're going for somethin' you hope exists." And, "Bobbin' [is] about as basic as you can get. You're as close as what you are when man first started fishing."

But a primary attraction seems to be more subtle, even spiritual. It can't be appreciated from the shore, where passersby see only ice, a wintry scene, nothing more than Wisconsin in winter.

If you've arrived several miles from land after arduous preparation and effort, you see differently. "It's a wonderful wilderness, no fences, no boundaries," artist Alexander observes. "Almost as deadly as walking surrounded by fire."

Others agree. Quite a few mentioned solitude, or if not being alone, at least having elbow room, a quality often lacking when ice fishing in Chequamegon Bay or in smaller inland lakes. "I like being out there; being in the open . . . I like a little space around me," one remarked.

There are those who seek company, those who prefer to not be alone, but bobbing is an activity that calls to those who can be alone with their thoughts. Those who, in their own way, ask the lake to speak to them.

One angler reads books on the ice, sitting in his tent, waiting for a bite: "What better time to read Shackleton than [at] . . . 22 below frickin' degrees."

Is it a stretch to compare Lake Superior's far-out expanse to the Antarctic? What is a wilderness, anyway, if not a personal encounter with nature unadorned? My dictionary defines a *wilderness* as "an unsettled, uncultivated region left in its natural condition." Certainly, that describes the ice of the greatest lake: unsettled, uncultivated, lacking any sort of civilization, unknowable, really, except from hour to hour. It's a place where nature calls the shots, and those who visit need to be attuned with all their senses.

It seems to me that there is always an element of danger in any true wilderness, because danger is an authentic element in a human's place in the world. Our entire advanced society has been constructed to lessen those dangers—to be safe from disease, from predators, from human enemies, from hunger and the elements. The degree to which you take these safety measures with you—cell phones in the Boundary Waters, GPS in the Badlands—is the degree to which you devitalize the wilderness and remove some essential quality, making it less inclined to teach its lessons of silence, solitude, and self-reliance.

The lessons of Lake Superior's ice are not lost on the anglers who haul their gear miles from shore, no matter how wild and crazy they talk. "The lake," says Alexander, "is a misunderstood beauty. She takes people every year who don't respect her." Adds someone who ended up in the lake, who admittedly takes risks, but who also "religiously" has ice picks around his neck each time he steps onto the ice, "It was almost a spiritual experience to me [breaking through bad ice and crawling two miles to shore] . . . because I looked at Lake Superior as if She, Lake Superior, humbled me but also let me live."

I will admit that I have changed my assessment of bobbers in the decades since I first spotted them out on the ice. Over the years I have seen that society's sense of safety is deceptive. The safeguards we cling to can only protect us so far. Beyond the safeguards lies the great expanse, the depths to be plumbed.

THE LAKE EFFECT

I gazed out the front window on a gray afternoon. It was still snowing. The year was 1983, our first in Ashland, Wisconsin. November had been dark but dry. Our toddler and I had taken my bicycle downtown every day to pick up the *Minneapolis Tribune*. It seemed like the brown of fall would go on forever, but then, just before Thanksgiving, things changed. A large system dropped a heap of wet, sloppy snow on us. Three days later, another storm brought sixteen inches.

It was now mid-December, and this latest storm was delivering well over a foot of snow. The snow had begun yesterday. By midafternoon today, I estimated there was another foot on the once-shoveled sidewalks, and according to the forecast, it was supposed to continue into tomorrow. I wasn't sad about this. One draw of Ashland had been the opportunity to cross-country ski, and the skiing had been great! We had hired a babysitter a couple of times to go on our own, but we also took Andy in a contraption called a "pulk"—a cupped wooden sled, low to the ground, with two poles extending forward and meeting at a belt that Tom buckled around his waist. Andy wasn't keen on it, but we went anyway. He had ultimate veto power by screaming when he had had enough.

I thought about going out to shovel. As a native Minnesotan, I had dealt with snow all my life. Here was how it worked: the snow began, fell, ended. Then you went out to shovel. To shovel mid-snowfall seemed masochistic.

But then I thought about what it would be like to move that snow with another twelve inches on top of it. And I remembered Tom was on call at the hospital tonight. It seemed best to get out there and shovel. I sighed, contemplating stuffing the toddler into his little blue snowsuit and boots. He would have to be outside with me. I couldn't trust him alone inside. At least it wasn't cold. He could practice walking as I shoveled. The snow piles lining the front walk were already over his head.

THE SOUTH SHORE of Lake Superior is perfectly situated to receive lake-effect snow. Lake-effect snow occurs when a cold air mass moves across a long expanse of warm water. The lower layer of air picks up water vapor from the lake and rises through the colder air above it. The vapor freezes and drops as snow. For a lake effect, the watery expanse, called the "fetch," must be at least sixty-two miles, and the temperature of air moving across the surface must be significantly cooler than that at the surface.

In the Midwest, cold air masses come from the north and west, so the South Shore usually receives lake-effect snow rather than the North Shore. We think of lake-effect snow occurring especially in the Upper Peninsula of Michigan, but other large bodies of water can also create the phenomenon. For example, Hokkaido, Japan, where the 1972 Winter Olympics were held, gets lake-effect snow from storms crossing the Sea of Japan. The other Great Lakes (think Buffalo, New York, on Lake Erie), the Great Salt Lake, the Black Sea, the Caspian Sea, and the Baltic Sea all can generate lake-effect snow.

Regions receiving significant precipitation are termed *snow-belts*. Pretty much the entire Upper Peninsula of Michigan is one big belt, but the Keweenaw Peninsula that reaches into Lake Superior like a beckoning finger is notorious for its "big dumps."

Highway 41 runs like an artery down the Keweenaw. Just outside the defunct mining town of Mohawk is a vertical billboard, shaped like an old-fashioned mercury thermometer, illustrating the tremendous regional snowfall. At the top of the bright red column is 390.4 inches (32½ feet), the record snowfall of 1978–79. The record *low* snowfall is 81.3 inches, received in the dust bowl years of 1930–31 (by comparison, Minneapolis averages 54 inches of snow each winter). The Keweenaw overall averages 187.4 inches per winter, about the height of a two-story house.

When I saw this thermometer, I gasped. The line was far, far over my head. Of course, the level of snow is tempered: once it lands, it settles. Residents are not burrowing out of two-story snows—usually.

Any cross-country skier worth her salt would be magnetically drawn to such a snow haven. We have spent many family vacations venturing first to Ironwood, Michigan, and the Porcupine Mountains, and then later, when the kids left home, farther up the Keweenaw to trails in Houghton and Calumet.

A few years ago, we journeyed to Calumet to ski the trails at the Swedetown Recreation Area, just outside the town's Swedetown neighborhood. Our intent was twofold: to ski and to see how Calumet handled the tremendous snowfalls.

We arrived in Calumet on a dark Sunday night. It had not been snowing in Houghton when we had skied on the Michigan Technological University trails, but by the time we reached Calumet, it was snowing heavily and had been for some time. The streets were marginally plowed. Snow piles were six feet high. We left our car in the parking lot of the motel and walked to the local pub, the Michigan House, the home of Red Jacket Brewing. The core community of Calumet was known as "Red Jacket" in the heyday of the mines, and the Red Jacket mine was adjacent to the residential area. We later learned there was a Blue Jacket and a Yellow Jacket, with mine shafts at Tamarack northwest of town, and other locations. The copper deposit was so vast that the Calumet and Hecla Company comprised many mines.

The next morning snow continued to pelt the Keweenaw. We drove out to the Swedetown Trails and discovered that they were freshly groomed. Swedetown grooms every morning at seven o'clock. When we arrived at the trails at nine o'clock, a small plow was clearing off the parking lot—which it would also do the next day, and the day after, because it just didn't stop snowing. The trails wound their ways through a mix of vegetation types on what had undoubtedly once been cutover land. When the mines had been in their heyday, the surrounding forests were devastated as wood was burned to drive the steam engines used in processing copper ore.

In the twenty-first century and when draped with snow, the landscape was a winter wonderland. Leading away from a warming hut, the trail ran to the major beginner's circle, the Greenstone Loop. With Tom's broad back ahead of me, a view I had had on the ski trail for forty-five years, I passed the shorter, hilly Len's, Valley Trail, and Cedar Loops, on my way to the Greenstone Loop.

It was warm, twenty-two degrees, a comfortable temperature for a leisurely ski. Tom headed off for the Bear Loops: Mama Bear, Baby Bear, and Papa Bear, and I explored the flatter Greenstone. Though warm, there was a wind, and I was happy to find that the Greenstone wended its way through woods. First, a red pine plantation, and then, an alder and tamarack bog. Both landscapes have their charm. Bogs are intimate, closed in and cozy. I prefer a natural forest to a plantation, but there is a certain stateliness to tall red pines, and a pleasing orderliness to the rows. I even like trails through clear-cuts. Snow covers scars and wounds, and the snow-decked piles of slag might be a good perch for a Snowy Owl. I am ever hopeful.

The snow continued to fall, and I found that I got good glide with my skin skis. These were new—lightweight Fischer skis with mohair strips on the bottoms, better than fish-scale bottoms, and like them, they do not need waxing. They were quickly becoming my all-time favorite skis. I believe I will never again wax another pair of skis.

The snow muffled ambient noise, but in the tops of the pines I heard chickadees chipping and the nasal honks of nuthatches. Bold, bright Blue Jays landed near me and jeered.

I made it around the loop and decided to head in. As I glided toward the chalet, I encountered a skier going out. After jubilantly agreeing with me that the snow was fantastic, he told me that he was eighty, that he had been born in South Range (a town south of Houghton), to Finnish parents: "They were all Finnish in South Range!" and that when he was born, his parents were apprehensive about the doctor's bill, it being the depths of the Depression. He said that the doctor eyed the scrawny, mewling baby and declared, "Why, he's not worth more than $2.50 and a sack of potatoes!"

I smiled and wished him a good ski. He said, "Thank you! You made my day!" And he had made mine. Such a small thing—and a big thing—to make someone's day.

Later, we poked around Calumet to bask in the prodigious snowfall. We had learned that the ski trails had received 217 inches (18 feet) thus far; they receive 331 inches in a normal year. What does 18 feet of snow look like? Tom took a photograph of me standing next to a pile shoved aside by a plow on a side street. It was 8 feet tall. Forget the sidewalks: we walked in the street. The business district walks might be shoveled in a few days, but it was still snowing heavily. The locals were under assault. We, on the other hand, were giddy.

Pickup trucks zipped by us, plows fronting their bumpers. They were no doubt busy working on private driveways and parking lots. We paused for a moment to watch the city plows. The method seemed to be to plow the snow away from the sidewalks and heap it in the center of the road. Then a contraption with a chute on it and a rotating device on a front plow tackled the central pile, sucking it up, and blowing it into a dump truck, which carted it away. The device was noisy and effective.

Many of the tourist attractions were closed. The large, red sandstone Catholic church, St. Anne's, now the Keweenaw Heritage

Center, was buried in snow. Drifts spilled over the central stairway and obscured the handrails. Likewise the outdoor patio of Carmelita's, a TexMex restaurant that buzzes with diners and generous margaritas in July. Were there tables under those drifts? We couldn't tell.

Cross Country Sports, an outdoor equipment store on Oak Street, was open. The owner greeted us and showed us his wares. He was white-haired and talkative, about our age, and a snow enthusiast. He sold Tom a pair of ski boots and two pairs of snowshoes, made in Wisconsin. We had not intended to buy snowshoes, but the shopkeeper made quite a case for them. The snowshoes were lightweight. The manufacturer claimed we would save a literal ton in lifting, compared to conventional snowshoes, with every mile we would walk. He told us that he hadn't believed that claim, so he got out a pencil and did the math.

We used the snowshoes the next day, tromping out to a waterfall west of Munising. The frozen waterfall creates an icy stalactite cavern that reflects the colors of the river and the air. It is a local favorite—the signs pointing the way were hand-lettered, and a ranger for the Pictured Rocks National Lakeshore told us that sixty cars had been parked at the lot leading to the path the prior weekend. Sited on the edge of the Hiawatha National Forest, the path to the cave crosses private land, a farm field. The waterfall was inaccessible on skis, but our snowshoes were nimble and light. The cleats on the bottom were particularly valuable in maneuvering the steep hills of the path and the slick ice lip at the cavern.

We have a lot of friends who have left cross-country skiing behind in favor of snowshoeing. I do not want to join their ranks. But sometimes snowshoeing is better than skiing. We're still enjoying winter.

CHANCE BROUGHT US to Paradise. There's something fitting about that, as if Paradise, Michigan, isn't a destination to be earned or planned for but rather an unexpected blessing.

One minute we were on a snowy highway headed for Sault Ste. Marie and the next we were ensconced in a Comfort Inn at Newberry, taking refuge from a storm that began seriously to obscure the road. We had gotten a late start out of Marquette, despite ample warning that a winter storm warning was in effect. The snow didn't trouble us much, but as the day grew old and night came on, we began to imagine how the road might be in the total dark. There would be no orienting the white median line, no intersecting roads, no towns for literally miles. Newberry was our last opportunity to abort the push to the Soo, so we took it. The Comfort Inn was hopping with snowmobilers who had also gotten off the road while they could. The motel had a room available, and we had leftover pizza for a modest supper. It was a good deal, so we took it.

The next morning the storm was over, and the sun was bright, but the road into Sault Ste. Marie was still not plowed to pavement. The county road to Paradise was, so we made a snap decision to visit the town and its state park, Tahquamenon Falls.

Would you know you were in Paradise without a sign announcing it? One buried to its neck in fresh snow proclaimed we were "Entering Paradise—glad you made it." Cartoons had led me to imagine St. Peter at a heavenly desk, not this, but the snow was a nice touch. Paradise seemed to have little going on (except snow removal), so we continued on to the state park outside town.

There we found a brew pub and a café inside the park, and a freshly plowed parking lot with a trail leading to the Upper Falls. Tahquamenon Falls actually consists of two parts—a dramatic fifty-foot-drop Upper Falls, and a stair-step Lower Falls. We were able to ski in to the Upper Falls. The Lower Falls, four miles downstream, we would save for another visit.

Refreshed by the recent storm, the Upper Falls were extremely picturesque. The second-highest waterfall east of the Mississippi River (Niagara Falls has it beat), the water cascades over a dolostone ledge in a creamy froth resembling Guinness stout. The river is colored by tannins, natural compounds picked up as it flows through boggy environs. The tannins give the water an umber color; swimming in tannic water, I look like I have acquired a pleasing dark tan.

Most waterfalls are created in areas where a softer rock underlies a hard rock. The relentless stream of water erodes the softer rock and undercuts the hard rock, which breaks off, causing the river to drop. In the Upper Falls, the hard rock is dolomite (similar to limestone), and the softer rock is sandstone—in the case of the Upper Falls, Miner's Castle Sandstone; at the Lower Falls, Chapel Rock Sandstone. Chapel Rock Sandstone tends to break along bedding planes (the different layers in which the sand is laid down). This produces smaller falls one right after the other.

The sandstones' names reflect rock formations within the Pictured Rocks National Lakeshore. Tahquamenon Falls is part of the same geological formation. There are a number of waterfalls in the surrounds, on different rivers flowing into Lake Superior. Knowing the difference now between Miner's Castle Sandstone and Chapel Rock Sandstone, the astute observer would be able to discern which generates each—a large drop or a series of small ones.

CLIMATE CHANGE threatens this snowy paradise, and we got a taste of the future as we skied trails in the Marquette area east of Calumet one weekend. Marquette had gotten fresh snow, but the initial precipitation was ice, as the upper atmosphere had been too warm for snow. We headed for the Noquemanon Trails outside Marquette. It's the site of a big ski race, the "Noque," somewhat on par with the famous Birkebeiner in northern Wisconsin. The ice had coated the tops of the trees, and they glistened in the sunshine. But it also made the conifer spires heavy, and I feared many would snap in a brisk wind. Snow, and lots of it, had followed the ice. Conditions on the trails were fine by the time we got to them, but the roads remained treacherous. Global warming is pushing the Lake Superior region ever closer to what I call unusable winter—winters where one deals with ice storms, slush and grayness, rather than the crisp, cold pleasure of snow to play in. Missouri winters, not South Shore winters.

What can be said of this future, the loss of something so fundamental to the appeal of Superior's South Shore? A generation ago Aldo Leopold lamented the loss of wilderness. Now it is our turn to mourn the death of something beautiful. "Man always kills the thing he loves," Leopold wrote, "and so we the pioneers have killed our wilderness. Some say we had to. Be that as it may, I am glad that I shall never be young without wild country to be young in."

This is a reflection of an older man, one who has the depth of experience to put such a profound loss into perspective. It comes from someone who has struggled against the dominant current of conventional society, someone who values something that most people do not. I think about this as I trudge along a ski trail in new snow, often a solitary pursuit and now a pursuit made lonely by this unnerving thought: the age of cross-country skiing is drawing to a close.

LOCKING THROUGH THE SOO

On a fine fall evening, Tom and I sit at a choice table overlooking the world-famous Soo Locks in Sault Ste. Marie, Michigan. We are dining at Karl's Cuisine on Portage Avenue. I gasped a little when, outside the restaurant, I looked up and saw the street sign. In the dark of an early evening, we weren't yet oriented to town, but here it was, proof of the historic path around the rapids, "Portage Avenue." It didn't occur to me that the portage would actually be the central street in town.

Karl's is busy for a weeknight. Most of the tables are occupied, whether with locals or tourists, I can't say. Tom and I are served crisp green salads, and I am savoring the first forkfuls of a piquant blueberry vinaigrette, when to my astonishment, the scene beyond the picture windows seems to shift. The background is moving, left to right. For a split second, I wonder if I am having vision issues.

I look again. What is really happening is that an enormous freighter, the MV *Spruceglen* of Canadian Steamship Lines, is nosing carefully into the Poe Lock, the largest lock of four that comprise the Soo Locks, run by the U.S. Army Corps of Engineers. Slowly, slowly, the big vessel eases forward, while lock workers on the platform walk briskly alongside.

The *Spruceglen*, we will learn later, is a gearless bulk freighter, meaning it carries cargo like taconite or grain, as opposed to crated goods; and it doesn't have the means to off-load its own cargo—it requires a crane or conveyor on the pier. Most freighters now are "boomed," allowing for a "self-unloading" operation.

Though a standard-sized freighter, the *Spruceglen* seems absolutely gargantuan. The pilothouse, situated aft, is a full five stories tall. I try to recall when I had been closer to a Great Lakes freighter and couldn't think of a time. We watch them come into port under the Aerial Lift Bridge in Duluth, and the SS *William A. Irvin,* once the flagship of U.S. Steel's fleet, is at anchor in the harbor. But actually seeing a freighter moving, one hundred yards away? Never.

From what I can see from our table at Karl's, the *Spruceglen*'s arrival is an unremarkable event. On an evening in October, there are no crowds in the viewing stands. No tourists gawking. A solitary lock worker moves purposefully on the pier alongside the boat. I think I can hear some garbled communication between the lock and the boat. The *Spruceglen* is locking through. This event happens many times a day.

WHEN THE ECONOMY of Lake Superior was based on furs and, later, barrels of fish, a portage sufficed to get goods around the rapids at Sault Ste. Marie. But those who invested heavily in the copper mines of the Keweenaw Peninsula had their ore shipped out in small, weighty barrels, portaged over the rapids by an adjacent railroad of sorts, powered by horses. It was laborious and time consuming. They clamored for a lock.

The North West Company had constructed a modest lock of thirty-eight feet by eight feet nine inches on the Soo rapids in 1797, an enclosed box that filled with water. It was large enough to accommodate an upbound Montreal canoe, raising it to the water level above the rapids. The company was owned by the British at the time, but lock technology dates to around 1000 CE, when the Chinese developed an operating lock. By the eighteenth century, locks were in operation throughout Europe. In fact, the design in which a pair of gates closes off the lock was first drawn up by Leonardo da Vinci. As far as is known, the North West Company lock was used until U.S. troops dismantled it in the War of 1812.

The State of Michigan was interested in seeing a canal and locks built at the Soo in 1837, and the legislature granted seed money for the project. However, the plan encroached on federal land near the rapids. The encroachment was not an intentionally aggressive move on the young state's part, but the U.S. Army halted construction by sending soldiers with muskets and bayonets. That canal and locks were never built.

Finally, in the 1850s, the federal government granted land, and Michigan passed legislation for funds for locks that would be 350 feet long, longer than any boat then plying the waterway. The locks were a challenge to build, with three hundred to four hundred workers sweating through the summer, and work continuing throughout the dark, snowy, and bitterly cold winter.

In the 150 years since, there have been various improvements, with new locks added and the narrow St. Marys River dredged to facilitate navigation. Today, there are four locks, only two of which are regularly used. The "new" Poe Lock, which replaced an older version and opened in 1968, is 1,200 feet long, the only lock that can accommodate the "thousand footers" that ferry ore and other cargo through the Great Lakes. These big boats are confined to Lakes Superior, Michigan, Huron, and Erie; the locks at the Welland Canal circumventing Niagara Falls between Lakes Erie and Ontario are too short for the behemoth boats. That means that ships from foreign ports, the so-called salties, seem diminutive at less than 800 feet long, compared to the ore boats.

The other lock, the MacArthur, built during World War II to ease the transport of Mesabi Range iron ore to steel mills farther east, is 800 feet long. Salties will sometimes lock through via the MacArthur Lock.

Locks are built to get around a barrier in a river, like a rapids or a falls. In theory, they are simple. They consist of three parts:

a watertight chamber, part of the canal; a gate, or often a pair of gates, one at each end; and a set of lock gears, usually a simple valve.

A boat going downstream enters the chamber. Recall, the river is dropping in elevation (a rapid or falls) at this point. The gates shut, and a valve is opened to let out water. The water level in the chamber drops, and the boat rides the water down. When the water level in the chamber is the same as the water level of the river below the rapids, the gates open, and the boat continues on its way.

The procedure is just as simple for upbound boats. The boat enters the chamber, and the gates shut. A valve is opened, letting in water from above. The water level rises, and the boat rises as well. When the water level is equal to that of the river before the rapids, the gates open, and the boat is released. On average, the process takes ten to twenty minutes, depending on the size of the chamber.

To get an idea of what it is like to guide a giant freighter through the Soo Locks, I asked a high-level crew member, James Bittner, first mate (second in command) of the *Roger Blough*. James is also my first cousin, and I am not surprised that he is at the helm of a massive vessel on Lake Superior. As a little boy in Duluth, he and his younger brother kept tabs on ore boats coming in and out of harbor, some from across the ocean! He has a clear memory of being drawn to a wooden toy freighter, of choosing it to play with over the array of attractive new toys on his first day in kindergarten.

He spent a stint in the U.S. Coast Guard and later crewed sailboats in races from Duluth to ports on Superior's South Shore. He also once spilled me from a sailboat into the Duluth Harbor, heeling just a bit too far, but that is a story for another day.

James is a hard man to characterize. A true intellectual living the life of the mind, he might start his morning with practical physicality, splicing a cable onboard, and end it with philosophy, reading Hegelian metaphysics in his cabin, as the freighter sails through the night on its way to Gary, Indiana.

The *Roger Blough* is a classic Great Lakes freighter, painted mahogany red with the diagonal gray and black stripes on her hull that signify membership in the Great Lakes Fleet, based in Duluth. The shipping company has a history in Duluth dating to 1901, the only major shipping company headquartered on Lake Superior. It consists of nine vessels, the names of which are familiar to tourists who hang around Canal Park gawking at the big boats: the *Arthur M. Anderson,* the *Cason J. Callaway,* the *Philip R. Clarke,* the *Edgar B. Speer,* the *John G. Munson,* the *Edwin H. Gott,* the *Presque Isle,* and the *Great Republic.* In his twenty-six years on the Great Lakes, James has served on all of these, except the *Munson.*

Great Lakes Fleet is closely tied to U.S. Steel. The *Blough* picks up taconite pellets at Two Harbors and delivers the cargo to steel-making plants in Gary, Indiana, and Conneaut, Ohio. Occasionally, the boat will pick up cargo in Duluth or Superior or, even more rarely, Silver Bay, but generally, the *Blough* does a loop between Two Harbors and one of those two steel mills.

The *Roger Blough* was built in 1972 and is a grand old lady at forty-eight years, but vessels on the Great Lakes have longer life spans than do oceangoing ships. Fresh water doesn't corrode like the briny sea. She's a hefty 858 feet long; Great Lakes Fleet has only three thousand-footers: the *Speer,* the *Gott,* and the *Presque Isle.* The *Blough* is a sturdy boat, with plenty of steel, according to James. He feels confident on her in a storm. He noted that he has not seen any crew don survival suits in high seas on the *Blough*— although other boats have made sailors nervous.

The *Roger Blough* rode through the storm that sunk the famed *Edmund Fitzgerald* in 1975, and she assisted in the search for the doomed ore boat, recovering one of the life rafts. James was not working on the Great Lakes at the time.

More recently, and infamously, the *Roger Blough* made news when in 2016 she ran aground at Gros Cap Reefs light in Whitefish Bay. James was onboard as first mate. The boat had been feeling her way across the lake through heavy fog—Whitefish Bay is historically notorious for fog in spring and fall. James terms fog "tedious." You can't see anything around and must watch the radar continually. But as he ended his shift that day in the wheelhouse, he was hopeful that as they approached the St. Marys River and moved away from the chill of the lake, the fog would dissipate.

So he was mighty surprised several hours later when he heard an untoward noise. Startled, he thought they were dropping anchor, then he paused, reassessed, and realized they were running aground with a belly full of taconite, 45,000 tons worth. One can't slow a vessel with that momentum.

"It was quite a thrill," James remarked dryly. "I ran up to the pilothouse and thought, 'Oh, my lord.' We were way out of whack. What are we doing over here?"

The *Roger Blough*'s escapade on the reef cost the Great Lakes Fleet four and a half million dollars. Two of her fleet mates, the *Arthur M. Anderson* and the *Philip R. Clarke*, helped off-load some of the cargo. Even so, it took a week before she was refloated and limped down Lake Michigan for repairs in Sturgeon Bay.

James expressed surprise that I wanted to hear about a non-eventful passage through the Soo Locks. The *Roger Blough* locks through eighty to eighty-five times in a shipping season. For him and his crewmates, it is routine, all in a day's work.

Nonetheless, there is considerable skill involved. The approach to the locks starts early for a freighter headed downlake. At about Caribou Island (approximately the same longitude as Grand Marais, Michigan), the mate switches the radio over to Channel 12 to monitor "Soo Traffic." Soo Traffic controls the VTS, Vessel Traffic System. The lockmaster, in turn, monitors the locks on Channel 14. In this way, the mate—James, on the *Blough*—gets an idea of other traffic vying for slots at the Soo—competition for the lock.

At Whitefish Point, the boat calls in to Soo Traffic, the first of many call-in points on the route. Soo Traffic terms it a "pre-call," and it might sound like this: "This is the *Roger Blough*. We're down one hour above Ile Parisienne with a load of taconite pellets for Gary, Indiana. Our draft today is twenty-eight feet." A freighter's draft is how far it is submerged in water. Soo Traffic will answer, giving the *Blough* water levels and the traffic configuration, so the crew knows what vessels they will encounter.

At Ile Parisienne, the mate is looking for the lighthouse, a point at which he will make a little turn, starting to line up the boat to go into the river. Freighters don't turn on a dime. The process begins miles out. Again, the boat notifies the lockmaster of her progression downlake. At this call-in, they inform the lockmaster if crew members are coming onboard at the Soo, because they need to clear security to enter the lock area.

The pilot then looks for a succession of markers: a green quick-flashing light that is Buoy 39, the last green buoy in the channel; the Birch Point Range, a pair of lights on shore that ships use to determine their position in the channel; the light at Gros Cap, situated on the treacherous reef; after Gros Cap, Light 26. These aids to navigation help guide freighters through the increasingly narrow channel, away from reefs.

At Pointe Louise, and then at Old Lookout #6, the freighter is pointed at the Soo, and the mate is reducing speed continuously. The *Roger Blough* clips along at 16.7 miles per hour on open water. In the harbor at the Soo, the speed is reduced to 4 miles per hour.

At Big Point, so close to town, now, that Sherman Park can be seen on shore, the lockmaster assigns the lock. The *Blough* only fits in the Poe Lock, but the crew members are told at this point whether they have competition for the Poe, whether they get priority or will have to wait for another boat, say, one coming up from the lower lakes. Up to this point, there has been subtle competition to arrive as quickly as possible to the lock, because the wait could easily be an hour and a half.

At Big Point, too, the captain is at the window and instructs the wheelman on how to guide the boat in. The window, up high, offers a panoramic view of where the boat is headed. James, as first mate, then goes on deck and communicates by walkie-talkie to the captain to help her position the freighter into the lock.

Freighters respond to the confined lock chamber idiosyncratically. The *Blough*, for example, likes to come away from the lock wall as she enters, and to ride the other side, but it's tricky. The lock is 110 feet wide, and the *Blough* has a 105-foot beam. There's not a lot of leeway. James tells me he might say, "OK, Captain, she's coming away, one foot, two feet, three feet, coming away . . . four feet, four and a half, five . . ." And five is all she can do.

If the boat comes into the chamber perfectly in the middle, there is 2½ feet on each side, and maybe 5 feet of water under her. It takes a lot of skill to maneuver an 850-foot vessel carrying 45,000 tons. "Yeah," adds James. "If you screw something up, that can get pricey pretty quick. To do a hundred, two hundred thousand dollars [worth of damage] isn't hard at all."

The captain of the *Roger Blough* is Lori Reinhart, who took command a few months ago. She is the only female captain in Great Lakes Fleet but has been a captain for years and was with American Steamship Company for much of her career.

"How does she get along with the crew?" I asked, curious.

"Oh," James assures me, "she's one of the guys. She can cuss to make a sailor blush."

Wind can affect the easing of a big boat into the lock chamber, and—because this is Lake Superior—so can ice. The shipping season goes through December into January, long after average daytime temperatures register below freezing. Ice can mess several things up. One way is floating on the surface. A boat nosing into a lock might push quantities of ice ahead of it. This can put a lot of pressure on the lower gates, the blockade, and lock workers try to avoid that.

Sault Ste. Marie has historically served as the Lake Superior freighters' post office and still does today. After the gates close and the valve opens, letting water out of the chamber and lowering the boat, the deckhand goes to the post office and exchanges outgoing mail for mail and packages coming in. On deck, James goes up to the bow to watch the gate. When it opens, there is a little flooding of water rushing in that serves to shift the ship astern. The crew stands by to counteract this. Then the lines that had held the *Blough* in place during the process are pulled in, and as James says, "Off we go!"

Below the locks, the Great Lakes Fleet takes on supplies stored in the Soo Warehouse. A supply boat, the *Ojibway,* with its crane, ties up alongside the *Blough* and transfers cargo aboard. This might be kitchen or engine room supplies. Sometimes there are other kinds of mail. If the *Roger Blough* is taking on passengers or has been carrying them, they get on or off at this point.

Task completed, the two vessels move apart. The *Ojibway* blows a salute, the *Roger Blough* returns an acknowledgement, and the boat heads down the St. Marys.

The trip down the river takes about four and a half hours, from Mission Point (still in town) to DeTour Reef, where the river ends. At that point, boats make a choice: right, to head down Lake Michigan—the *Blough* will be going to Gary—or left, down Lake Huron and to Conneaut, Ohio. The lock process going up river is similar.

James takes a prosaic view of life on an ore boat. "People view it as kind of romantic . . . it's more like driving to work every morning." I told him I found that reassuring—that storms would make me nervous. Not James. "It would take an awful lot to sink the *Blough.*" As retirement looms for him, he claims he wants nothing to do with water or boats. After decades of standing watch every twelve hours from March to January, he is ready for a different life. Yet, I would be surprised if Lake Superior doesn't call to him in new ways. He was born on its shores, and the wide, glimmering lake has been a seductive presence most of his life.

TOM AND I have finished our meals. I had whitefish, fresh from the lake, and we both drank local wine from Karl's vineyard. The *Spruceglen* has left the lock and is on her way downriver, but the

Army Corps has an informative display in a museum on the grounds of the locks. We decide to go through security—check the purse, answer questions—and see what we can learn.

A big whiteboard behind the information desk lists the vessels expected through the locks during the next twenty-four hours. We see that the *Cason J. Callaway* is due in at ten tomorrow morning, and the *Roger Blough* will be coming upriver from Lake Michigan at noon. Noon is too late for us—we are on our way to Quebec and need to meet a bike shuttle at a specific time on Monday. But we might be able to see the *Callaway*.

As we arrive at the locks the next morning, the *Clyde S. Van-Enkevort* with her barge, the *Erie Trader,* has just left the locks and is headed toward Lake Superior. The Great Lake Fleet's *Callaway* had been waiting outside the locks for the Poe to open. As the *VanEnkevort* inches away, leaving a puff of black diesel smoke in the air in a goodbye toot, the *Callaway* creeps forward, slowly, slowly. Time has a different rhythm with behemoths.

We don't stay to watch the *Callaway* lock through. It could be hours, and we need to get on the road. As we drive over the international bridge that arcs over the St. Marys River connecting the two Sault Sainte Maries, we see a big boat on the far horizon. It's the *Roger Blough*, right on schedule.

WHEN THE QUEEN IS RILED

We have a blue-and-white placemat at the cabin titled "Shipwrecks of Lake Superior." It features the familiar wolf's head outline, with little ship symbols—schooner, propeller, steamer—depicting the type of craft and location of its sinking. Every square inch of the outline is covered with little ships, save for a curious open area on the Canadian north shore directly south of the town of Marathon. Family members have spent many meals poring over this placemat, munching grilled cheese sandwiches and contemplating the numerous and varied ways boats have gone down in the big lake.

This is not to say that Lake Superior is particularly treacherous compared to the other Great Lakes. Of the estimated six thousand to twenty-five thousand shipwrecks on all the lakes (the estimates vary widely), only 550 have been tallied in Lake Superior. Lake Erie, with 2,000 wrecks, is feared because the shallow lake can whip up a fury in short order. Lake Michigan has strong currents running parallel to its elongated shorelines. Lake Huron has a similar fetch to Superior's, allowing waves to build under a northwest wind. Still, Lake Superior sets itself apart. Its vast size inspires more than a little fear, and its northernness conveys more than a little wildness.

The sinking of the freighter *Edmund Fitzgerald* in 1975 is the Superior shipwreck most alive in people's imaginations. I remember being astounded and horrified when I woke that November day and learned that an ore boat was missing in a storm and presumed sunk. How on earth could that be? To our twenty-first-century understanding, that tragedy epitomizes Lake Superior shipwrecks: a November gale, the geographical doom of Whitefish Point, the non-briny depths, the total loss of the crew, and the reputation of a lake who never gives up her dead.

Yet the story of the *Fitzgerald* is hardly representative of all wrecks on the lake. While it is true that autumn storms have taken many ships to the bottom, disasters have also occurred in the spring and summer when a fine gauze of fog hangs over the water. Although boats have sunk in deep water, perhaps more have foundered on the abundant shoals that lurk beneath the surface, their basalt ridges obscured by water, or on sandbars that form when the capricious lake pushes its substrate around. As for the legendary loss of life, for every dramatic account of mass drowning, there is an equally compelling, often heroic story of rescue.

The history of shipwrecks in Lake Superior opens in 1816, a short two hundred years ago. Economic activity on the other Great Lakes goes back to the 1600s, but entrance into Lake Superior was cinched by the St. Marys rapids (in French, the Sault Ste. Marie), which made it impossible for most watercraft to enter the lake. Craft had to be carried or constructed on Superior's shores.

Marquette-based historian Frederick Stonehouse records the 1816 wreck as a huge, thirty-six-foot Montreal canoe owned by the Hudson's Bay Company and carrying prisoners HBC had taken when it seized the North West Company's fur-trading post at Fort William (now Thunder Bay). This massive canoe could carry three to four tons of cargo and had been cruising under a sail in Whitefish Bay when it capsized, killing ten or so men. Undoubtedly, other canoes under the guidance of native Ojibwe had similarly swamped or been battered and sunk, but the tragedies were not recorded.

The first documented ship to wreck was the little *Invincible,* a schooner that foundered near Whitefish Point during a storm also in 1816. She had been built on the lake at Sault Ste. Marie in 1802 from timber carried over the portage around the rapids, and at the time of her sinking, had been carrying goods bound for Fort William. All the crew made it safely to shore.

It is not a coincidence that these earliest records come from the vicinity of Whitefish Point, at the far eastern end of Lake Superior. Of the 550 known Superior wrecks, more than 200 occurred along the shoreline from Whitefish Point to Munising, what Stonehouse terms the "shipwreck coast," a "graveyard" where more lives have been lost than anywhere else on the lake.

A look at a map of the lake explains why. The lake narrows at the eastern end, and traffic both upbound and downbound is forced into constricted shipping lanes, increasing the odds of collision. Many a boat has gone down through inattention. In 1892, the downbound steamer *Vienna,* headed to the Soo, carrying iron ore and towing a barge, spied the upbound *Nipigon,* towing two schooner barges. The boats belonged to the same company, and so they moved into a position to say, "Hi!" The *Nipigon* inexplicably swerved and hit the *Vienna* portside. It promptly sank, but all crew members were rescued.

Sometimes it is not inattention but sheer bad luck that causes a wreck. Lake Superior is so frigid that in spring and summer, as air warmed over the land hits the cold air over the lake, thick fog often hangs over the water. Fog is particularly troublesome in the narrow confines of Whitefish Bay. Stonehouse adds snow squalls and smoke from forest fires as hazards in the bay at other times of the year. All of these, before radar, increased the risk of collision.

A thick fog in June 1889 caused two nearly new freighters, the *C. J. Sheffield,* upbound for Duluth, and the *North Star* to crash. The *North Star* rammed the *Sheffield* hard, nearly cutting it in two, but was able to rescue all crew while the two boats remained in contact. An investigative report blamed the fog but noted that both vessels were traveling at a pretty good clip.

Whitefish Bay is also subject to winds that can blow up to three hundred miles unimpeded, whipping up waves to fearsome heights. The night the *Fitzgerald* went down near Whitefish Point, winds clocked in at eighty miles per hour, gusting to ninety-two miles per hour, and creating thirty-foot waves. Modern weather forecasting now informs captains of the severity of intense gales, but Great Lakes mariners still must deal with the consequences of high winds.

Even today extreme winds and waves instill a healthy respect on the modern, 1,000-foot ore boats (the *Fitzgerald* was "only" 729 feet long), so imagine their effects on the smaller vessels of the nineteenth century. The earliest boats were masted schooners, like the *Invincible*, a diminutive 60 feet long. Schooners were popular for commercial shipping. Later, when shipyards developed higher-tech alternatives, schooners were often towed by newer, steam-propelled boats, to carry more cargo. The tows are referred to in shipping literature as "consort barges." These barges usually retained their sails and could be cut free from the lead boat in high seas, when the captains thought that each vessel would fare better on its own.

One schooner-barge that didn't fare so well was the *Eureka*, in tow with two other schooner-barges of the *Prentice*, a steamer. Imagine this: four in a row. In retrospect, such a configuration in late fall seems foolhardy, and this is an example of when a good weather forecast would have been useful. The train of four had left Marquette's dock loaded with iron ore on October 20, 1886, when a seasonal storm blew up. They were nearing Whitefish Point—if they could get in the lee of the point, they would be protected from the northwest wind—when the train broke up. The *Eureka* was lost from view, and since there were no survivors, there were no witnesses to its demise. No bodies ever washed ashore, but in 1983 divers located the remains of the boat.

Bulk freight steamers carrying cargo such as copper and iron ore, wheat, coal, and limestone began to appear on Lake Superior in 1869. By that time, iron mines in Ishpeming and Negaunee, Michigan, were shipping ore north to the dock in Marquette, multitudinous copper mines on the Keweenaw Peninsula were shipping out of various ports, and the deforestation of the Great Lake states had begun. This cargo was conveyed differently. Raw logs generally went to market in big rafts, held together by chains. Lumber was shipped by boat.

The mining of the onetime resources in Lake Superior's watershed went hand in glove with the introduction of vessels that were bigger, more powerful, and more reliable. The *William F. Sauber,* a 291-foot wooden-hulled steamer loaded with iron ore from Ashland, Wisconsin—Michigan's Gogebic Range shipped out of Ashland—left port bound for Lake Erie in late October 1903. An intense storm blew up; mammoth waves washed over the decks, and water flooded the hold. A nearby steamer, the *Yale,* saw the *Sauber* in distress and positioned itself between the stricken boat and the northwest wind, with the intent of moving toward the shelter of Whitefish Point.

But the *Sauber* didn't make it. Near midnight on October 26, the crew abandoned ship, shimmying down a rope to a lifeboat sent by the *Yale.* The captain refused to leave and went down with the ship. One of the crew also died, crushed between the lifeboat and the hull of the *Sauber,* but fifteen survived.

Iron ore is considered stable cargo, but if it shifts, it can spell disaster. During another October storm, in 1907, the steel-hulled *Cypress* was headed downlake carrying a load of iron ore in the hold. Along the "shipwreck coast" it was pushed sideways by strong winds blowing parallel to the huge waves. The ore shifted, and the ship flipped—"turned turtle" in nautical parlance—and sank, drowning twenty-one of twenty-two crew members. The tragedy stung because the *Cyprus* was only twenty-one days old, on its second voyage downlake.

Whitefish Point and the shore extending west are not the only dangerous coast on the lake. The Keweenaw Peninsula has submerged shoals and a geographic position that ensures its north shore gets pounded by strong prevailing winds. Such winds battered Douglass Houghton's small boat as he and his survey team made their way from Eagle Harbor to Eagle River one stormy October night in 1845. Mercilessly pummeled by the surf, the boat was only two hundred yards from shore when it capsized. Two men and the dog made it to shore, but Houghton did not, a swift curtailing of a promising scientific career.

On Thanksgiving Day, November 26, 1919, the steel-hulled steamer *Tioga* got hung up on Sawtooth Reef beyond the outlet of the Eagle River. It had left Superior, Wisconsin, carrying wheat, bound for Buffalo, New York. Alerted to its foundering, the U.S. Coast Guard based in Eagle Harbor came to its aid. When they arrived, the captain of the *Tioga* invited them to Thanksgiving dinner. The boat was stable on the reef and not going anywhere— yet. After the meal, the crew went ashore with the Coast Guard. Several days later, the *Tioga* broke up under the battering of another storm, and its pilothouse floated to shore—where it remains today, under care of the Keweenaw County Historical Society.

When ships ran aground just offshore, the distress of the people onboard was visible. This was true whether the wreck was on the seacoast or the Great Lakes. Earlier wrecks in the 1700s, for example, off Long Island in New York and the Jersey Shore, had demonstrated the need both for lighthouses and for some sort of rescue operation. Both people and valuable cargo needed rescuing, but it was 150 years before the first government lifesaving teams were organized and supplied with equipment and training.

The Life-Saving Service, forerunner of the Coast Guard, was set up on the Great Lakes in 1876. It took a particularly disastrous winter in 1870–71 to jump-start the program. That season the East Coast was hit hard, and so were the Great Lakes: 1,167 wrecks with 214 lives lost. Legislation and funding from Congress followed. The Eastern Seaboard and the five Great Lakes were bestowed manned and unmanned stations, depending on the perceived need.

By 1877, Lake Superior had four manned lifesaving stations, all on the "shipwreck coast," at Vermilion Point, Crisp's Point, Two-Hearted River, and Sucker River. In the years to come, lifesaving stations would be added at the west end of the mouth of Portage Lake and Lake Superior Ship Canal (the base of the Keweenaw Peninsula), Marquette, Duluth, and, lastly, Eagle Harbor.

Every station had a keeper to oversee operations, which included 24/7 watch duty in addition to rescues. The keeper hired his crew, six or eight men (depending on whether the lifeboats had six or eight oarlocks), and organized them into rank and duties. The crews generally were drawn from the local population, as was the keeper. The head of the service, Sumner Kimball, wrote of selecting a keeper:

> In the vicinity of nearly all stations there are numbers of fisher-
> men and wreckers who have followed their callings from
> boyhood and become expert in the handling of boats in broken
> water, and among them there is usually someone who, by
> common consent, is recognized as a leader par excellence.
> He is the man it is desirable to obtain for keeper.

Plying Lake Superior is different than traversing the ocean. First, harbors are frozen for at least a third of the year. Lifesaving stations were unmanned in winter. When the water opened up, it could be tranquil and serene for days on end. One sailor wrote, "there are weeks in the summer when these great bodies of water sleep like placid woodland ponds."

But this can change within minutes. Squalls with high winds launch themselves with fury. Waves pile high, with shorter troughs than in the ocean, so recovery is difficult. At the end of the season, ice accumulates on boats, on decks and rigging. Rescuing any crew in trouble requires stamina, skill, and courage. And that was why the keeper drew from a pool of local sailors well versed in Superior's capricious moods. The job required lifesavers to head out whenever someone needed rescuing, no matter what the conditions. Men who did not respond were immediately fired.

There were several ways lifesavers could rescue the stranded.

Often, the stricken boats were caught on a reef or sandbar close to shore. During fierce storms, the powerful surf and floating debris in the water slamming into shore prevented a simple exit from the boat to a raft, or merely wading ashore—though the desperate did that, too, and sometimes drowned. One method was termed a "breeches buoy rescue." A Lyle gun, whose sole function was to pitch a length of heavy rope out to a stranded ship, was fired. When successful, the rope reached the ship, and the crew grabbed and secured it. Meanwhile, the lifesavers on shore had set up a pair of crossed poles that guided the rope through to an anchor in the ground. A type of swing was then employed, which the crew rode, one by one, to safety. The ride was harrowing, though, dangling those being rescued over fomenting water.

While this seems like an improbable means of rescue, it was often used. Lifesavers drilled on the technique once a week and were very skilled. After practice, teams were expected to perform a rescue within five minutes. Stonehouse notes that since lifesaving stations were sited in vacation areas, tourists often came to watch the drills. A breeches buoy drill became a way for the crew to impress the ladies and was often part of a community's Fourth of July celebration.

Lifesavers had two different kinds of rescue boats at their disposal. The lifeboat was heavy bottomed and could be sailed or rowed. Over the years, its design was perfected to make it self-righting and self-bailing. Only those stations in protected waters, like Eagle Harbor, had lifeboats, since the craft were too heavy to be pulled over long stretches of sand to reach a point of launching. They were, however, very useful in giant waves. If possible, a lifeboat would be towed by a tug out to the wreck, allowing the crew to stay rested rescuing those aboard ship.

A more nimble vessel was the surfboat, a lightweight (700 pounds) skiff that was rowed out to a wreck by six or eight men. Horses could haul it over a sandy beach to the wreck site, where it was launched amid the breaking waves. Crews rowed furiously to get beyond the surf, where the agile vessel worked to avoid debris and outsize waves to reach the stranded ship.

Every member of a lifesaving team was assigned a specific place in the boat, and they were ranked, one through eight, each with clear duties, which they practiced weekly.

The lifesaving stations greatly curtailed the loss of lives in the early years. Lake Superior data isn't broken out from the tallies, but for the Great Lakes as a whole, from 1876 to 1914, 9,763 ships were wrecked and 55,639 people rescued. Only 275 people died from these wrecks, less than one percent of those in need of rescue. As shipping activity increased to meet growing demand, there came more stories of heroism, courage, and disaster. Stonehouse believes one of the best examples of the lifesavers' skills was the rescue of the crew of the *Charles J. Kershaw*, just east of Marquette on September 29, 1895.

The *Kershaw*, a wooden steamer, was headed uplake, towing two schooner-barges, when the captain detected a change in weather. By 2:00 a.m. the trio was approaching the protection of Marquette's harbor when a pipe cracked in the boiler room, rendering the steam-powered engine useless. The vessels were suddenly at the mercy of an intensifying wind, which pummeled them toward shore. The towlines were cut, under the assumption that the barges might fare better, and certainly no worse, than if linked to the *Kershaw*. This proved true: the schooner barges were blown far enough on the beach east of Marquette that the crew could hop ashore to safety.

Sadly, that was not true of the *Kershaw*, which foundered on Chocolay Reef at the mouth of the Chocolay River, listing badly with a good-sized hole in the hull. The lookout in the tower of Marquette's lifesaving station detected the disabled vessel, and the lifesavers swung into action. They loaded the surfboat onto its wagon and got a team of horses to haul it to the launch site on the beach. The waves crashing ashore were ferocious, carrying logs and stumps from the eroded coastline, any of which could smash the lightweight surfboat.

Timing the launch of the boat to coincide with advantageous waves, the keeper, Henry Cleary, a legend of maritime Marquette, stood astern in the boat and manned the steering oar while deftly maneuvering around towering waves and floating debris to reach the wreck. Onlookers stood on the beach witnessing the harrowing scene unfold. Nine men were rescued and brought ashore. It was at this point that the first casualty occurred: a surfman in the water, clearing a path for the boat to land, was crushed between the boat and a log.

Keeper Cleary pulled a volunteer from the onlookers to man the injured man's oar, and the stalwart crew headed back to the *Kershaw* amid the roar of the wind and the toss of the waves. As they approached the ship, a trio of monstrous waves hit them in quick succession, and they capsized, righted, and capsized again. The roiling water then battered the lightweight surfboat beyond use, and keeper and crew rode the waves into shore. Two more crew members were injured. Indefatigable, Cleary headed back to the station for the heavy lifeboat.

Meanwhile, the remaining crew of the *Kershaw* feared the ship was breaking up, and they launched a raft from the ship. All scrambled aboard. Cleary returned, enlisted the aid of four more volunteers, and launched the heavy lifeboat. The tank-like craft plowed through the heaving water to reach the raft and take everyone on board. The rescuers, some of whom had been at it for eight hours, were too exhausted to even row to shore. To assist them, Cleary employed a device called a drogue, which was trailed behind the boat to slow its beaching. The local paper termed the rescue "a plucky and skillful . . . piece of work."

But Lake Superior has a way of balancing gallant tales like the *Kershaw* rescue with stories that haunt, even to this day. Eighteen years later along that same length of shoreline, the *Henry B. Smith*, a wood-hulled propeller, left Marquette's harbor, laden with iron ore. It headed into a November storm and at some point north of Marquette met its demise. All twenty-five lives onboard were lost, and no trace of the *Smith* has ever been found, no wreckage, no bodies, nothing.

My favorite shipwreck story, however, is more lighthearted and stars, in a secondary role, not people but fancy automobiles as cargo. On November 30, 1926, The *City of Bangor* had 220 new Chryslers (with a handful of Whippets) lashed on its deck and tucked into its hold as it headed to Duluth, where buyers awaited their new cars. The run was made late in the shipping season, and the freighter encountered a raging storm as it made its way around Keweenaw Point. Clearing the point, the *City of Bangor* felt the full brunt of the wind and driving snow. The captain turned the ship around and was retracing the route back to the protection of Keweenaw Bay when the steering gear broke and the boat was pushed onto a reef just two miles from the point.

Luckily, the *Bangor* grounded near shore. Protected from the wind by the boat, the crew members launched their life rafts and made it to land. The twenty-four men and five captains spent a miserable night huddled around a fire, expecting a rescue that didn't come. The next day, they decided they needed to rescue themselves and began a six-mile trudge through knee-deep snow to Copper Harbor. They had misread certain landmarks from the deck of the ship in the storm and set out in the wrong direction before recognizing their mistake and rectifying it.

One day later, the Coast Guard crew based in Eagle Harbor was returning from a different rescue when they spied the *Bangor* crew plowing through the snow. They made haste to Copper Harbor, unloaded survivors, and went back for the crew of the *Bangor*. The twenty-nine men were in tough shape but were delivered to town, where local residents fed and housed them while also hosting the other shipwrecked crew.

Eventually, the crew of the *Bangor* was transported to Calumet by horse and sleigh (no plowed roads that far up the Keweenaw), where a railroad could carry them home.

But the story didn't end there, because there were still around 220 Chryslers and Whippets lashed to the deck or stowed in the hold of the stranded *City of Bangor*. Eighteen of them had been blown off the deck and into the deep by the wind. And after the snow and the wind and the waves, the remaining cars were fully encased in ice.

Chrysler was most anxious to recover its loss. In December, the cars on deck were chiseled free and lifted out. Via a ramp, the cars inched their way off the boat and onto the ice. Teams of horses graded a snow road to Copper Harbor, where the cars were driven and tidily lined up, all 202, awaiting spring snowmelt, when Highway 41 from Copper Harbor to Phoenix would be passable.

In March, plows from Houghton and Keweenaw County, as well as a crew from Albert Lea, Minnesota, worked on the road for two weeks, making it navigable for the rescued vehicles. Chrysler paid local drivers, including Calumet teenagers, five dollars a car to deliver them to the train station. By April 1, most of these cars had been returned to Detroit to be refurbished and sold.

But not all. One elegant Chrysler found its way to the Keweenaw County Historical Society's museum in Eagle Harbor. It dominates the display, intact and jaunty, never a hint that it had survived a shipwreck, a winter in Copper Harbor, and a trip down the snowy peninsula.

In 2019, Eagle Harbor residents thought the car would be a great addition to their annual Fourth of July parade. But the Chrysler did not perform well. It coughed to a halt before leaving the museum, then broke down six more times in the four-block route, before it was towed back to its home. Visitors can see it in summer, when the museum welcomes guests. It holds court in a building right behind the lighthouse, an odd and quirky emblem of what can happen to an innocent bystander when the queen is riled.

THE LAKE BREEZE HOTEL

The phone rang once, twice, then someone picked up, and a pleasant voice said, "The Lake Breeze Hotel."

So they're still open, I thought to myself, *how wonderful.* "I'd like to book a room for the third week in August," I said.

There was the slightest of pauses, then the voice asked, "Have you stayed with us before?"

Now I paused and then replied, "Well, actually, I have, but it was a long, long time ago. Close to thirty years now."

I thought back to August 1987, when Tom and I had stumbled on the Lake Breeze while in Eagle Harbor on the Keweenaw Peninsula, looking for a room for the night. We had two small children in tow, ages four and two, and a newborn. The summer of 1987 had been uncommonly hot, and the little bodies I tended had suffered heat rash, sunburn, and sweaty discomfort for days on end. On our vacation, we had fled our home outside the Twin Cities, seeking relief from the heat, and headed to Lake Superior and the sand beaches of the Keweenaw.

Our four-year-old that summer had developed a mania for lighthouses. The allure was partly the rotating light, I think, and partly the frisson of shipwrecks. Wearing his lighthouse-print shirt made by Grandma, he and his sister (wearing a matching dress) had eagerly toured the lighthouse at Ontonagon earlier in the week. The lighthouse at Eagle Harbor beckoned.

Eagle Harbor's lighthouse was very fine—red brick, small-scale, perched on a rock at the mouth of the harbor, with a revolving light that was still operational. Its next-door neighbor was the hotel, so we thought it would be great if they had a room available and we could be close to the lighthouse that night.

A family of five with a preschooler, a toddler, and a newborn is a lot to handle. We discovered that the Lake Breeze patrons were a geriatric bunch. Tom and I had our hands full tamping down the noise of excited children's voices, the occasional skirmishes, and the cries of an incessantly hungry baby. Maybe the elderly clientele liked our youthful presence. Maybe they were relieved it was us and not them who had to corral the little animals. But even with these distractions, Tom and I were entranced by the tranquil, courtly ways of the Lake Breeze. Decades later, we wanted to return. I closed my eyes and imagined the front reception area to the hotel, the pine floor, and the wooden staircase next to the desk.

"Yes!" the voice on the other end broke through my reverie. "I believe we do have something open during that week. Would a yard view be OK? How many nights are you looking for?"

THE LAKE BREEZE HOTEL of Eagle Harbor hunkers on the top of a perfectly protected C-shaped harbor on the rough northern coast of the Keweenaw peninsula. Michigan's first state geologist, Douglass Houghton, sailed past the site in October 1845 as he and his team wound up the surveying field season. He camped in the harbor and passed the point again the next morning, headed for Eagle River. It was a fateful passing, for that night a terrific storm blew up that swamped his little Mackinaw boat. Houghton perished in the storm.

Speculators had found profitable copper deposits at Eagle River in 1844, and soon there was mining action in Eagle Harbor. The Copper Falls Mining Company organized in 1845 and sunk several shafts along Owl Creek southwest of Eagle Harbor. These were fissure mines, pulling pure copper out of a vein.

The town became a popular destination for commerce on Lake Superior's South Shore. About equidistant between Sault Ste. Marie and Duluth, it was a customary stop for "wooding"—to refuel steamships that burned wood in their boilers. The natural harbor was a place to off-load goods and supplies for the mines exploiting the lodes running down the Keweenaw's ridge. There were now several, and the nearby communities of Delaware, Mandan, Central Mine, and Phoenix all accessed the lake at Eagle Harbor. The town had a large hotel, the Eagle Harbor House, and a general store.

Warehouses soon became necessary. In the 1850s, a depot was built on the site and ran an L-shaped dock into the water near the harbor's mouth. Other warehouses also with docks now lined the C. Supplies of all kinds were trundled in from boats. Mining supplies, necessary chemicals, and explosives were kept apart from other goods (food staples like flour, coffee, and sugar, as well as horse tack and liquor) in their own special warehouse over the water. The last shipment of the season, before the lake froze, was meat to last the winter. Sometimes the meat was "on the hoof," the animals shoved into the icy water and forced to swim to shore, before being corralled and maintained until slaughter.

The arrival of a cargo-bearing ship was a big event in the tiny hamlet. The warehouse had a sizable bell that was rung upon the sighting of a boat. A shipment of goods was imminent, and fresh vegetables and fruits would be available to purchase down at the dock. The bell was rung to let would-be passengers know that their ride was arriving. It was rung to call dockworkers in to unload the boat. The town had several bells—the schoolhouse bell, church bells—and in quiet times, they were the primary means of communication.

Once unloaded, the boats took on more cargo—barreled copper ore in need of stamping, or hunks of mass copper that had been brought to the warehouse and piled in the adjacent yard, often during the winter, when it was easier to convey heavy loads with horse and sled. The copper masses formed towering mounds before being shipped to East Coast smelters upon ice-out in spring.

Owned by a partnership, the Raley-Shapley warehouse made life in Eagle Harbor possible as goods moved in and out. By 1860, the barnlike, two-story warehouse was the pulsating heart of the town. The copper mining towns on the Keweenaw were utterly dependent on boats arriving from Detroit and other cities for crucial food items and equipment. There was no railroad and no wagon road through the dense and rugged terrain. Moreover, once the lake froze in November or December, what people had on hand would have to last until spring.

In November 1860, calamity struck Eagle Harbor when a warehouse caught fire and burned, igniting several others. The blaze was fueled by the ignition of gunpowder that had been stored for blasting in the mines. In a matter of hours, the certainty that residents could withstand the coming winter was thrown into doubt.

The owner of the warehouse, William Raley, watching the calamity unfold and feeling the weight of responsibility, quickly organized a party to head for Detroit to replenish supplies. Time was of the essence—it was nearly mid-November, and the harbor would freeze in a few weeks. Furthermore, November storms were notorious on the big lake. The voyage through the Soo and back could be upended at any time.

Raley chartered a boat, traveled to Detroit, and headed back. By November 24, the party was in Marquette. The temperature stood at twelve degrees below zero, and the snow was already two feet deep. Nevertheless, they pushed onward, arriving safely in Eagle Harbor with enough supplies to last the winter. The townspeople held a dinner in honor of Raley that night.

William Pettit Raley was both singular and archetypal of the nineteenth-century Americans drawn to the copper scene. A Quaker from Ohio (some early investors in mines around Copper Harbor had also been Quakers), he attended Oberlin College from 1848 to 1850, then headed to the Keweenaw Peninsula on the advice of an uncle. He acted as a bookkeeper for a copper mine on Isle Royale and later worked at a copper mine on the peninsula before settling in Eagle Harbor and subsequently opening his warehouse. A long-term marriage produced eight children. The family lived in Eagle Harbor in the summer and moved to a larger town, nearby Laurium, Michigan, or Duluth, Minnesota, for the school year. The Raley children were raised in a Quaker home with a strong sense of identity and addressed each other using "thee" and "thou." Most would not stay on the Keweenaw as adults.

Raley was a young man when he embarked on his business in Eagle Harbor, and his life followed the rise and fall of the copper boom. After Raley's legendary trip on the cusp of winter to replenish supplies, the town continued to prosper. Raley rebuilt his warehouse, a structure that stands today. He was appointed a judge of probate for Keweenaw County in 1861 and bought out his partner in 1879, assuming full control of the warehouse. The federal government replaced the frame lighthouse with a new red-brick one, still in operation. A telegraph line linked the small community to the wider world, and in 1880, townspeople gathered around a new device using the telegraph wires to hear a voice speaking in Hancock, thirty-five miles away. The telephone had broken the isolation of Eagle Harbor.

The mines along nearby Owl Creek never produced ore in quantities as large as the Cliff mine of Eagle River, but anywhere else in the world, they would have been celebrated. The Hill mine, sited in the vicinity of numerous ancient mining pits, was an early producer—245,000 pounds of pure copper. The Agency mine, an experimental venture by the Eagle Harbor Copper Mining Company, produced sufficient ore to be bought out by Calumet and Hecla in 1899. The Ashbed mine produced reliably, and in 1899 several tons of mass copper were removed, but eventually it, too, went the way of all mines and closed in 1907.

Throughout the decades, elephantine copper masses accumulated beside the Raley warehouse and were shipped east through the Soo, the piles rising and falling with the seasons. Raley was aging, and by the time the Ashbed mine closed, he was an old man. He died four years later at age eighty-five.

His son closed William's estate and sold off the warehouse. Act 1 of the Raley warehouse ended, and there was a pause, an intermission. Then the curtain rose on Act 2.

By 1909, the towns that had depended on Eagle Harbor to ship out copper were spent—ghost towns. Mining communities foundered, lacking a solid economic base, but they still had logging, commercial fishing, and meager farming. In the Roaring Twenties, since the Keweenaw Peninsula had scenic beauty and sparkling water in spades, local towns turned to recreation and tourism.

The first summer cottage in Eagle Harbor appeared in 1908. Others followed, and a bit later, William Raley's warehouse assumed a new life. Raley's youngest child, Austin, bought back the building, which had spent the interim decade or so as a garage for families occupying adjacent summer cottages.

Austin had married a Keweenaw native, Alice Getchell, and the couple, now in their early thirties, had a young son. Alice, a small dynamo with curly hair and an eye for business ventures, proposed establishing a tearoom in the now empty warehouse. The couple gave the building a new name, "The Lake Breeze," and a new identity. This single gesture set the stage for an eating establishment that tracked the trends and became a hallmark of genteel dining.

The Roaring Twenties swept over America in a wave of jazzy giddiness. In the years following World War I, women got the vote, cut their hair, and abandoned corsets and long skirts. Henry Ford's Model T rolled off the assembly line and at $260 was within reach of most middle-class Americans. Paved roads were laid down to accommodate cars and gas stations. American wealth doubled during the decade, and middle-class folk, experiencing a new prosperity, took vacations. Prohibition became reality on May 1, 1918, in Michigan, a state that went dry before the nation did.

A TEAROOM BRINGS TO MIND proper ladies in hats, daintily sipping from china cups, pinkie fingers extended. But tearooms in the

1920s were deceptively feminist ventures. They were almost always owned by women, and in an age when respectable women seldom, if ever, frequented restaurants and then only in the company of a man, a tearoom was a place where women could meet, share a light meal, and partake in the public scene.

Tearooms sold more than tea. Chicken salad was a popular item, as was something called "cheese dreams," grated cheese, mustard, and cayenne spread on bread and toasted under a broiler. They offered desserts, such as cakes and ice cream, and other delectables, like charlotte russe, a sponge cake filled with berries and custard.

One of the features of conventional restaurants prior to Prohibition was, of course, alcohol. Tearooms were strictly dry; in fact, they were sometimes referred to as "T rooms"—for Temperance. Temperance and feminism were naturally paired in the early twentieth century: activist women supported both causes. The Lake Breeze's tearoom opening in 1922, four years into Prohibition, meant it was unquestionably dry, even though elsewhere on the Keweenaw might see a brisk black-market trade in spirits coming from Canada.

Alice launched her tearoom in partnership with a friend and, of course, with the backing of Austin, who, raised Quaker, was something of a feminist himself. She was a good baker and furthermore collected and displayed antiques in the dining area, another characteristic of a tearoom. Women diners could admire and scrutinize the antiques on their visit. A relative would later recall a large, ornate porcelain coffee urn prominently displayed—pink and gray with sterling silver ornamentation, quite the piece.

It was perhaps in this first year of running the tearoom that Alice honed her skill at remaking leftovers into edibles for the next round of dining. This skill proved invaluable in the next stage of the continually evolving Lake Breeze, when in 1923 the Raleys expanded the tearoom into a dining room, initially serving dinners only and then expanding to three meals a day.

The newly christened Lake Breeze retained the form of the erstwhile warehouse, long and low slung, with cedar shakes and white trim. A porch extended across its front entry and eventually wrapped around the east side fronting the open lake. The L-shaped dock reached into the harbor. Cargo-laden boats no longer docked there, but excursion boats were frequent visitors. Some were headed to Isle Royale, but others brought tourists, often suffering from hay fever, to Eagle Harbor. As early as the 1800s, hay-fever sufferers fled to the Great Lakes—Mackinac Island in Lake Huron was an early destination—for relief from the miseries of allergies. Austin Raley's business card touted the "Lake Breeze Resort Hotel . . . where hay fever is unknown."

The dining hall proved so popular that diners asked for overnight accommodations. After all, even with Model Ts to ferry folks around, Eagle Harbor was an isolated village. How much easier to return to a room after a fine dinner in the dining hall.

The Raleys began adding rooms to the warehouse, building a second floor and bumping out dormers as they did so. First two, then four, then six dormers appear on successive photographs of the hotel. The rooms were spacious, some paneled in pine, and all with large windows that let in sunlight and the cool lake air. Those on the lake side offered the long view of Lake Superior in all its moods. Those on the other side now opened to a parking lot where Model Ts clustered, replacing the barrels and masses of pure copper that had once waited to be shipped out.

The enterprising owners added cabins to rent, buying and moving some and building others. At the resort's zenith, seventeen cabins were available to visitors, in addition to the rooms on the hotel's second floor.

The Lake Breeze dining hall became famous for fish dinners— fresh lake trout and whitefish, caught locally in the spring and stored in freezers cooled with ice cut from the harbor in March. The cold-water fish were easy to net in spring, much harder in August, when the surface water warmed and the fish were driven into the depths. Chicken dinners were also popular, the chickens raised locally in an age when large poultry operations were unknown.

Turning out three meals a day was an immense undertaking. The breakfast menu was simple. Twenty-five cents would get one toast and coffee. But one could also order a cooked breakfast of juice or prunes, oatmeal, bacon and eggs, or wheat cakes. In a locale where fresh fruit, even in summer, was an inconsistent commodity, dried breakfast prunes were indispensable. Lunch items included several different sandwiches, including peanut butter (ten cents). For dinner, in addition to the fish and chicken, the Lake Breeze offered T-bone steak, the priciest item on the menu.

The twenty-five tables in the dining hall were decked in white linen. The house china was white and green. Alice's antiques still added ambiance, and there were views of the restless lake. The restaurant was very, very busy. Menus were, at one point, hand-lettered, with a charming sketch of the hotel on the front, a full complement of rooms with dormers atop, indicating the hotel was at its pinnacle.

Austin and Alice were delightful hosts, and people gravitated to them. The Lake Breeze's popularity grew. Early on, the couple introduced dancing on Wednesday and Saturday nights, with a live band. The old warehouse sparkled on summer nights with warm lights, laughter, and music drifting out over the still water of the harbor.

The hotel markedly influenced the quiet town's economy. It employed cooks, cleaners, salad chefs, and pastry chefs. It was a badge of distinction to be a waitress. Girls from out of town bunked in one of the cottages. In addition to managing the kitchen, marketing the hotel, and overseeing its maintenance, the Raleys presided over a small payroll.

A changing of the guard occurred in 1946 when the Raleys' only child, Frank, and his wife, the red-haired Helen Carlson, took over the hotel. Austin and Alice were in their midfifties. Frank and Helen, in their twenties and recently married, were vigorous and young and eager to maintain the sterling reputation of what had become an institution.

Frank and Helen Raley were the first generation to not live full-time on the Keweenaw Peninsula. Eagle Harbor had become a summer residence for most of the families of the town. Over the span of their tenure, Frank completed a doctorate in industrial engineering and held a succession of teaching posts in the Midwest; Helen, a nurse by training, devoted herself to raising two daughters, Alison and Marcia.

This Raley generation assumed operations at the onset of the American prosperity brought by the end of World War II. They were acutely aware that the restaurant business was fiercely competitive and relentlessly trendy. They dined out frequently to see how other businesses ran things. How did they present their salads? Their desserts? What was on the menu?

They experimented. In the 1950s, there was a trend toward English clotted cream, which was added to some store-bought confections. Incredibly, the clotted cream they added to the dessert menu was locally sourced from nearby Calumet, perhaps a legacy of the Cornish miners who once filled the town. "Molded Fruit Salad," aka "Jell-O," appeared on the menu. In the 1960s, customers asked for "Minute Burgers." Grilled Minute Steak on Toasted Bun (99 cents) joined the old favorites of Oven Baked Chicken ($2.00) and Broiled Lake Trout ($2.50) in 1965. Salad bars became popular. The Raleys set up a salad bar. Also a dessert bar.

Frank was known for his soups and had a penchant for unusual recipes, skipping over a standard chicken noodle for Chicken Mulligatawny or Norwegian Fruit Soup to head up the menu. The Raleys ran through a rough patch with cooks, and Frank made the decision to become a trained chef at the Dunwoody Institute in Minneapolis. This venture paid off in several ways. They no longer worried about a cook quitting unexpectedly in midseason, and with quality control in the kitchen, the Lake Breeze earned a coveted Duncan Hines travel guide listing in 1959 and retained it for the rest of the years the dining hall operated. They proudly hung the Duncan Hines sign from the hotel's front porch: "A Haven and Oasis for the Traveler."

There was no denying it was a tough business. Close to the tip of the Keweenaw peninsula, their stop was nearly the end of the road. The Lake Breeze submitted food orders, but sometimes got "whatever was left on the truck," Marcia Raley told me. Often, Frank or Helen made an emergency run into Laurium, twenty-three miles away, to supplement their dinner supplies. They had a good relationship with Quality Market in town.

In 1961, Eagle Harbor observed its centennial year, and Helen thought it would be festive and appropriate to have the staff dress in period costumes. Thus, the waitstaff found themselves in long calico skirts and freshly starched aprons. Even the Raley girls played a part—they had worked in some capacity at the restaurant since early childhood. Marcia thought she may have learned how to make change running the cash register—as a first-grader.

By the mid-1960s, it was time for a change, and the Raleys closed the restaurant and began selling off the cottages. Frank and Helen were in their forties. They continued to run the hotel, much more manageable without its dining hall or cottages. Tom and I met them when we dropped in with our young children in 1987. We had no idea we were conversing with living legends. In 1989, they turned over the hotel operations to Marcia, who became the fourth generation of the Raley family to run a business on that site.

The curtain opened on Act 3.

"CHECK-IN IS AT THREE," Marcia Raley, the owner of the pleasant voice told me. "No pets, please. There are places to eat meals in town. We provide coffee in the morning."

Marcia and her husband, Chris Kvale, assume most of the work in operating the Lake Breeze in a limited way. They are open only in August. They don't advertise and rent mostly to people who have been coming to the hotel for years. When we visited in 2015, there was a father-daughter pair in a room adjacent to ours who had been spending Augusts there since 1961. The father was ninety, frail and bent; the daughter about our age, blonde and solicitous. I watched them make their way across the hotel yard one afternoon and wondered if they shared memories of the Lake Breeze when he was slim and vigorous, maybe carrying a little girl on his shoulders, and she thrilled to the crash of waves from the big lake and scampered on the rocks out in front.

Tom and I have since been back to Eagle Harbor several times. We like the rooms away from the water, overlooking the side yard and a big red oak, in which migrating warblers sometimes flit. We don't spend a lot of time in our room, but there are comfortable chairs and a good reading light in each pine-paneled room, and no televisions. Also, no air conditioning, but the windows actually open, and at night, gentle breezes waft in, lifting the cotton curtains.

The clientele of the Lake Breeze has not changed much. It's still an older crowd, but now the people are mostly our age. The Lake Breeze has aged out of lively evenings filled with dancing and saxophones. Its visitors gather in the lounges. The inner lounge, with chairs clustered around a brick fireplace, glows warmly, as people tell stories, laugh together, and share the adventures of the day. In this room one can admire the bell that once perched atop the warehouse and was rung to call laborers to work.

The sun parlor is fully glassed in, with a view of the harbor and the big lake immediately outside its windows. The rotating cyclopic eye of the lighthouse can be seen out its west window, flashing throughout the night. People play cards in this room, or board games. The Lake Breeze supplies all the standards: Monopoly, chess and checkers, Clue, Risk. On our last visit, a young couple sparred over a cribbage board. I take my morning coffee in its blue ceramic "Lake Breeze" mug to the sun parlor to write, watching the late-summer sun rise out of the water.

The upbound shipping lane runs close to the north side of the Keweenaw. The thousand-foot-long freighters look uncommonly large as they ply the waters, heading toward Duluth or Two Harbors.

But many evenings, the guests simply lounge about outside, loath to surrender a view of Superior to the confines of four walls.

They drape their forms over deck chairs or gently rock the porch swing, making it creak. It has been warm on the Keweenaw in the past five years since we have resumed our visits, uncommonly warm. People are happy to receive the evening's cooling air.

Many of our memorable experiences at the Lake Breeze occur in the evening, just before bedtime. We often are at Eagle Harbor in mid-August at the time of the meteorite shower Tears of St. Lawrence, and have spent hours in the dark on the front lawn, looking for shooting stars. On one night, they failed to materialize, but a fantastic show of flashing lightning out over the lake entertained. That same night, we witnessed an odd phenomenon of ghostly pale Ringbilled Gulls drifting in to the harbor long after dark, silently floating without flapping on the night air. I surmised that they spent their day over the open water, perhaps quite a ways out, and returned to the protection of the harbor after the sun went down.

One year, Tom and I pondered dark, shadowy forms flitting about in the twilight, too big for Chimney Swifts and not buzzing like nighthawks would. Our host, Chris, thought they might be bats, but that didn't seem right, either. After much thought, we decided they must be nighthawks that were migrating and were perhaps silent in their journey. But then we wondered where they all came from—there wasn't much land mass on the Keweenaw thrusting out into Lake Superior, not enough to collect all those birds. Could they possibly have flown south over open water?

Last year, one of the guests brought his telescope, and Marcia let it be known that there would be an astronomy opportunity that evening on the front lawn. Many of the guests gathered to peer through the optic at the craters of the moon and the rings of Saturn. Eagle Harbor isn't well lit. The night was inky, and crickets chirped from the grass.

Marcia and Chris know their guests uncommonly well. Some remember her parents and her grandparents. They recall her as a girl. They ask about her sister. The Lake Breeze offers a unique but probably once common example of a close relationship between innkeepers and vacationers. Guests return year after year, warm and loyal, getting older, having babies, losing elders, weaving their summer vacation spot into the whole of their lives. The innkeepers, for their part, see their guests as complete people, not a night's rental or an occupied room to enrich their bottom line. Over years, the relationship grows rich and complex. The tapestry of the former warehouse is faded but beautiful.

We have lost something in our restless mobility, a new Super 8 every night, incessant forward motion. Being on vacation—taking a holiday—might be viewed as a sacred act, setting aside days to be apart from one's ordinary routine for rejuvenation. It isn't something you would leave to just anyone. Signing up for a week in a small hotel, you are entrusting yourself to the innkeeper's care. At the Lake Breeze, we open ourselves to interaction with the others occupying the upstairs with a common hall, where the light goes out at ten thirty every night, and where Marcia or Chris brings fresh coffee every morning, and we drink it in rounded mugs.

What binds us, besides an appreciation of quietude, relationship, and simplicity, is undoubtedly a love of Lake Superior. No one travels hundreds of miles to a remote little village and a non-air-conditioned hotel in an old warehouse without being irrationally, incessantly, passionately pulled by the restless big sea water.

When I last met up with Marcia, she was overseeing the final demise of the long, L-shaped dock that her great-grandfather had installed and that her own father had shored up, every generation restoring to wholeness what has been relentlessly battered by the waves. It seemed momentous to me, a retreat of human claim to this particular inlet of Superior.

Marcia recalled sitting with her dad and having him ask her—perhaps he already knew the answer—what it was that she loved about the Lake Breeze and its harbor.

"Oh," she said, "that's easy. It's the water . . . no, the trees . . . no, the rocks . . . I guess, it's the weather."

Which is to say, everything.

PART V

Superior Redux

A RETREAT FROM THE CLIFF

During the winter of 2018–19, the large spruce tree that shaded our picnic table succumbed to erosion. Incessant wave action wore away the soil around its roots, and it toppled into the lake. The loss was a slow-motion process. We observed the exposure of the roots facing the lake while eating lunches at the picnic table. Just a few roots at first, then more. The tree remained upright with half of its roots anchored, but gradually the inevitable happened, and we lost it.

When we looked out the kitchen window toward Lake Superior, we felt shockingly exposed. There was nothing between the cabin and the big lake. When we had bought the cabin thirty-one years before, we had stood on the cliff's edge and looked down on a large red sandstone boulder directly beneath us. Now that boulder was seventy feet from shore. I became acutely aware that our well was situated even closer to the edge.

Tom and I began to entertain the unthinkable, that our cabin would fall into Lake Superior in our lifetimes. It was, perhaps, in its last days. A friend asked us if knowing that the cabin was "terminal" diminished our pleasure in being there. It was an interesting question, and the answer was yes. There was always a background uneasiness, especially when it rained and waves pounded the cliffs.

We had seen how our neighbors had dealt with their shoreline erosion. Those directly west of us had tried remediation with hardware cloth and boulders placed at the toe of the cliff to protect it from waves. That hadn't worked. Farther down the shore, neighbors had somehow yanked their simple structure back from the cliff's edge. They had apparently solved the issue, at least temporarily. To our east, on a narrow lot, a couple in their seventies had torn down a childhood cabin and built a handsome new one as far from the water as possible, which put it nearly to Highway 13's verge. This option was attractive, but privately we wondered about spending that kind of money so late in life.

We cast about for other options. What if we were to sell the place and find another elsewhere on the South Shore, on land that wasn't eroding? What if we were to sell the cabin and buy another on a large northern lake, like Lake Vermilion or Lake Owen? What if we were to do nothing, live as fully as we could on our beloved land, watching the cliff edge creep closer, then tear the cabin down and walk away, calling it good enough? That would mean, probably, that at some time before we were done living, we would sever our ties with Lake Superior.

For one reason or another, we rejected these scenarios. The south shore was eroding almost everywhere. Superior's record-high levels were eating away beaches as well as red clay cliffs. On a visit to Sault Ste. Marie, we had seen how a flooded St. Marys River below the rapids had inundated suburban lawns just south of the locks.

We tried to imagine cabin life on a smaller lake. Appealing as that might be, we knew we would always wonder what was happening on Lake Superior.

I recalled our desolation after our move away from Ashland, so long ago. I remembered that after returning to Minnesota, I tried to orient toward a shining sheet of water that wasn't there, how I felt I had lost a point of reference. Gradually, I came to realize that our lives would be diminished without an ongoing relationship with the big lake. We had made that mistake once. We oughtn't make it again.

Despite the erosion, the property we owned on the lake had

some advantageous features. It was very deep. We could easily meet Bayfield County's 235-foot setback from the cliff and not site a new cabin right next to the highway. Also, there was a small, unnamed creek flowing through the property that had always provided us a way down to the beach without having to scramble over the red clay cliff. This creek's banks were not eroding, and we could place the cabin overlooking it.

TWO YEARS AFTER LOSING the protective spruce, Tom and I sat down at the beach and began to discuss our future life on the property we already owned. Well, we weren't exactly on the beach. Lake Superior was at a record-high level, and there was no beach that year. We sat on sand chairs atop the pile of driftwood blocking the mouth of the creek, facing the water. Tom was melancholic. He saw impermanence everywhere. A recent major storm had snapped the tops of three of our mature white pines. In addition to having no beach, we were losing the cliff. Our affectionate sheltie had recently died of cancer. Our two twenty-year-old cats were dying. We ourselves were noticeably declining. We were six months into the pandemic, and it had been hard on us, the incessant worry, the constant vigilance. We had known several people who had died after weeks on ventilators. And Tom's job as a family practitioner meant he was continually at risk of exposure.

We had earlier experienced a false start. We had hired an architect—our daughter Katie, who worked for a firm that designed many lake cabins—and asked her to draw up plans for a simple new cabin. We gave these to a prospective builder and met with him in Duluth two days before Minnesota shut down for the pandemic. His bid was almost twice as much as we thought we could afford. Discouraged, we had retreated from the plan to build.

Now, regrouping, sitting atop the driftwood, we agreed that a $400,000 cabin was not appropriate on our eroding property, but thought there might be a way to whittle down the cost. We didn't need a second story with a loft overlooking the lake. We might be able to compromise on building materials. I wanted pine paneling, but it didn't have to be tongue-and-groove. Perhaps a rough siding would be acceptable.

We had more lakeshore footage than we really needed. With that in mind, we put the western two parcels on the market. It was slow to sell, but we dropped the price, and this time, we attracted a buyer. Tom thought she had gotten a real bargain, but I was ecstatic. We had seen the same "for sale" signs for years on some lakeshore properties. With the sale we had perhaps a quarter of the new cabin paid for.

We pondered further on financing. We decided not to draw on our savings but on an inheritance from my mother. My mother had lived a modest life but had squirreled away her salary as a church organist by investing astutely in stocks and bonds. She did this entirely on her own and bequeathed to her children a tidy sum. Through this project, her reach would extend to her grandchildren and great-grandchildren, giving them a retreat from a fast-paced life in a warming world. Tom and I would be the conduits of this gift.

We had to reframe the project psychologically as well as financially. We were nearing seventy. We hoped for ten more good years, but one never knew. Tom had seen enough dire diagnoses in forty-three years of practice to know that, as he put it, "the other shoe could drop at any time." We could not think of a new cabin as being an end in itself. Rather, we were going to have to simply enjoy the process of planning and dreaming. It would give us an ongoing relationship with Lake Superior.

Over the years, Tom's medical practice had aged with him. Now he saw mostly geriatric patients. One who wintered in Florida, possibly at his wife's preference, called that state "God's Waiting Room." We were not going to spend the remainder of our lives in any waiting room. We were going to live, as fully as we could, in a life-affirming present, moving forward into the future without too many backward glances.

WE HIRED A NEW BUILDER, Joe Hokanson of Herbster, Wisconsin, one town down the shore from Port Wing. Tall and lanky, Joe had a good-natured personality, a wealth of experience, and a can-do attitude. Although I had trepidation as I placed the phone call to offer him the job, I also could feel a pull toward the future. If we had decided not to accept his bid, our dream would have died that day. But with Joe at the helm of our project, all sorts of possibilities opened to us, including a renewed romance with Lake Superior.

Tom and I had turned inward during the pandemic. We had long observed that worlds become smaller as people age, but our worlds had shrunk prematurely due to pandemic restrictions. With the new cabin project we would be moving upward and outward into a more hopeful future.

About this time, my brother tore down our childhood cabin in central Minnesota, preparing to erect his own place. He rescued two beautiful leaded-glass windows before demolition, windows that had come from Little Falls, my mother's hometown, and asked me if I wanted them. I took them in a heartbeat and asked Katie if she could find a place for them in her design. I was thrilled that a small part of Mother's past would transfer sunlight into our new cabin.

KATIE'S PLAN that we asked Joe to build, the scaled-down version, is just over a thousand square feet, about the size of our old cabin. It is slab-on-grade, with electric in-floor heating, a place we can use year-round. This means we will have to keep it heated all the time, a circumstance I find wasteful, but we hope that with smart technology, we can adjust the heat remotely and run it efficiently. Many of the state-of-the art green features Katie had originally called for were relinquished to stay on budget. This grieved her, but at the same time she acknowledged that merely building to 2022 code produces a more energy-efficient home than the twenty-six-year-old house we were currently living in. This was emphasized when the plumber asked us if we wanted a tankless water heater, rather than storing hot water in a holding tank. When we built our house a quarter century earlier, a system that heated water on demand was a pie-in-the-sky dream. Today, it is standard in new construction.

Tom's chief desire for a new cabin was a good view of the lake. Katie gave him a deck and a bank of windows facing northwest over the creek to the lake beyond. I asked for sunshine in as many rooms as possible. The kitchen and a corner "writing room" are flooded with light. In fact, every room has large windows overlooking either the lake, the woods, or the creek. As I did when I first occupied the old cabin, I move from room to room in the unfinished new one, looking out windows and admiring the view.

One feature we regretted not having is a heart-stopping, up-close-and-personal view of the water, nor will we hear its roar or feel the wind rattle the windowpanes. The reason? A 235-foot setback.

Because we were building smaller, Tom and I did not give up the dream of some sort of masonry stove, like the old ceramic ones we had seen in northern Europe, and we got extraordinarily lucky. On a call to a Duluth woodstove firm, Tom was offered a Finnish Tulikivi soapstone stove at a nice discount because it had been on display in the store. The store even offered to keep it for us until it could be installed. I am going to mourn the old cabin's fieldstone fireplace (inefficient as it was), but the handsome gray stone Tulikivi will ease the sense of loss.

Everything in the new place is powered by electricity. This includes a charger for the electric vehicles that we and a couple of our children own. Fossil fuels have no place in our future. We will add rooftop solar panels next spring and hope that future panels will be efficient enough to cover our electrical use.

Joe Hokanson had not worked with an architect before and was continually delighted with the level of detail in Katie's drawings. Indeed, in her plans she revealed herself to be more type A than I had recognized, accurate to one-quarter inch in every aspect. As parents, we have been delighted to see her function as a professional. She is good at what she does, envisioning three-dimensional space, thinking of practical needs (will the cabinets allow the refrigerator door to swing widely open?), imagining creative solutions to design problems, and communicating ideas to her clients and colleagues.

I FOUND THE DECISION to build breathtaking. One day as we gazed out over the site of the new cabin, Tom said, "You are going to hate cutting those trees." There were not any really big ones, just some slender aspen trees and a deformed and broken white pine, but I agreed with him. I am always objecting to Tom's plans to cut any trees—those too close to the cabin or the house, those that are dead and in danger of falling. I had requested that site preparation begin in the fall and not summer. The Ovenbirds that nested in this area would have migrated by then. They and our other nesting warblers would miss the disruption of early construction. When they returned the next May, they would have to be flexible.

The trees were cut in September, and the site cleared and graded. Footings followed, and the slab was poured before the ambient temperature could sink below forty degrees. Tom and I went to inspect one day and brought a lunch. We hauled chairs from the old cabin and sat overlooking the lake, our first meal atop the slab of the new cabin.

The slab did not look too small, but it didn't look too big, either. We thought maybe it was like trying to judge the size of a Christmas tree before you cut it—you just can't gauge its true dimensions.

Joe wanted to get the place framed and enclosed before the weather turned really cold, so that in winter, his crew could work inside. The trusses arrived, and on a brisk November day, a forty-mile-per-hour wind blowing off the lake, the men attempted to affix them to the frame. They positioned the first ones, but as the wind intensified, it became too risky for the men. Joe had to call off the work. "It's a brutal site," he observed to us in a phone conversation. For some reason, this amused us. "Brutal," we would tell each other when someone commented on the temperature, or wind, or rain at the cabin, when we viewed photographs of family members hunched over a beach fire in winter jackets, when we recalled snow on Memorial Day or ice chunks in the water in late May.

Katie and I made a trip to the project in early December to assess its progress and do a walk-through with the electrician. The electrician met us at the front door. He was Katie's age, maybe younger. He had a question for her, and together they bent over the blueprints. They were colleagues on this project, collaborators. These young people, these millennials, were running the show. It occurred to me that some time ago, when I wasn't aware of it, I had become old. And so had Tom. We were no longer in charge.

Snow fell, and the air became frigid. Tom drained the pipes in the old cabin, probably for the last time. He ran the water out of the hot water heater and the holding tank. We poured antifreeze in all the traps. This had been a fall chore for us for thirty-three years, one that we were probably never going to have to do again. We thought we had heard flying squirrels in the crawl space over one of the bedrooms, and for once, we didn't fret. We didn't need to somehow remove them. The days of the old cabin were numbered.

To run their power tools, the crew had tapped one of the outlets in the old cabin and was drawing power from the line. A long, one-inch-thick insulated electrical cord snaked out of the bathroom of the old cabin, across the backyard, and down the driveway to the new one. I hoped that Joe was right that it was safe to step over it, take a shower, use the sink, or even accidently step on it, because it would surely be instantly lethal if it leaked current. Our very young granddaughters did not visit the cabin this summer.

Slowly the blueprints became reality. There were delays due to the pandemic. One week, Joe's entire crew was sick with Covid. The windows from Marvin were late in arriving, either due to illness or supply chain issues, or perhaps just heavy demand from builders. We felt most fortunate to have the work proceed without major hitches. Katie had another project near Lutsen Resort on the North Shore. There, builders had told her clients that they could not get to their project for two years.

Tom and I made infrequent trips up throughout the winter. We chose flooring and other materials from a design studio in Ashland, so every time we drove up, we swung by the cabin for a look-see. I got over being jarred by the sight of new construction taking place in our woods. Indeed, it was gratifying to discover that every time I laid eyes on the new cabin, my inner self yelled, "Perfect! It's perfect!"

The scale of the place was pleasing. It looked like my preconception of a cabin. The profile didn't dominate the site. I was happy we hadn't opted for a second story. I could imagine sitting on the deck on summer afternoons, basking in the sun. We had planned for a little yard to the west of the building, protected from the wind, where we could eat at a picnic table and not get chilled. My mind's eye replaced the construction site's red clay with green grass and a bird feeder.

The pine paneling that I desired was achieved by using a lesser grade of wood, a mix of pine, spruce, and fir. These soft woods are still moving about even as they form the walls of the cabin. Joe said they would continue to react to their environment, expanding and contracting, for some time. It pleases me that the cabin embodies a living, functioning organism.

The reframing of the project away from a goal-oriented new cabin and toward a more relationship-oriented life on Lake Superior has been immensely helpful for me. The new cabin is so exquisite, I regret to think we could have less than ten years to live in it. It is true, no one knows how long they will live, but since starting the project, both Tom and I have developed medical conditions that decrease the odds we will live to see eighty. Instead, we are grateful for the opportunity to have something new to think about. It has provided us with useful distraction when we felt we were sinking beneath the weight of doctor appointments, medical scans, and testing.

In a few short weeks, we will move into the new place, and the old cabin, the cabin that I thrilled to before I even stepped inside it, will be taken down. A friend advised me not to be present when that happens. I think that's good advice. As much as I love the new cabin and anticipate living there, I can't quite believe that we will no longer have the old one. I will not wash dishes at the white enamel sink where I bathed my last baby. I won't sit at the writing table in the low-ceiling bedroom, watching nuthatches on the spruce tree. The old cabin will be gone.

Our time here on Lake Superior has been brief. How could I transform from May to November in such short order? It seems like last month we had towheaded children paddling about on inner tubes and building forts out of driftwood on a wide and sandy beach. In fact, it feels like just a short time ago that the Greyhound bus was pulling into Ontonagon and the driver was hauling our bicycle boxes out of the bus's underbelly. See, Tom is now getting out his wrench, ready to reattach the brakes and the pedals. It is near midnight, and the city streets are dark. When Tom is finished, we will get on our bikes and with very little light to guide us, head out into the night.

EPILOGUE

New Views

On a golden day in October, Tom and I turned off Highway 13, drove down our driveway toward Lake Superior, and parked in front of the new cabin. The aspens were a brilliant yellow, the sky bright blue. We paused before opening the car doors. I turned to him and said, "It doesn't get any better than this." We were still strong and able, thinking well and hopeful. A passage from Annie Dillard's *Teaching a Stone to Talk* came to mind:

> You know what it is to open a cottage. You barge in with your box of groceries and your dufflebag full of books. You drop them on a counter and rush to the far window to look out. I would say that coming into a cottage is like being born, except that we do not come into the world with a box of groceries and a dufflebag full of books—unless you want to take these as metonymic symbols for culture. Opening up a summer cottage is like being born in this way: at the moment you enter, you have all the time you are ever going to have.

Then we got out, unlocked the cabin door, and set about moving our possessions from the old to the new. It was perhaps a two-minute walk down the driveway to go between cabins, our morning's task, back and forth.

I walked down to the old place and opened the unlocked front door. Several weeks before, the power company had switched service from old to new, so I stepped into an interior that was cold and dark. We had, of course, stopped trapping mice, and mouse dirt covered the kitchen countertops. An overwhelming odor of mustiness assailed the senses. The old cabin had always smelled musty. On a weekend visit, our clothes would come home smelling like the cabin, and the scent had intensified as the cabin grew older. The cold air and the dim light, the damp smell and the filthy kitchen all combined to make the place surprisingly unappealing. I had not expected this.

Tom bustled about, loading the car with tables and lamps and boxes of food, while I stood in the kitchen, wrapping glassware in newspapers and putting plates and bowls in boxes. We made countless trips, and soon I switched to a post in the new kitchen, with its south exposure, now flooded with sunlight. I unwrapped the glasses and considered where best to put them, and the plates, and the mixing bowls.

We worked all day, ceasing only at supper. I put a hot dish into the oven, and we opened a bottle of wine. The day had turned cold; a stiff wind blew in from the northwest. From the front windows, we watched the waves racing in to shore.

The new cabin with its in-floor heating was warm, despite the wind that howled outside. I thought of the immense stone fireplace in the old cabin, the sole source of heat. It took over a day to get the living room warm enough to sit in comfortably. "I feel like we are too humble to have such luxury as warmth," I told Tom. "Like we don't deserve this."

"You mean, you're not suffering enough?" he asked. Well, yes, sort of.

The next day, our builder, Joe, stopped by and helped Tom move the heavy furniture—the couch, the trestle table, the bed. He didn't charge us for this because, he said, we had become neighbors. It was a friendly gesture.

Now the old place was truly emptied. Tom came back to where I was organizing the shelves in the new kitchen and reported that it felt like the old cabin had "lost its soul" with the furniture gone. I thought about this. Does a building have a soul and can it lose it? Or has the soul already transferred to the new cabin? Another unexpected feeling.

I was loath to tear the old cabin down immediately, as Joe (and Tom) had suggested. I thought I needed time to adjust to the change. I wanted to be able to go into the place and walk about, imagining the little children wrapped in blankets on chilly mornings, sipping cocoa and watching *Sesame Street*. I wanted to recall the time when our Volkswagen's car alarm suddenly sounded at 2:00 a.m., the emergency lights flashing and lighting up the woods (its key had been submerged in the Brule River when we tipped a canoe the day before).

I also wanted time to have people salvage materials. Joe had found men who would take out all the pine paneling and reuse it. Joe himself wanted the corrugated steel roof. I advertised at the convenience store in town and sold the pine kitchen cabinets and the fairly new low-flush toilet. Tom sold the electrical panel spontaneously. Apparently, such panels had become scarce in the pandemic.

It pleased me to think of the custom-crafted cabinets having new life in someone else's place. It was not unlike the phenomenon of organ donation in the event of an untimely and sudden death. The whole is gone, but the parts play new roles in someone else.

I think I will be sanguine in the face of demolition. It probably will not happen until spring. For now, the old place is our nearest neighbor. I can look out our bedroom window and see its familiar form. It anchors me as I adjust to the new scene. But I still think it best not to witness the destruction.

From the first evening, the new cabin has felt like home. We are becoming acquainted with its sounds, its own unique music. We hear the hum of the air-to-air exchanger, ventilating the tightly constructed house. The refrigerator and the boiler click on and off. After a disastrous first lighting of the Finnish stove, the Tulikivi, when smoke poured into the living room setting off smoke detectors, Tom has learned how to operate it. The stove kicks out a lot of heat with very little wood, and its flame is a cozy flicker as we sit and read.

By far, the biggest surprise of the new cabin has been the scenes outside the windows. Far from being denied a view of the lake, we enjoy a spectacular panorama that extends for 360 degrees. We see the lake, we see the creek, we see the woods in all its splendor, from the dark conifers to the transformed aspens with their buttery autumnal color. Because, situated on the creek bank, we are higher in elevation, we can see the waves breaking on the beach or frothing in whitecaps farther offshore. Such a perspective was wholly unexpected. One never knows when turning a corner, what kind of world opens up.

Tom and I turn seventy next year. Seven decades. As we approach this milestone, I find myself gauging the passage of time differently from how I used to. Time no longer yawns expansively in front of me. Time is assessed in discrete chunks: five years, ten years. It is a realistic way to think of time for any seventy-year-old. No one really knows how long they will live. I think that maybe Tom and I were given a gift to be forced into this point of view.

A day or two after the move, a brisk wind and a night of rain took down the remaining aspen leaves. What had been spun gold in the air surrounding us became a carpet of amber strewn across the driveway and forest floor. The yellow leaves resembled coins, a great multitude of coins. It was as if we had come unexpectedly upon a cache of gold doubloons. Unable to believe our good fortune, we had caught them up and spent the coins with abandon. We had cast them about generously, without a bit of hesitation, and now they lay scattered all around us, and we basked in the glow of our extravagance.

ACKNOWLEDGMENTS

People like to talk about Lake Superior, and I am fortunate that they do. Over the course of writing this book, I relied on the expertise and experience of so many others in all walks of life. No one person can comprehend all the different ways of experiencing the big lake. It was endlessly fascinating to converse with people and hear their stories.

In particular, I am indebted to wildlife artist and Ashland, Wisconsin, resident Greg Alexander, who welcomed me into his studio in the old Beaser School in Ashland to talk to me as an emergency medical technician and a reflective "bobber"; Chris Andersen, who read selected essays and shored me up when I needed it; Tom Anderson, North Branch; Don Arnosti; James Bittner, retired first mate of the *Roger Blough* and his wife, Peggy, who urged him to let me write about him; Mary Childs of the Port Wing Historical Society, who allowed me to take PWHS books home for the winter, when their library is closed; Paula Nourse Cunningham, Ashland, for her many insights into the Apostle Islands; Dr. Peter David, retired wildlife biologist with the Great Lakes Indian Fish and Wildlife Commission (GLIFWC); Dr. Therese Durkin; Dr. Gretchen Ehresmann, who cheerfully visited Superfund sites with me on the Keweenaw Peninsula—to this day, her only exposure to the UP; John Esposito, formerly of Ashland, whose remarkable book *Lake Superior: Blood on the Ice* gave me a little frisson of terror every time I opened it; Dr. Faith Fitzpatrick, hydrologist with the U.S. Geological Survey (USGS) for insight into erosion of the Lake Superior clay cliffs; Lisa Melberg French, whose love of Frog Bay keeps those memories alive; Andrew Leaf, also of the USGS; Ben Lewis; Sue Mackenzie-Smith, Ashland; Marcia Mason, summer resident of Eagle Harbor, Michigan, who first suggested I write on wild rice; Bob Nelson of Bayfield, Wisconsin, for all his ponderings on the Apostle Islands; Mark and Erica Peterson, also of Bayfield, for so many kindnesses (I owe you big time. Dinner at the Fat Radish?); Marcia Raley, for loving and sharing the Lake Breeze Hotel; Ruth Sablich, Mason, Michigan, a displaced Yooper, for her remarkable memory in recalling old Calumet; April Stone of the Bad River Band, for good conversation and a generous spirit; Ed Swain, who stood at the ready to answer wild rice questions; Shanda Waller; and Mike Wiggins, Tribal Chairman of the Bad River Band, Lake Superior Chippewa, who took time out of his busy schedule to take me down the Kakagon River to the wild rice beds and who made the Ojibwe stories come alive with his passion and eloquence.

The Ashland Historical Society and the Wisconsin Historical Society Archives, housed in the David R. Obey Northern Great Lakes Visitor Center, Ashland, allowed me access to old newspapers and photographs so I could read local history and relive our time in Ashland. The Keweenaw County Historical Society provided information on the mislaid anchor of the *John G. Munson*.

The University of Minnesota Press has once again crafted a beautiful book, gussying up my words with stunning covers and handsome text. Editor Kristian Tvedten, with a family cabin on the South Shore, was endlessly supportive and brimming with creative ideas. Copy editor Mary Keirstead with her eagle eye has once more produced flawless copy; Laura Westlund, managing editor, again guided a smooth production of my book; Rachel Moeller, production and design, kept the book moving forward; and publicist Heather Skinner is vigorous and unflagging in lining up events for me to bring my book to the wider world. Thank you all. I feel so lucky to be in your capable hands.

Susan Narayan of Minneapolis and Patti Isaacs of Marine on St. Croix have been my writing partners for twenty-five years. We read each other's work, edit, and comment on content and clarity. Sue N. is an amazing copy editor. She makes my writing so much better. Patti, a cartographer by training, has wanted to draw a map for my past three books, and, at last, she now has her chance. Thank you both forever and a day.

Let's hear it for my four children, Andy, Katie, John, and Christina Leaf. They never asked for a mother who continually exposes them to public scrutiny through the written word. Thank you for your tolerance and good humor. You are the absolute best.

And to my dear husband, Tom, who pulled me along to bike the South Shore, shared the dream, and made it come true: it has been fun building a life with you.

Books on Lake Superior abound. Many of these are on our book-shelves, and I reread all or part of them while writing this book. For a general, inexhaustible source on Lake Superior, particularly its North Shore, *North Shore: A Natural History of Minnesota's Superior Coast* by Chel Anderson and Adelheid Fischer (University of Minnesota Press, 2015) should be on every Superior lover's shelf. *Sustaining Lake Superior: An Extraordinary Lake in a Changing World* by Nancy Langston (Yale University Press, 2017) offers solid commentary on abuse the lake has suffered and what needs to be done to keep it healthy. *The Death and Life of the Great Lakes* by Dan Egan (W. W. Norton, 2017) looks at all the Great Lakes and their environmental threats, though I note that when all five lakes are taken together, Superior seems to get shorted. Norman Risjord provides an informative account of the lake, *Shining Big Sea Water: The Story of Lake Superior* (Minnesota Historical Society Press, 2008). Erika Alin offers nice essays in *Lake Effect: Along Superior's Shores* (University of Minnesota Press, 2003). Mike Link and Kate Crowley walked Lake Superior's perimeter, described in *Going Full Circle: A 1,555-Mile Walk around the World's Largest Lake* (Lake Superior Port Cities, 2012). I consulted many times the classic *Lake Superior* by historian Grace Lee Nute (Bobbs-Merrill, 1944). And lastly, for a breath of fresh air, see Eric Olmanson, *The Future City on the Inland Sea: A History of Imaginative Geographies of Lake Superior* (Ohio University Press, 2007).

The Place for Us

An account of James Hansen's appearance before the U.S. Senate Committee on June 23, 1988, can be found in Ben Block, "A Look Back at James Hansen's Seminal Testimony on Climate" (three-part series), grist.org, June 16, 2008, https://grist.org/article/a-climate-hero-the-early-years/.

For information on the Leech Lake cormorants, see John Enger, "Minnesota Pulls Out All the Stops to Protect Walleyes," MPR News, May 8, 2015, mprnews.org/story/2015/05/08/walleye; and Stephanie Hemphill, "Managing Cormorants on Leech Lake," Minnesota Public Radio, May 27, 2005, http://news.minnesota.publicradio.org/features/2005/05/27_hemphills_cormorants/.

The Bill Holm essay "Horizontal Grandeur" appeared in *The Music of Failure* (1985; reprinted by University of Minnesota Press, 2010).

Red Clay Cliff, Sandy Beach

The story of the lawsuit brought against Concordia University by its neighbors is profiled in Bryan Polcyn, "Bluff Failures Accelerate near Concordia University after Jury Finds Rock Wall a 'Nuisance.'" fox6now.com, October 18, 2015, https://www.fox6now.com/news/bluff-failures-accelerate-near-concordia-university-years-after-jury-finds-rock-wall-a-nuisance. See also "Stabilizing Concordia University's Bluff," Great Lakes Coastal Resilience Planning Guide, 2013, https://greatlakesresilience-floodscience.hub.arcgis.com.

The Linchpin

For the history of Sault Ste. Marie, see Bernie Arbic, *City of the Rapids: Sault Ste Marie's Heritage* (Allegan Forest, Mich.: Priscilla Press, 2003).

John Johnston's memoir is quoted in *Lake Superior* by Grace Lee Nute (1944; reprinted by University of Minnesota Press, 2000).

For information on the life and writings of Jane Johnston Schoolcraft, see *The Sound the Stars Make Rushing through the Sky: The Writings of Jane Johnston Schoolcraft*, edited by Robert Dale Parker (University of Pennsylvania Press, 2008).

Commentary on voyageur families appears in *The Voyageur,* by Grace Lee Nute (1931; reprinted by Minnesota Historical Society Press, 1987).

Charles Whittlesley's description of the portage appeared in *National Magazine,* February 1846, https://chequamegonhistory .wordpress.com.

Ozahaguscodaywayquay's reaction to her pending marriage is recorded in http://riverofhistory.org/index.php/articles/ozhahgus codaywayquay-c-1772–1843/.

Information on the shipyard at Pointe aux Pins is available at sootoday.com, November 27, 2016, a publication of the Sault Ste. Marie Public Library and Archives, https://www.sootoday .com/columns/remember-this/remember-this-pointe-aux-pins -474834.

Copper, Part I

Information on the Cass party and the Ontonagon boulder can be found at https://en.wikipedia.org/wiki/Ontonagon_Boulder. See also Hope Pantell, "The Story of the Ontonagon Copper Boulder," *The Mineralogical Record* 7, no. 5 (September-October 1976): 207–10. The Cass party tried to move the boulder but was unsuccessful.

Information on the Treaty of La Pointe 1843 is available at https://en.wikipedia.org/wiki/Treaty_of_La_Pointe.

Information on the American Fur Company's fishery at Madeline Island is included in Thomas K. Backerud, "American Fur Company Fishing on Lake Superior, 1835–1841," MNopedia.org, www.mnopedia.org/event/american-fur-company-fishing-lake -superior-1835–1841.

Steve Lehto has written an informed biography of Douglass Houghton, *Michigan's Columbus: The Life of Douglass Houghton* (Royal Oak, Mich.: Momentum Books, 2009).

For a detailed account of the Cliff mine, see Donald Chaput,

The Cliff: America's First Great Copper Mine (Kalamazoo, Mich.: Sequoia Press, 1971); and Angus Murdoch, *Boom Copper: The Story of the First U.S. Boom* (Drier and Koepel, 1964).

For statistics on the incredibly productive Calumet and Hecla mines, see https://en.wikipedia.org/wiki/Calumet_and_Hecla _Mining_Company.

For information on the Finnish communities on the Keweenaw, see Michigan Technological University Archives and Copper Country Historical Collections, J. Robert Van Pelt Library, "Keweenaw Ethnic Groups: The Finns," http://ethnicity.lib.mtu.edu/groups _Finns.html.

Copper, Part II

For descriptions of the various kinds of pollution, see "Environmental Impacts of Mining in the Keweenaw," Keweenaw National Historical Park Michigan, National Park Service, https://www.nps.gov /kewe/learn/nature/environmental-impacts-of-mining-in-the -keweenaw.htm.

For information on Torch Lake, see Brooke Singer, "Torch Lake, Ste Rte 26 N of Quincy Mills," at ToxicSites.us, https://www.toxic sites.us/site.php?epa_id=MID980901946.

For PCBs and mercury in Torch Lake, see "PCBs in Torch Lake: What's the Story?," Michigan Sea Grant, https://www.michigansea grant.org/wp-content/uploads/2019/02/16–723-PCBs-in-Torch -Lake-Whats-the-story-rev5.pdf; and "Mercury in Torch Lake: What's the Story?" Michigan Sea Grant, https://www.michigan seagrant.org/wp-content/uploads/2019/02/16–716-Mercury-in -Torch-Lake-2016-rev3.pdf.

For mercury in Keweenaw wetlands, see Eric Freedman, "Mining Legacy, Wetlands Expansion Fuel Concern over U.P. Mercury Levels," *Great Lakes Echo*, September 4, 2018, https://great lakesecho.org/2018/09/04/mining-legacy-wetlands-expansion -fuel-concern-over-u-p-mercury-levels/.

For information on the threat of stamp sands to the spawning beds of Buffalo Reef and recovery action, see Mary Kate McCoy, "Legacy Mine Waste Threatening Lake Superior's Buffalo Reef," Wisconsin Public Radio, October 15, 2018, https://www.wpr.org /legacy-mine-waste-threatening-lake-superiors-buffalo-reef; and "Buffalo Reef Task Force to Reveal Plan for Stamp Sands at July 12 Public Meeting in Houghton County," Michigan Department of Natural Resources, press release, June 27, 2022, https://www .michigan.gov/dnr/about/newsroom/releases/2022/06/27/buffalo -reef-stamp-sands-plan-to-be-revealed-at-july-12-meeting.

The cleanup of the Eagle River is covered in Sean Gohman's epilogue to Donald Chaput, *The Cliff: America's First Great Copper Mine* (Quincy Mine Hoist Association, 2015). The quotation beginning "We dig in the earth" is on page 192.

You Can't See the Forest

Dr. Suzanne Simard's remarkable book is *Finding the Mother Tree: Discovering the Wisdom of the Forest* (New York: Knopf, 2021).

The history of Port Wing, Wisconsin, is from the Chequamegon Region Who's Who Edition, *Ashland Daily Press,* 1929, by Postmaster Carl V. Dahlstedt. See also Okerstrom Reunion at Port Wing, Wisconsin, July 3, 1976, by Paul Okerstrom; and *History of Port Wing* (undated) by Carl Bystrom. All three are available at the Port Wing Historical Society.

For an assessment of the northern Wisconsin cutover, see Eric Olmanson, *The Future City on the Inland Sea: A History of Imaginative Geographies of Lake Superior* (Athens: Ohio University Press, 2007).

On tree communication, see Edward Farmer, plant biologist, University of Pausanne, Switzerland, on voltage-based signaling system: https://onetreeplanted.org/blogs/stories/how-do -trees-communicate. German forester Peter Wohlleben, author of *The Hidden Life of Trees,* is profiled in Richard Grant, "Do Trees

Talk to Each Other?," *Smithsonian Magazine,* March 2018, https://www.smithsonianmag.com/science-nature/the-whispering-trees-180968084/.

The Two-Hearted River

For accounts of the Duck Lake fire of May 23–June 15, 2012, see https://en.wikipedia.org/wiki/Duck_Lake_Fire. Photographs of the fire are accessible at https://www.mlive.com/news/2012/05/duck_lake_fire_exceeds_20000_a.html.

Also informative is John Barnes, "Life Slowly Reborn amid U.P. Wildfire Ash, Devastation," *Detroit News,* June 3, 2016, https://www.detroitnews.com/story/news/local/michigan/2016/06/03/life-reborn-upper-peninsula-wildfire/85381152/.

Ernest Hemingway's "Big Two-Hearted River" can be found in *The Nick Adams Stories* (New York: Scribner, 1972).

The Piping Plovers of Long Island

For basic information on piping plovers in the Apostle Islands, see Sumner Matteson, "Past, Present, and Future of Piping Plovers in the Apostle Islands," Apostle Islands Stewardship Symposium, March 30–31, 2021, https://friendsoftheapostleislands.org/2021/04/01/past-present-and-future-of-piping-plovers-in-the-apostle-islands/.

Frog Bay

For information on Frog Bay Tribal National Park, see the website of the Red Cliff Band of Lake Superior Chippewa, https://www.redcliff-nsn.gov/frogbay/.

Melanie Radzick McManus, "Frog Bay in Wisconsin Is the First-Ever Tribal National Park," *Star Tribune,* February 18, 2022, https://www.startribune.com/frog-bay-in-wisconsin-is-the-first-ever-tribal-national-park/600148209/.

For information on tribal work on wild rice restoration in the Lake Superior region, see the website of the Keweenaw Bay Indian Community Natural Resources Department, https://nrd.kbic-nsn.gov/wild-rice-management-and-restoration.

The Kakagon Sloughs of Mashkiiziibii

For information on the Kakagon Sloughs, see James Meeker and N. Tillison, "Kakagon (Bad River Sloughs), Wisconsin (USA)," chapter 32 in *The Wetland Book,* edited by C. Finlayson et al. (Dordrecht, Netherlands: Springer 2018). This is Meeker's doctoral thesis taken at University of Wisconsin, Madison.

For information on the fight to save the Penokee Hills, see the website of the Bad River Tribe, Ashland, Wisconsin, http://www.badriver-nsn.gov/natural-resources/threats/.

Mark Anthony Rolo, "My Tribe's Stand against Corporate Mining," *The Progressive Magazine,* October 31, 2016, https://progressive.org/magazine/tribe-s-stand-corporate-mining/.

The Sacred Act of Ricing

A version of the migration story can be found at "On the Shores of the 'Great Water': The Ojibwe People's Migration to Gichigamiig," by Mattie Harper (Bois Forte Band of Ojibwe), May 29, 2018, at https://growlermag.com/author/mattie-harper/.

For information on April Stone's lovely baskets, see the website of the Native Arts and Cultures Foundation, Portland, Oregon, https://www.nativeartsandcultures.org/april-stone.

Making a National Lakeshore

For the Apostle Islands Ojibwe creation story, see Gerry DePerry's account in *Jewels on the Water,* by Jeff Rennicke, published by Friends of the Apostle Islands National Lakeshore (2005).

For a comprehensive account of the history of the Apostle Islands and how they became a national lakeshore, see James W. Feldman, *A Storied Wilderness: Rewilding the Apostle Islands* (Seattle: University of Washington Press, 2011).

For a discussion of summer life on Rocky Island and Air Haven restaurant, see *Apostle Islanders: The People and Culture*, by Robert J. Nelson (Bayfield: Blue Box Press, 2011).

Plumbing the Depths

To read entertaining and sometimes harrowing firsthand accounts of bobbing, see John Esposito, *Blood on the Ice: Ice Fishing and Adventures in the Apostle Islands Region of Lake Superior* (self-published). The author can be reached at jespowisconsin@gmail.com.

The Lake Effect

For information on the Swedetown Trails, see https://next.swedetowntrails.org/conditions/.

To read about Tahquamenon Falls State Park, see https://www.michigan.org/property/tahquamenon-falls-state-park.

For more information about Noquemanon Trails, and especially the Forestville trails and campground, see the website of the Noquemanon Trail Network, https://noquetrails.org/forestville/.

The Aldo Leopold quotation is from *A Sand County Almanac and Sketches Here and There.*

Locking through the Soo

On February 1, 2021, the MV *Roger Blough* suffered a fire that started in the engine room and spread to the conveyor system, causing more than one hundred million dollars of damage. The boat is currently laying in Conneaut, Ohio, awaiting a decision on whether it will sail again.

James Bittner, who swore that upon retirement he was done with Lake Superior, has bought a sailboat, aptly named *Destiny,* by which he plies the great lake.

When the Queen Is Riled

The history of Great Lake shipwrecks is retold in several fine sources. Any of Frederick Stonehouse's books, and especially his history of the Life-Saving Stations, *Wreck Ashore: The United States Life-Saving Stations on the Great Lakes* (Lake Superior Port Cities, 1994), are worthy reads.

Mac Frimodig's *Shipwrecks off Keweenaw,* published by the Fort Wilkins Natural History Association and the Michigan Department of Natural Resources, is engaging in its recounting of wrecks along the treacherous coast of the Keweenaw. The Annual Reports of the Life-Saving Service, available at https://uslife-savingservice.org /publications/annual-reports-2/, are terrific. The website boatnerd .com has an exhaustive compilation of every wreck documented in the Great Lakes: http://www.boatnerd.com/swayze/shipwreck/.

The quotation from Sumner Kimball is from Stonehouse, *Wreck Ashore,* page 28.

The Lake Breeze Hotel

For an account of Eagle Harbor's 150-year celebration, see Paul Freshwater, "Keweenaw County Sesquicentennial History Part II: The Second Half Century of Change and Re-invention, 1911–1964," in *The Superior Signal* 26, no. 2 (May 2011), the quarterly magazine of the Keweenaw County Historical Society. For more on tearooms, see Cara Strickland, "The Top-Secret Feminist History of Tea Rooms," *JSTOR Daily,* March 6, 2019, https://daily.jstor.org /the-top-secret-feminist-history-of-tea-rooms/.

Sue Leaf has written the memoirs *The Bullhead Queen: A Year on Pioneer Lake* (2009) and *Portage: A Family, a Canoe, and the Search for the Good Life* (2015), as well as the biographies *A Love Affair with Birds: The Life of Thomas Sadler Roberts* (2013) and *Minnesota's Geologist: The Life of Newton Horace Winchell* (2020; winner of a Minnesota Book Award), all published by the University of Minnesota Press. She is also author of *Potato City: Nature, History, and Community in the Age of Sprawl*. Trained as a zoologist, she writes on environmental and natural history topics. She and her family have owned a cabin outside Port Wing, Wisconsin, on Lake Superior's South Shore for thirty-five years.